ORGANISATION & MANAGEMENT

Series Editor
Brian Coyle

PASSWORD ORGANISATION AND MANAGEMENT

First edition January 1990

ISBN 1 871824 08 7

Published by
BPP Publishing Ltd
BPP House, Aldine Place,
142/144 Uxbridge Road, London W12 8AA

Printed by Dotesios Printers Ltd, Trowbridge

A CIP Catalogue reference for this book
is available from the British Library

CONTENTS

Page

Preface. v

How to use this book. vi

SECTION 1:
NOTES AND QUESTIONS

Page

1. Organisational structure and culture. 3
2. Marketing and distribution. 16
3. Production. 28
4. Authority, responsibility and delegation. . 40
5. Communication and co-ordination. 48
6. Planning and control. 59
7. Motivation and discipline. 72
8. Management and leadership. 84
9. Teamwork. 94
10. Managing change. 102
11. Manpower resourcing. 112
12. Manpower development. 124
13. Work environment. 136
14. Theories of management. 147

SECTION 2:
MARKING SCHEDULES
AND COMMENTS

Page

. . . . 157
. . . . 164
. . . . 170
. . . . 176
. . . . 180
. . . . 188
. . . . 194
. . . . 201
. . . . 207
. . . . 213
. . . . 220
. . . . 228
. . . . 236
. . . . 243

PREFACE

Password is a series of multiple choice question books on business and accountancy topics. If you are studying for an examination, or would just like to test your knowledge on one of these topics, Password books have two special features which are designed to help you.

1 They contain about 300 multiple choice questions, with answers provided later in the book. You can get an objective idea of your strengths and weaknesses, and whether your standard is as high as you would like it to be.

2 We explain most solutions in some detail, to show why one answer is correct and the others are wrong. Our comments should help you to learn from any mistakes you have made, and to improve your understanding of the subject.

Objective testing is an increasingly popular method of examination. An answer is right or wrong, and there are no 'grey areas' or 'in-between answers' that are half-right or arguably correct. Multiple choice questions (MCQs) are the form of objective testing that is now most widely used. Professional bodies that have adopted MCQs for some examination papers include the Institute of Chartered Accountants in England and Wales, the Institute of Chartered Accountants of Scotland and the Chartered Institute of Management Accountants. The Chartered Association of Certified Accountants has recently taken a first step in the same direction.

MCQs offer much more than exam practice, though. They test your knowledge and understanding. And they help with learning.

- The brevity of the questions, and having to select a correct answer from four choices (A, B, C or D), makes them convenient to use. You can do some on your journey to or from work or college on the train or the bus.

- We know from experience that many people like MCQs, find them fun and enjoy the opportunity to mark their own answers exactly.

- Being short, MCQs are able collectively to cover every aspect of a topic area. They make you realise what you know and what you don't.

If you're looking for the fun and challenge of self-testing, or preparing for an examination - not just a multiple choice exam - Password is designed to help you. You can check your own standard, monitor your progress, spot your own weaknesses, and learn things that you hadn't picked up from your text-book or study manual. Most important, Password books allow you to find out for yourself how good you are at a topic, and how much better you want to be.

Good luck!

Brian Coyle
January 1990

PASSWORD. MULTIPLE CHOICE

HOW TO USE THIS BOOK

Aims of the book

This book is designed:

- to familiarise you with a type of question that you are increasingly likely to face if you are studying for examinations (although not yet in this subject)

- to develop your knowledge of Organisation and Management through repeated practice on questions covering all areas of the subject. There are more than 300 questions in this book.

The multiple choice approach

A multiple choice question is in two parts.

- The *stem* sets out the problem or task to be solved. It may be in the form of a question, or it may be an unfinished statement which has to be completed.

- The *options* are the possible responses from which you must choose the one you believe to be correct. There is only one correct option (called the *key*); the other, incorrect, options are called *distractors*.

There are various ways in which you may be asked to indicate your chosen response. If you meet with MCQs in an examination, you should obviously read the instructions carefully. In this book, you will find that the options are identified by the letters A, B, C, D. To indicate your choice, draw a circle round the letter you have chosen.

The notes

In Section 1 of this book each chapter begins with brief notes which are designed to refresh your memory of the subject area and get you thinking along the right lines before you begin to tackle the questions.

The notes are *not* a substitute for a textbook: Password assumes that you are already broadly familiar with the topics covered in the chapter. Nor do they give you answers to all the questions.

- The notes are a *reminder* of the some points in each topic area. If your studies have left you feeling that you can't see the wood for the trees, the notes may help to bring the important issues into focus.

- They provide brief *guidance* on particularly knotty points or areas which often cause problems for students.

- They *comment* on areas of current interest in the field of management, and draw your attention to the views of influential writers whose work might be useful.

The questions

The questions are arranged roughly in the order of the key areas highlighted by the notes. But it is difficult, and undesirable, to keep topics completely separate: there's a great deal of overlapping. Also, the range of factual knowledge required in management or business studies exams is very wide.

The general principle has been for questions *on each topic* to get progressively harder. The result of this is that within a single chapter the level of difficulty will rise, and then fall back to begin rising again. So if you have trouble with two or three questions, don't assume that you have to give up on the whole chapter: there may be easier questions ahead!

Try to work through a whole chapter before turning to the solutions. If you refer to the marking schedule after each question you will find it almost impossible to avoid seeing the answer to the next question, and the value of the book will be lessened.

Finally, don't rush your answers. Distractors are exactly what their name suggests: they are meant to look plausible and distract you from the correct option. Unless you are absolutely certain you know the answer, look carefully at each option in turn before making your choice.

The marking schedules

The marking schedules indicate the correct answer to each question and the number of marks available. You should add up the marks on all the questions you got right and compare your total with the maximum marks available.

At the foot of each marking schedule there is a rating, which is intended to be helpful in indicating the amount of work you still need to do on each topic. You'll need to use your discretion in interpreting your rating, though. The book may be used by a very wide range of readers, from GCSE students, through students of college or professional business and accountancy courses, to qualified personnel with years of practical experience. A mark of 10 out of 35 might be worryingly low for an experienced accountant or manager, while representing a very creditable achievement for someone at an earlier stage of his studies.

The comments

The answers to purely factual questions generally need no explanation, but for others there is a commentary, often detailed. This is particularly necessary for management topics, where there are many 'grey areas' and points of interpretation.

These comments will usually describe why a particular option is correct. Distractors are usually chosen to illustrate common misconceptions, or plausible, but incorrect, lines of thought. The comments will often highlight what is wrong about particular distractors and this should help in clarifying your ideas about topics that you may have misunderstood. You should expect to learn more from getting a solution wrong than getting it right.

Conclusion

Password Organisation and Management is designed as an aid both to learning and to revision. It is not primarily aimed at those who are already expert in the subject. So don't expect to score 100%. And don't despair if your marks seem relatively low. Choosing the wrong answer to a question is not a failure, if by studying the solution and comments you learn something you did not know before. This is particularly relevant if you are using the book at an early stage in your studies, rather than in the final stages of revision.

And if you *do* score 100%? There are 14 other Password titles to get through...

SECTION 1

NOTES AND QUESTIONS

CHAPTER 1

ORGANISATIONAL STRUCTURE AND CULTURE

> This chapter covers the following topics:
>
> ● The organisation
> ● Organisation structure
> ● Organisational culture

1. The organisation

1.1 An organisation may be defined as a complex social system which brings together a number of individuals to fulfil certain objectives.

1.2 It may be helpful to focus on three elements of this definition. An organisation:

(a) is made up of *people* (which sounds obvious, but identifies the root of many problems, uncertainties and opportunities in organisational functioning);

(b) may be viewed as a *system*, which interacts with its environment, absorbing inputs (finance, labour, information, raw materials, equipment and machinery etc) and releasing outputs (finished goods, services, information, finance etc). There are also sub-systems of the overall system; technical (technology, methods of working, task structure) and social (human relationships, group dynamics), for example;

(c) has *objectives*. Each person in the organisation has his or her own personal goals, but the organisation as a whole has objectives which it must attain if it is to be considered 'effective'. (If possible, individual and organisational objectives should be reconciled, in order to secure maximum commitment from employees.)

1.3 An organisation is given definition and 'shape' by the formal *structure* which orders the various tasks and relationships so that they are directed towards the fulfilment of the organisation's objectives.

However, there co-exists with the formal organisation structure a pattern of *informal* relationships, communication and authority, known as the 'informal organisation' - or, more properly, 'organisations', since each social group, clique or communication network is an organisation in its own right, with its own customs and norms, authority structure and goals.

1.4 The informal organisation may operate for or against the interests of the formal organisation. It can usefully:

- improve communication by means of the 'grapevine'
- co-ordinate the activities of individuals and groups without 'going through channels'
- establish 'unwritten' but practical ways of doing things.

On the other hand, informal organisations may absorb energy and loyalty that should (from management's point of view) belong to the company and the task. They may even have objectives (eg having fun!) which run counter to the requirements of the formal organisation.

2. Organisation structure

2.1 The main issues in organisation design are:

- division of labour (ie who does what?)
- source of authority (ie who has the right to tell them to?) and
- relationships (ie how does the whole thing hang together)

'Organisation structure' therefore includes:

- the division of work and grouping of activities
- the allocation of formal responsibilities
- linking/co-ordination mechanisms, if necessary
- communication channels
- the interaction of roles and people

2.2 The classical approach to organisation structure concentrates on the channels and extent of delegation of authority in the organisation. So, for example, you have considerations such as centralisation and decentralisation (how much delegation should there be?), the scalar chain (who is responsible to whom?) span of control (how many people report to each superior?) and unity of command (one man one boss).

2.3 One of the more interesting organisational dilemmas, arising in classical organisational structures, is the relationship between 'line' and 'staff' management. The terms are used to denote both function (a distinction between 'doers' and 'advisers/supporters') and authority (a distinction between direct 'positional' and indirect 'expert' power). Staff or 'functional' managers - in Accounts, Personnel, Data Processing etc - have a constant political battle in most organisations to impose their authority on situations requiring their expertise but under the direct control of 'line' managers.

2.4 There has, for some years, been a move away from prescriptive, 'one best way' theories of how organisations should be analysed and designed, and towards a *contingency* approach which says, in essence, 'it all depends'. In other words, the structure which will enable optimum efficiency in an organisation will not conform to universal principles, but will vary according to the internal and external conditions of the organisation, including its:

- market/environment, and its stability
- size
- task/product
- type of personnel
- technology
- 'culture'

2.5 This awareness of internal and external influences on organisational structure and functioning has contributed to the important emphasis on *flexibility* and adaptability in recent years, particularly since the pace of technological change and the competitive environment in which businesses operate put organisations under increasing pressure to innovate.

- Bureaucracy, the classical formal structure, has come under fire for its inability to adjust to change

- Burns and Stalker contrast 'mechanistic' (bureaucratic) organisations with more responsive 'organic' (or 'organismic') systems, which are suited to conditions of rapid change

- There is a trend towards task-centred structures eg multi-disciplinary project teams, to facilitate flexibility and innovation. In particular, 'matrix' organisation has emerged, dividing authority between functional managers and product/project managers/co-ordinators - thus challenging classical assumptions about 'one man one boss' and the line/staff dilemma.

3. Organisational culture

3.1 *Organisational culture* is the complex body of shared and accepted values, beliefs and informal practices of an organisation. It manifests itself in:

- underlying assumptions eg quality is important, innovate or die

- overt beliefs eg mottos, mission statements, legends about the history or leader of the organisation, sense of the heroic ('the winning team') etc

- visible artefacts eg style of offices, dress 'rules', informality, rewards

3.2 Peters and Waterman (*In Search of Excellence*) suggest that the culture of an organisation can be controlled by management and made a vital source of staff satisfaction and motivation, non-coercive control ('central faith' or 'guiding values' replacing measures which forbid autonomy and stifle entrepreneurship) and enhanced performance.

3.3 Handy (following Harrison) adds that culture is intimately related to organisation structure, and identifies four variations.

- *Power* culture (where influence stems from a central source) fosters informal structures centred on key figures

- *Role* culture (based on jurisdiction and defined roles) fosters formal bureaucratic structures

- *Task* culture (centred on contribution of skill and effort to get the job done) fosters flexible structures with matrix elements

- *Person* culture (centred on the gratification of personal interests) may exist where individuals 'use' the organisation for their own ends, but a full-blown organisation based on it is rare; an example might be a partnership where a few individuals do all the work themselves.

Some common forms of organisational structure, with notes on their cultural characteristics, are illustrated opposite.

Some organisation structures

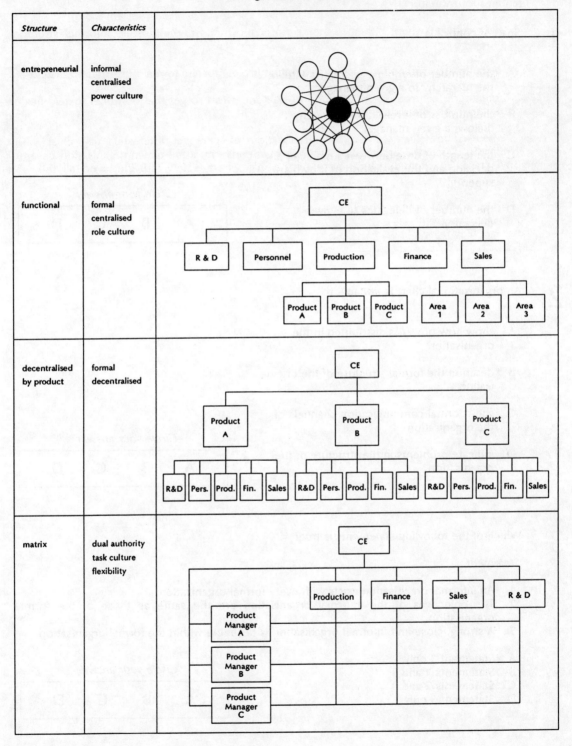

Structure	Characteristics	
entrepreneurial	informal centralised power culture	
functional	formal centralised role culture	
decentralised by product	formal decentralised	
matrix	dual authority task culture flexibility	

QUESTIONS

1 Span of control is

A the number of employees subordinate in the hierarchy to a given manager

B the number of levels in the hierarchy 'below' a given manager

C the length of time between a manager's decision and the evaluation of it by his superior

D the number of delegates to a given delegator

Circle your answer

A	B	C	D

2 An organisational chart is *not* able to

A show how power is distributed in the organisation

B describe the formal structure of the organisation

C show formal communication channels of the organisation

D indicate problems in the structure of the organisation

Circle your answer

A	B	C	D

3 Which of the following statements is true?

Statement

1 An informal organisation exists with every formal organisation.
2 The objectives of the informal organisation are the same as those of the formal organisation.
3 A strong, close-knit informal organisation is desirable within the formal organisation.

A Statement 1 only
B Statements 1 and 3
C Statements 2 and 3
D Statement 3 only

Circle your answer

A	B	C	D

Data for questions 4 - 6

B Z Ness Ltd is an organisation with a strongly 'traditional' outlook. It is structured and managed according to classical principles: specialisation, the scalar chain of command, unity of command and direction. Personnel tend to focus on their own distinct tasks, which are strictly defined and directed. Communication is vertical, rather than lateral. Discipline is much prized, and enshrined in the rule book of the company

4 From this scenario, one may assume that B Z Ness Ltd is *not*

A   a bureaucratic organisation
B   a mechanistic organisation
C   an organismic organisation
D   a role-culture organisation

Circle your answer

A   B   C   D

5 From the information given, B Z Ness's structure is likely to offer advantages for

A   innovation
B   motivation
C   communication
D   control

Circle your answer

A   B   C   D

6 From the information given, we can infer that the management of B Z Ness Ltd models itself on the theories of

A   Charles Handy
B   Henri Fayol
C   Abraham Maslow
D   Elton Mayo

Circle your answer

A   B   C   D

7 Which of the following commonly recognised features of bureaucracy could most clearly be identified as a *disadvantage* of the system?

A   Insensitivity to feedback
B   Rigidity of behaviour
C   Delegation of authority
D   Rules

Circle your answer

A   B   C   D

8 Which of the following is likely to occur if an organisation increases in size?

Consequences

1   It will be able to take advantage of economies of scale
2   Its span of control will increase
3   It will no longer have an informal organisation
4   It will tend towards formalisation

A   Consequence 2 only
B   Consequences 1 and 4 only
C   Consequences 1, 2 and 4
D   Consequences 1, 2 and 3

Circle your answer

| A | B | C | D |

9 Nysslit Lerner plc, an organisation of some 400 employees has an average span of control of three, throughout its management structure. From this, one might infer that:

A   the work is systematic and routine
B   job satisfaction is high
C   the level of complexity in the work is high
D   the organisation structure is flat

Circle your answer

| A | B | C | D |

10 A mechanistic organisation is associated with

A   conditions of rapid change
B   automated processes
C   task culture
D   bureaucracy

Circle your answer

| A | B | C | D |

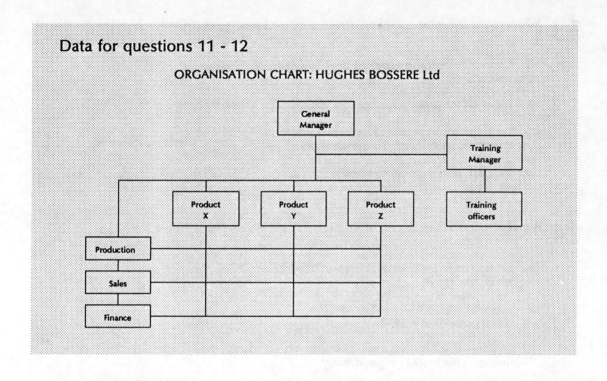

Data for questions 11 - 12

ORGANISATION CHART: HUGHES BOSSERE Ltd

11 In the Hughes Bossere chart the authority of the Training Manager would be defined as

A   line only
B   staff only
C   functional and staff
D   line and functional

Circle your answer

A   B   C   D

12 The chart features all but one of the following. Which is the exception?

A   Dual authority
B   Staff management
C   Matrix organisation
D   Span of control

Circle your answer

A   B   C   D

13 Which of the following would *not* create pressure towards centralisation of decision-making?

    A A computerised management information system

    B The need for product/service uniformity

    C The reluctance of trade union representatives to deal with middle management

    D The cost of managerial overheads

Circle your answer

A	B	C	D

14 A market oriented firm is one which plans its activities on the principle that

    A consumers know (and buy) a 'good thing' when they see it

    B a 'good thing' is by definition one that consumers will want to buy

    C consumers will buy whatever the sales function tells them is a 'good thing'

    D consumers will not know (or buy) a 'good thing' *without* being told by the sales function

Circle your answer

A	B	C	D

15 If the chain of command in an organisation is short, problems will most likely arise with

    A management succession
    B management development
    C crisis management
    D communication

Circle your answer

A	B	C	D

16 The greater the proportion of non-supervisory (but routine) work in a manager's work load

A   the wider the span of control should be

B   the narrower the span of control will be

C   the greater his delegation of authority should be

D   the less his delegation of authority should be

Circle your answer

A   B   C   D

17 The organisation of a conscript army of infantry men into divisions is an example of organisation by

A   matrix
B   territory
C   function
D   numbers

Circle your answer

A   B   C   D

18 Federal decentralisation involves

A   the division of a business into autonomous regional or product units

B   setting up integrated units with responsibility for distinct phases of the business process

C   superimposing functional and product authority structures

D   the application of management by objectives

Circle your answer

A   B   C   D

19 Dedd (Boring) Ltd, an oil refinery company, acquires a company which operates a petrol tanker fleet. This is an example of expansion by

A   horizontal integration
B   backwards vertical integration
C   forwards vertical integration
D   diversification

Circle your answer

A   B   C   D

20 If management wanted to change the culture of an organisation, the *least* direct way of doing so would be to alter

A   staff selection
B   reward policies
C   management style
D   the product

Circle your answer

A   B   C   D

21 Which of the following types of organisation has/have a separate 'legal personality'?

Types

1   Sole trader
2   Partnership
3   Public limited company
4   Private limited company

A   Type 1 only
B   Types 2 and 3 only
C   Types 1 and 4 only
D   Types 3 and 4 only

Circle your answer

A   B   C   D

22 'Private enterprise' would *not* describe:

A   a sole trader
B   a professional body
C   a partnership
D   a public limited company

Circle your answer

A   B   C   D

23 Which of the following is *not* a feature of co-operative societies?

A   Constitution as corporate bodies with limited liability

B   Distribution of surpluses in proportion to the value of member's purchases

C   Political or religious affiliation

D   Democratic control of the society's affairs

Circle your answer

A   B   C   D

24 The environment of organisations consists of several aspects

Aspects

1   Political/legal environment
2   Economic/commercial environment
3   Social/ethical environment
4   Technological environment

An organisation's policy on Health and Safety at work, for example, would be affected by:

A   Aspect 3 only
B   Aspects 1 and 3 only
C   Aspects 1, 2 and 3 only
D   Aspects 1, 2, 3 and 4

Circle your answer

A   B   C   D

25 Which of the following factors would not generally impose social responsibility on organisations?

A   The need for new products
B   Organisational ethics
C   The organisation's self-interest
D   Membership of a professional body

Circle your answer

A   B   C   D

CHAPTER 2

MARKETING AND DISTRIBUTION

This chapter covers the following topics:

- Marketing and the marketing concept
- The marketing mix
- Marketing research
- The marketing function

1. Marketing and the marketing concept

1.1 "Marketing is the management process which identifies, anticipates and supplies customer requirements efficiently and profitably." *(Chartered Institute of Marketing)*

"Marketing is not only much broader than selling, it is not a specialised activity at all. It encompasses the entire business. It is the whole business seen from the point of view of its final result, that is, from the customer's point of view. Concern and responsibility for marketing must therefore permeate all areas of the enterprise." *(Peter Drucker 1958)*

Marketing and organisational objectives

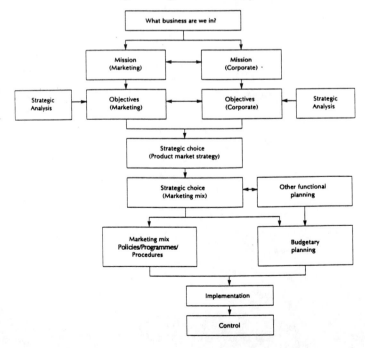

1.2 The *marketing concept* may be defined as a management outlook that accepts that the key task of the organisation is to determine the needs, wants and values of a target market and to adapt the organisation to delivering the desired satisfaction more effectively and efficiently than its competitors.

Alternative outlooks or 'orientations' may be towards:

● production: concentrating on manufacture, cost and volume;
● product: concentrating on product design and quality;
● sales: concentrating on selling product in the face of assumed customer inertia.

1.3 'Modern' marketing recognises that while consumer needs and wants must be taken into account, there is also a wider 'marketing environment' made up of the values and attitudes of consumers, social and ethical trends and other influences on consumer choice. For example, consumers may buy the product they want - *consistent* with looking after the natural environment (is it lead-free/ozone friendly?) or conforming to social ethics (is it South African? Does a percentage of the price go to charity?) The *'societal marketing concept'* suggests that marketing should aim to maximise customer satisfaction within the constraints of responsibility for the well-being of the consumer, society and environment. An organisation may adopt this view out of self-interest (preserving its image and product attractiveness to socially conscious buyers), but also out of an ethical code.

2. The marketing mix

2.1 The marketing mix is defined as "the set of controllable variables and their levels that the firm uses to influence the target market." *(Kotler)*

(Note that there are different types of market: *consumer* markets, consisting of people who purchase goods/services for personal consumption, and *industrial* markets, consisting of those who purchase goods/services for use in business or manufacture, or for resale.)

2.2 The marketing mix may be simplified into the four Ps:

● Product - planning, development, modification, branding and packaging
● Price - cost definition and calculation, profit margins, policies (quality, market positioning etc.)
● Place - channels of distribution, customer service, inventory, transport, direct marketing
● Promotion - advertising, sales promotion, personal selling, publicity

Nowadays, the 'marketing environment' (discussed above) would be added to this formula.

2.3 The marketing mix is the basis for a variety of strategic choices that the organisation will have to make, about:

● which markets (or segments of markets) to be in
● which products/services to offer, and where they should be 'positioned' in the market (eg value-for-money or quality branding?)
● the relationship between the quality and price of the product
● what type of distribution channel to use
● what type of promotion to use etc

2.4 These decisions will be complicated by the fact that the organisation will, as it grows, develop a portfolio of different products in different markets. Product/market strategies may therefore include:

	Existing products		New products
Existing markets	Consolidation or 'segment protection' (capitalising on existing strengths)	Market penetration (increased competition for market share)	Product development
New markets	Market development or extension (eg by more detailed market segmentation and targeting, generating new demand through promotion or finding new customers on the strength of product improvements)		Diversification

2.5 Strategic decisions will be further complicated by the fact that products and product groups 'behave' differently over their saleable lifetime. This can be illustrated as the *product* lifecycle.

The product lifecycle

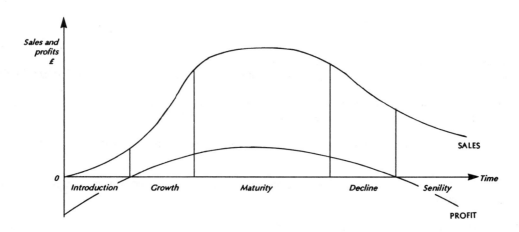

2.6 The process is still further complicated if the organisation has objectives related to *market share,* which may be declining or growing, in a market which itself may be declining or growing. A market growth rate/market share matrix (such as that designed by the Boston Consulting Group) can be used to indicate how a product is 'doing' in these terms. If it has a low market share of a fast-growth market, for example, it's clearly falling behind. A high share of a slow-growth market will offer a ready source of revenue, which can be used to finance products with more work to do - eg one with a low market share of a high-growth market.

These notes have given a general overview of the strategic features of marketing management. Bear in mind, though, that for the purposes of your exam, you may need to get down to some details of how these strategies are implemented in practice.

The questions in this chapter do address some of these detailed aspects.

---

3. Marketing research

3.1 Statistical information is used for strategy formation and for evaluation of the effectiveness of marketing effort.

3.2 *'Marketing research'* is 'the objective gathering, recording and analysing of all facts about problems relating to the marketing of goods and services'.

'Market research' is the aspect of marketing research which is concerned with assessing potential sales, ie the size of the overall market, size and nature of 'segments' within the market (based on distinguishing characteristics of a group of consumers, and how they perceive and differentiate between available products/brands) etc.

4. The marketing function

4.1 The marketing function may be organised in various ways, oriented towards:

- *sales.* The sales force and administration, with 'marketing' as intelligence-gathering backup and promotion emerging as part of customer service activity.

- *marketing.* Sales subordinate as part of the marketing function, which has responsibility for a wide range of product development, promotion and sales activities.

- *product/brand.* Product/brand managers act as general management responsible for the success of the product or product line, including 'marketing' activity.

QUESTIONS

1 Which of the following activities are 'marketing'?

Activities

1. A 'Retailer of the Year' competition as an incentive to retail outlets to stock and display the company's product.
2. Keeping abreast of technology in related product areas.
3. Budgeting for expenditure on advertising.
4. After-sales service and repair.

A Activity 1 only
B Activities 1, 3 and 4 only
C Activities 1, 2 and 3 only
D Activities 1, 2, 3 and 4

Circle your answer

A   B   C   D

2 Which of the following products could be identified as the fruit of a 'marketing orientation' to business?

A The Sinclair C5
B Concorde
C The personal stereo
D Double glazing

Circle your answer

A   B   C   D

3 Fairley Greene plc has just sent its senior managers on a training course, where they have heard about the 'societal marketing concept'. They've now got to look at a set of proposals for:

1. a new factory - to be carefully landscaped on reclaimed land;
2. a price rise on several of their ranges of bottled drinks;
3. a new product: an easy-to-open medicine bottle;
4. an extension of their soft drink ranges to include low-calorie and caffeine-free varieties.

The societal marketing concept might make them think twice about:

A proposal 1 only
B proposal 3 only
C proposals 2 and 3 only
D proposals 1, 2 and 4 only

Circle your answer

A   B   C   D

4 There are three main categories within the consumer market. These do *not* include

    A non-durable products
    B durable goods
    C capital goods
    D services

Circle your answer

A   B   C   D

5 Pro-Duct Mick's is a popular drain manufacturer. The management team decides to sell more heavily through agents and trade distributors. It will reduce its own sales force. At the same time, it will increase its advertising expenditure to reach small trade users as well as personal 'DIY' consumers. These plans will directly affect the marketing mix through:

    A promotion only
    B promotion and place only
    C promotion, place and price only
    D promotion, place, price and product

Circle your answer

A   B   C   D

6 Pro-Duct Mick's has diversified. It uses its metal-tube technology to manufacture bicycles. The Pro-Duct Cycle has many rivals in a mass market. Management's objective is to defend the existing market share of the product. Distribution is intensive. Sales are growing slowly and cash in-flow is high. The marketing budget is aimed mainly at fostering brand loyalty. Profits are actually declining, as the price of the Cycle is lower this year than last, and bigger discounts are being given to retailers. R & D are looking into the possibility of modifying the cycle as a 'BMX'-style model.

What stage of the product life cycle has this bike reached?

    A Introduction
    B Growth
    C Maturity
    D Decline

Circle your answer

A   B   C   D

7 The subdivision of a market into identifiable buyer groups, or sub-markets, with the aim of reaching such groups with a particular marketing mix, is:

    A market fragmentation
    B market segmentation
    C product positioning
    D quota sampling

Circle your answer

A   B   C   D

8 Which is the 'odd man out' among the following market strategies?

A Segment-specific marketing strategy
B Niche marketing strategy
C Differentiated marketing strategy
D Product-market strategy

Circle your answer

| A | B | C | D |

Data for questions 9 & 10

	Existing products		New products
Existing markets	Consolidation	X	Product development
New markets	Market development		Y

Ansoff's product-market matrix

9 Product-market strategy X is:

A market development
B market penetration
C market segmentation
D diversification

Circle your answer

| A | B | C | D |

10 Product-market strategy Y is:

A product positioning
B market penetration
C market segmentation
D diversification

Circle your answer

| A | B | C | D |

11 Based on the Boston Consulting Group matrix of market growth rate/market share, a 'cash cow' is a product where there is:

A low market-growth rate, high market share

B high market-growth rate, high market share

C low market-growth rate, low market share

D high market-growth rate, low market share

Circle your answer

A   B   C   D

12 Which of the following would *not* be true of a 'question mark' or 'problem child' product?

A A question mark is a low market share activity in high growth markets

B Question marks consume finance supplied by cash cows

C A question mark that fails to fulfil its potential becomes a cash cow

D A question mark may be developed into a star by increasing market share

Circle your answer

A   B   C   D

13 Backer de Laurie Ltd sells household goods of consistent medium quality at consistently low prices. Their price-quality strategy might be called:

A an average price-quality strategy
B a value for money strategy
C a cheap goods strategy
D a penetration strategy

Circle your answer

A   B   C   D

14 Old Crocks Ltd sells pottery items, through mail order catalogues, advertising (with product-description and order form) in local newspapers and 'mailshotting' letters and brochures through the post. This is a form of:

23

A   merchant supply
B   direct supply
C   short channel distribution
D   long channel distribution

Circle your answer

A   B   C   D

15 Old Crocks Ltd has now grown, and switched to new methods of distribution. But they're not altogether happy. They find that administrative and transport costs are still high, because they have a large number of separate retailer accounts to supply. They suffer from payment default and bad debts. Lately, too, they have had problem with companies which buy in bulk demanding large trade discounts and ordering fluctuating quantities which disrupt the flow of production. It is fairly clear from these problems that Old Crocks is selling via:

A   merchant supply
B   direct supply
C   short channels
D   long channels

Circle your answer

A   B   C   D

16 A channel network which has more than one outlet but less than the total number of intermediaries who could/would like to carry the manufacturers' products offers adequate market coverage, with control and cost advantages. This is called:

A   short channel distribution
B   intensive distribution
C   exclusive distribution
D   selective distribution

Circle your answer

A   B   C   D

17 Hugh Needsham & Son has two main elements in its promotional mix. It advertises in the national newspapers (through an agency), and it sponsors a football club (through Hugh's personal friendship with the chairman). Which of these activities is a 'below-the-line' method of promotion?

A   The advertising only
B   The sponsorship only
C   Both
D   Neither

Circle your answer

A   B   C   D

18 Which of the following sales promotion techniques would you expect to be most frequently used in industrial markets?

A   Exhibitions
B   Point of sale display
C   Sponsorship
D   Consumer incentives

Circle your answer

A   B   C   D

19 Sloe Cellar Ltd is a gin manufacturer. It has just done an appraisal of its advertising. Expressed as 'cost per thousand people reached by the medium', it's doing rather well. Audience research has also shown that people who've seen the ad have a good recall of it: they even talk about the ad campaign in conversation. Sloe Cellar's market share is growing. The only snag is that it's costing them a fortune, and eating into profits badly. The campaign obviously has a problem with:

A   reach
B   frequency
C   wastage
D   impact

Circle your answer

A   B   C   D

Data for questions 20 & 21

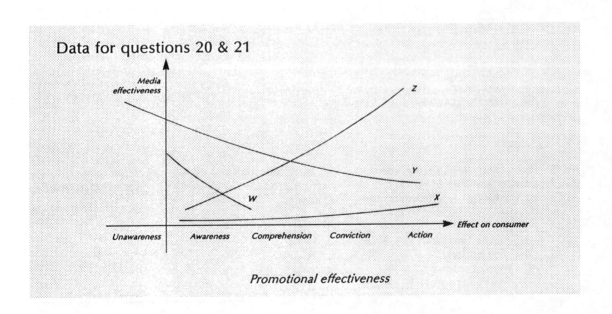

Promotional effectiveness

20 Advertising may be represented by:

A W
B X
C Y
D Z

Circle your answer

A   B   C   D

21 Personal selling may be represented by:

A W
B X
C Y
D Z

Circle your answer

A   B   C   D

22 Which of the following would not be a 'trade description' under the Trades Description Act 1968, section 2?

A

B £6.95
C Solid silver
D Only one previous owner

Circle your answer

A   B   C   D

23 'The objective gathering, recording and analysing of all facts about problems relating to the transfer and sale of goods and services from producer to consumer or user' *(British Institute of Marketing)*, is a definition of:

A product research
B distribution
C market research
D marketing research

Circle your answer

A   B   C   D

24 An estimation of a product's performance (expressed as sales volume, revenue and profit) in a future period, at a given price and using a stated method of promotion is:

A a sales forecast
B a market forecast
C the marketing mix
D the promotional mix

Circle your answer

A   B   C   D

CHAPTER 3

PRODUCTION

This chapter covers the following topics:

- Production
- Quality control
- Purchasing and supply

1. Production

1.1 Production is the process whereby various 'inputs' (eg plant and machinery, materials and labour) are transformed by various operations to provide 'outputs' (ie products and services) which have *added value* over that of the inputs.

1.2 The task of production or plant management can be very wide, embracing:

- product design (although this may be subordinated to the research and development - R & D - department)

- methods of production

- production control (monitoring production, comparing actual progress/output/quality/cost with planned or standard levels, and investigating and correcting any divergence)

- materials handling (although this may be subordinated to a purchasing/supply department which might not report to the production director)

- production administration (eg production planning, collection and reporting of production information, plant location and layout, capital expenditure decisions)

- process engineering, (ie technical planning: work study and ergonomics, tool and equipment supply, technical awareness and training, cost reporting and control).

1.3 You probably don't need to know a lot of technical detail about production methods, but you should be aware of three main *types of production*, classified in terms of their economic character.

- Job production, ie separate identifiable jobs, or 'one-off' projects. This requires versatile plant and labour, special stock ordering and flexible planning (since there is no regular 'rhythm' to production)

- Batch production, ie the production 'in one go' of a quantity of the same product, where the items are not intended for sale to a specific single customer. Efficient planning is required to route batches from one machine or process to the next

- Flow production, ie where a product is made on a continuous basis, with an unbroken flow from one process to the next. Sufficient continuous demand is required to justify the expenditure on highly specialised plant (usually highly automated)

1.4 Recent years, however, have seen fundamental changes in the approach to and economic character of production. World Class Marketing (WCM) is a term used by Professor Schonberger in 1986 to describe the trends. WCM is a very broad term, but can be taken to have four key elements.

(a) *A new approach to product quality.* Instead of a policy of trying to detect defects or poor quality in production as and when they occur, WCM sets out to identify the root causes of poor quality, eliminate them, and achieve zero defects - ie 100% quality. Eliminating waste is likely to involve building better quality into the product.

(b) *Just in Time manufacturing (JIT).* This is a system of manufacturing that aims to eliminate waste. Waste can be described as the use of resources that fail to add value to the product. Wasteful activities include inspection of goods, shopfloor queues, re-working of defective items, excessive storage and unnecessary movement of materials. The best-known feature of JIT is that it is a system for reducing stocks of raw materials, components and finished goods: items should be delivered or produced 'just in time' for when they are needed, rather than sitting around tying up capital and space, and not making any money.

This will mean that:

- the manufacturer will need to develop a close relationship with *suppliers,* who will also deliver 'just in time';

- with low stockholding, the *quality* standard will need to be high, because their is no safety margin if items are defective. Checking and worker *training* will be important;

- the production process may need to be shortened and simplified, and made more *flexible* .

(c) *Managing people.* The aim of WCM is to utilise the skills and abilities of the work force to the full. Employees are given training in a variety of skills, so that they can switch from one task to another. They are also given more responsibility for production scheduling and quality. A *team approach* is encouraged, with strong trust between management and workers.

(d) *Flexible approach to customer requirements.* The WCM policy is to develop close relationships with customers in order to

- know what their requirements are

- supply customers on time, with short delivery lead times

- change the product mix quickly and develop new products or modify existing products as customer needs change

1.5 Flexible manufacturing systems (FMS) are another new trend. They are highly automated computer-controlled manufacturing systems that enable manufacturers to achieve small batch production, without the loss of machine operating time caused by set-up times between batches. This helps to provide the flexibility needed for just in time manufacturing.

2. Quality control

2.1 Quality control has re-emerged as a central issue in the production of goods and services. It has become an important:

- *marketing tool.* High quality brands have been increasingly added to the upper end of product ranges and sold at a premium, positioning the brand in a different segment from popular, value-for-money 'own brands'

- *competitive advantage.* Consumer expectations have been rising, particularly in high-profile areas such as health, safety and environment-friendliness. The competitive market has created a climate where quality is not perceived as a 'luxury': poor quality may severely damage brand loyalty and repurchase rate - as well as eliciting buyer protest

- *cultural attribute.* Participation in quality assurance is increasingly perceived as a source of job satisfaction and motivation. Peters and Waterman *(In Search of Excellence)* argue that commitment to a job comes from believing that it is inherently worthwhile. "Owing to good luck, or may be even good sense, these companies that emphasise quality, reliability and service have chosen the *only* area where it is readily possible to generate excitement in the average down-the-line employee."

2.2 *Quality circles* are a fashionable approach to quality control, which fits in well with World Class Manufacturing concepts. They seem to have emerged first in the USA, but were adopted most enthusiastically in Japan; they are now re-appearing in the West, following the conspicuous success of Japanese business. A quality circle consists of a voluntary grouping of employees which meets regularly to discuss problems of quality and quality control with varying degrees of authority for recommendation and implementation of improvements.

3. Purchasing and supply

3.1 Purchasing and supply has traditionally been a somewhat underrated function, given responsibility for the primarily administrative aspects of supply (locating and selecting suppliers, purchase, maintenance of stock levels and records of availability/quality/ price/suppliers, maintaining relationships with internal departments etc). World Class Manufacturing and JIT manufacturing have, however, re-affirmed the crucial role of purchasing in controlling stockholding and goods inwards quality, and developing relationships with suppliers so that 'just in time' order requirements can be consistently met.

> "Some of the largest buyers - for instance, in the automobile companies - have become highly sophisticated materials managers and fully integrate design and purchasing. But most manufacturers have to learn what some of the large retailers grasped thirty or forty years ago; buying is as important as selling, and the best selling cannot make up for a mediocre buying specification." (Peter Drucker: *Managing for results*)

QUESTIONS

1 Which of the following is the 'odd man out'?

A Flow production
B Process production
C Mass production
D Batch production

Circle your answer

A B C D

2

Production activity	Technology
(1) Shipbuilding	(w) batch production
(2) Chemicals manufacture	(x) flow (process) production
(3) Car manufacture	(y) job production
(4) Bakery	(z) flow (mass) products

Match the production activities (1)-(4) with the technologies (w)-(z) by which they are most likely to be dominated.

A (1)(y) ● (2)(w) ● (3)(z) ● (4)(x)
B (1)(y) ● (2)(x) ● (3)(w) ● (4)(z)
C (1)(w) ● (2)(x) ● (3)(z) ● (4)(y)
D (1)(y) ● (2)(x) ● (3)(z) ● (4)(w)

Circle your answer

A B C D

3 Swettent Oil Ltd is a large oil refinery with a high degree of automation in its specialised plant. It has continuous 'outlets' for its product, continuous supplies of raw materials, and continuously running plant, which is serviced and controlled by highly-skilled technicians and specialists.

Which of the following is/are *not* a feature of Swettent Oil?

Features

1. Capital-intensive organisation
2. Labour-intensive organisation
3. Flow process production
4. Automation

A 2 only
B 3 only
C 1 and 4 only
D 2 and 4 only

Circle your answer

A B C D

4 Modern manufacturing systems are being built on the principles that

(1) companies must be able to produce a much wider product range, with many variations in product design, in the same factory premises

(2) manufacturing should be capital-intensive, using robotics and computer-aided manufacturing techniques

(3) production systems must be more flexible, capable of switching efficiently from one job to another without hold-ups in work flow.

These changes have various implications, one of which is

A the need for larger stockholdings
B the need for shorter production runs (smaller batches)
C higher unit costs of production
D less need to train production workers

Circle your answer

| A | B | C | D |

5 Just in Time (JIT) techniques of production management operate on the principle that stocks should be kept to a minimum so as to avoid the various costs of stockholding and tying up resources in idle assets. Three elements of JIT are:

(1) prompt delivery of materials and components from suppliers
(2) scheduling production runs to meet specific customer orders
(3) low stockholding of finished goods items

For JIT systems to operate efficiently, it will be important to have:

A a large number of raw materials and component suppliers for each material or component item

B centralised management of production operations

C a fairly limited product range, to facilitate stock control

D a high quality of raw materials and components, and high quality of production

Circle your answer

| A | B | C | D |

6

This diagram illustrates:

A   Mechanisation
B   Automation
C   A mechanistic system
D   A control system

Circle your answer

| A | B | C | D |

7   Fiddley (Bits) Ltd makes drill bits for mining operations, (jobbing work). Which of the following would *not* be a function of its production planning department?

A   Establishing production demand

B   Establishing requirements for materials, labour-time and machine time

C   Requisitioning materials and components from store

D   Scheduling work to be done in the planning period; preparing 'job' or 'route' cards

Circle your answer

| A | B | C | D |

8   The process concerned with ensuring that a product is manufactured so as to meet certain design specifications is most properly called:

A   Quality assurance
B   Quality control
C   Inspection
D   Value analysis

Circle your answer

| A | B | C | D |

Data for questions 9 - 10

Ondie (Cheapside) Ltd makes plastic mugs. Not very good ones. Production methods are notoriously unreliable, as is the Process Control officer. On the other hand, Marketing is of the opinion that people don't look for very high quality in mugs any more. It has been calculated that while 8% of current output has been identified as defective, the costs involved in reducing that proportion below 5% would be higher than the loss of sales - especially since the Reject Plastic chain of retailers is doing good business with 'slightly spoiled' items. Ondie currently inspects 10% of output.

9 Ondie would *not* want to operate its quality control by:

A 100% testing
B Acceptance sampling
C Quality assurance
D Monitoring customer complaints

Circle your answer

A   B   C   D

10 The AQL (acceptance quality level) in Ondie's case is:

A 3%
B 5%
C 8%
D 10%

Circle your answer

A   B   C   D

11 A manufacturer would need to operate careful goods inwards inspection if the supplier had:

A a supplier's quality assurance scheme
B a high vendor rating
C a high inspection sample for its output inspection
D a wide manufacturing tolerance

Circle your answer

A   B   C   D

12 A successful quality circle should be made up of:

A production (operational) workers only

B engineering (design) workers only

C production and engineering workers trained in quality control techniques

D production and engineering workers initially resistant to involvement in quality
control

Circle your answer

A   B   C   D

13 The 'purchasing mix' consists of four elements. Which of the following doesn't belong?

A Promotion
B Quality
C Price
D Delivery

Circle your answer

A   B   C   D

Data for questions 14 - 16

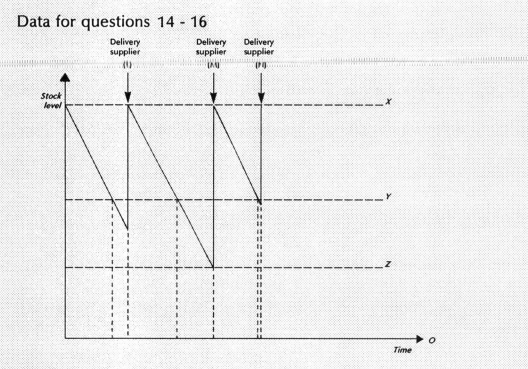

Stock control graph: Rhi Sauces Ltd

Rhi Sauces Ltd operates an efficient stock control system for its durable ingredients, illustrated above. Because of seasonal fluctuations in the market for these ingredients, Rhi purchases from a number of different suppliers over the year. The graph shows deliveries from three different suppliers; L, M and N. Rhi's rate of usage of the ingredients is constant.

14 Optimum re-order level is the stock level determined as the point at which orders should be made so that - allowing for delivery lead times - stock doesn't fall below the 'buffer' or safe minimum level. In the graph above it is represented by:

A X
B Y
C Z
D O

Circle your answer

| A | B | C | D |

15 Which of the following would *not* be a criterion for setting X?

A   Anticipated usage of stock
B   Storage space
C   Suppliers' lead time
D   Rate of deterioration of stock

Circle your answer

A   B   C   D

16 The quickest supplier over the period was:

A   L
B   M
C   N
D   Not identifiable from the graph

Circle your answer

A   B   C   D

17 The R & D department of Pat Pending & Son Ltd have a contract with the Ministry of Agriculture to formulate an anti-bacterial agent that will reduce the risk of listeria in poultry. Their function is:

A   Pure research
B   Applied research
C   Development
D   Method study

Circle your answer

A   B   C   D

18 Which of the following is *not* advisable in the long-term control of R & D?

A   Fix a separate cost and time budget for each research and development project

B   Identify the manager responsible for cost control and progress of each project

C   Suspend funding on projects when costs exceed budget

D   Develop a high cultural tolerance for error

Circle your answer

A   B   C   D

19 Which of the following design decisions would place the most explicit constraint on the design function's 'imagination'?

A Changing the front grill on the BMW
B Choosing materials for a sofa
C Developing the 'cheapest ever' hi-fi midi system
D Designing an 'easier to use' video recorder

Circle your answer

A   B   C   D

20 "The application of techniques designed to establish the time for a qualified worker to carry out a specified job at a specified level of performance" (British Standard 3138) is:

A work study
B method study
C job evaluation
D work measurement

Circle your answer

A   B   C   D

21 In an O & M study, the first set of questions to be applied to the activity under investigation is to do with:

A means (ie how?)
B place (ie where?)
C person (ie who?)
D purpose (ie why?)

Circle your answer

A   B   C   D

22 Rohrmatt Aerials Ltd reckons it currently has a standard manufacturing cost per aerial of £2.49. Within an acceptable tolerance of ±10p, it aims to ensure that costs do not exceed £2.49. Which of the following terms describe such a programme?

Terms

1. Cost control
2. Cost reduction
3. Value analysis
4. Budgetary control

A Term 1 only
B Terms 1 and 3 only
C Terms 2 and 3 only
D Terms 1 and 4 only

Circle your answer

A   B   C   D

23 Which of the following considerations is *not* characteristic of value analysis?

A How can we achieve the lowest production costs for the given product design?

B What is the function of each component
of the product?

C Can weight or embellishment be removed
without reducing the product's
attractions?

Circle your answer

D Can fewer or cheaper components be used
without loss of desirability?

| A | B | C | D |

24 What kind of 'value' is defined as a product's or service's worth on the market?

A Cost value
B Exchange value
C Use value
D Esteem value

Circle your answer

| A | B | C | D |

CHAPTER 4

AUTHORITY, RESPONSIBILITY AND DELEGATION

This chapter covers the following topics:

- Authority and responsibility
- Delegation
- Decision-making

1. Authority and responsibility

1.1 Authority and responsibility provide the basis for formal organisation structures, and the way in which they function. They define the relationships between people in the organisation.

1.2 *Authority* refers to the scope and amount of discretion given to a person to act and make decisions.

Responsibility refers to the liability of a person to be called to account for his actions and decisions.

With responsibility, we must associate *accountability*, the liability of a person to answer for his use of the authority delegated to him.

1.3 The inter-relationship of these elements is important, in the interests of performance and control.

Authority and responsibility should be balanced in the formal system so that:

(a) managers cannot exercise authority in a capricious way, feeling that they will not be held responsible; and

(b) managers are not held accountable for aspects of performance over which they have no control.

1.4 Authority may not be clear-cut in practice, however.

(a) There may be doubts about its *scope* (ie whether it is specific or general) or about its boundaries. Classical theorists such as Fayol argued that the chain of command must be clearly specified in terms of who holds what authority and who is accountable to whom and for what, according to a principle of *unity of command*. This principle is not accepted, however, by supporters of matrix management, inter-disciplinary teamwork etc.

(b) Authority is *subjective*. The way in which it is exercised will differ according to the environment, relationships and type of subordinates.

(c) Authority comes from different *sources* - not always conferred by the organisation or within the organisation's control. Formal 'legal', 'positional' or 'top-down' authority is conferred on a manager. But a 'leader' may acquire authority from his followers. In this context, *'power'* and *'influence'* are brought into play: they may reside in a number of personal and 'political' factors.

(d) Organisational *'politics'* is a range of behaviour broadly concerned with competition, conflict and power relationships. There are inevitable disparities of power and influence in hierarchical organisations, and political behaviour is aimed at resisting and enforcing authority, building and enhancing power bases. Cliques, alliances, pressure groups and blocking groups may be centred around values and objectives which are not reconcilable with those of the organisation.

2. Delegation

2.1 *Delegation of authority* occurs in an organisation where a superior gives a subordinate discretion to take actions or make decisions that are within the superior's own authority.

2.2 It is generally recognised that in most organisations management must delegate some authority, because increasing size and complexity calls for specialisation (both management and technical), and because there are physical and mental limitations to the work load of any individual or group in authority.

2.3 Again, however, it is not that simple.

(a) By delegating authority to perform some of his tasks to his subordinates, the superior takes on extra tasks of co-ordination and control.

(b) The superior delegates authority, but not *responsibility* for outcomes. The subordinate is responsible and accountable to the superior, but the superior is still responsible to his own bosses. There is therefore a managerial dilemma: the need to delegate and 'let go', and the need for control.

(c) Many superiors fear to delegate because it seems to represent the relinquishing of control, the divorce of the manager from 'real work', 'redundancy', or 'shirking responsibility'.

2.4 The culture and politics of the organisation, as well as the personality, training and experience of individual managers, will help to determine the extent to which authority is delegated in the organisation - as well as structural features such as span of control, job definition, geographical decentralisation etc.

You should be aware of the complexity of the superior-subordinate relationship as you revise issues such as 'decentralisation of authority', 'leadership' and 'co-ordination'.

3. Decision-making

3.1 Decision-making is in a sense the basic unit of all management functions. The delegation of authority is about: 'who makes the decisions about x?' The earlier management authors (eg Fayol) highlighted decision-making as one of the key differences between management and workers. Management are expected to take such decisions as necessary which fall within the scope of their authority.

3.2 There are many ways of categorising decisions, according to the type of problem that needs to be resolved, its complexity and seriousness, its time scale etc.

3.3 There are also different ways of looking at decision-making itself, and the main area of discussion is the extent to which decisions are:

● scientific, quantitative, and programmable, requiring, in the main, only information as opposed to
● qualitative, discretionary and non-programmable, requiring judgement.

In real life situations, both types of decision are used, often in unison. Decisions are made as scientifically as possible given the availability of information, but individual judgement and 'hunch' will be a major ingredient of many decisions, particularly where 'qualitative' influences such as risk and human behaviour and attitudes intervene.

The decision sequence

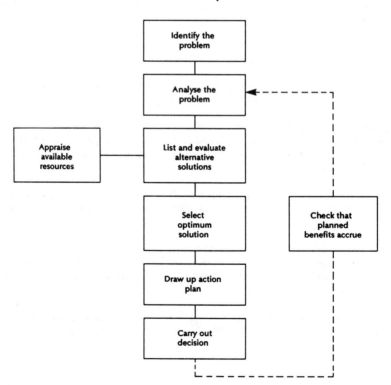

QUESTIONS

1 In which of the following organisations will leadership most likely be based on authority of a 'rational-legal' variety?

A   A trade union
B   A scientific research team
C   A local government department
D   An old-established family firm

Circle your answer

A   B   C   D

2 The 'right' to perform an action in an organisation is:

A   responsibility
B   authority
C   influence
D   power

Circle your answer

A   B   C   D

Data for questions 3 - 5

Warnaby-Bosse is a firm making chocolate bars. Mr Warnaby-Bosse himself is the founder of the firm, an almost mythical entrepreneurial figure; the staff swap stories of his canny deals and amazing generosity. Day-to-day running of the firm is in the hands of the Manager, who is responsible for operations, and also for deciding pay policy. One of the most important staff functions in the organisation is accounts, though the Chief Accountant is on the verge of being asked to take early retirement because the departmental heads never seem to get sensible information out of him. The Personnel Manager on the other hand, is acknowledged to be extremely competent: 'What a pity she's wasted in the Gibberish Department', seems to be the consensus.

Recently, one of the production mixers has been made redundant by the Manager. Fellow shop-floor staff are outraged: he was 'the only one who knew anything about chocolate' and they had relied on his judgement for years. Protests made to the Manager are ignored. A week later, cement is found in a batch of crunchy bars. Two weeks later, there is an over-time ban. Three weeks later, the mixer is reinstated.

3   Who in the scenario above has 'expert power'?

A   The Personnel Manager only
B   The mixer only
C   The Personnel Manager and the mixer
D   The Personnel Manager, the Chief
    Accountant and the mixer

Circle your answer

A   B   C   D

4   Which type of power is *not* illustrated in the scenario?

A   Resource power
B   Charismatic power
C   Negative power
D   Physical power

Circle your answer

A   B   C   D

5   Which type of power do the shop-floor workers and the Manager *both* exercise?

A   Negative power
B   Position power
C   Resource power
D   Expert power

Circle your answer

A   B   C   D

6   Which of the following forms of organisational politics will be detrimental to the organisation?

Form
1.   Dissent and challenge to authority
2.   Internal competition
3.   Withholding and distortion of information

A   Form 3 only
B   Forms 1 and 3 only
C   Forms 2 and 3 only
D   Forms 1, 2 and 3

Circle your answer

A   B   C   D

7 What is 'delegated' by a superior to a subordinate?

A Authority
B Power
C Responsibility
D Accountability

Circle your answer

| A | B | C | D |

8 Which of the following is *not* a feature of effective delegation?

A Specifying performance levels and results expected of the subordinate

B Obtaining the consent of the subordinate to the task and expected results

C Ensuring that the subordinate's decisions are confirmed (or ratified) by the superior

D Ensuring that the subordinate reports the results of his decisions to the superior

Circle your answer

| A | B | C | D |

9 Izzy Abel is manager of the accounts department. In which of the following situations would it be ill-advised of him to delegate decision-making to his subordinates?

Situation
1. Disciplinary action to be taken against a colleague.
2. Choice of a new word-processing package, where the subordinates are skilled WP operators.
3. Choice of a new word-processing package, where the subordinates are new trainees.
4. Determination of the nature and date of the office outing.

A Situation 1 only
B Situation 3 only
C Situations 1 and 3 only
D Situations 3 and 4 only

Circle your answer

| A | B | C | D |

10 Which of the following circumstances might contribute to a manager's reluctance to delegate?

Circumstance
1. His subordinates are obviously capable of doing any aspect of his job.
2. His subordinates are obviously not capable of doing any aspect of his job.
3. The organisation motto is: 'If you want it done well, do it yourself.'
4. The organisation motto is: 'The job of management is to manage'.

A   Circumstance 2 only
B   Circumstances 2 and 3 only
C   Circumstances 2, 3 and 4 only
D   Circumstances 1, 2 and 3 only

Circle your answer

A   B   C   D

---

11 The principle whereby a manager is only informed when results do not accord with plans, and some decision or corrective action (outside his subordinate's authority) is required is called:

A   reaction decisions theory
B   management by exception
C   management by objectives
D   programmed decision making

Circle your answer

A   B   C   D

---

12 The exercise of a high degree of 'discretion' is commonly associated with:

A   programmed decisions
B   non-programmed decisions
C   quantitative decisions
D   scientific decisions

Circle your answer

A   B   C   D

---

13 Ivor Hunsch is a manager for Egon & Dunnett Ltd. He is an intuitive - even impulsive - decision maker. He identifies a problem in his administrative function. Management reports are late, inaccurate and not flexible enough in their format and application. Ivor studies the existing system. The answer is clearly computerisation. He draws up alternative system specifications and a list of suppliers, compiles a buying checklist and has a computerised, Management Information System (MIS) up and running in no time. Unfortunately, shortly afterwards several of his clerical workers have resigned. He is way over budget on expenditure. Management reports are not noticeably improved, because the staff aren't quite 'on top of' the new computer system yet.

One day, a colleague mentions 'computer bureaux'. Ivor pales. 'I knew I'd forgotten something,' he says.

The critical stage of the decision sequence Ivor missed out was:

A Identify the problem
B Analyse the problem
C Appraise available resources
D Evaluate alternative solutions

Circle your answer

A   B   C   D

14 Which of the following is *not* a feature of the Japanese approach to decision-making?

A Focusing first on defining the question, rather than giving the answer

B Focusing on alternatives rather than the 'right' answer

C Encouraging dissenting opinion and argument

D Decisions taken swiftly and 'sold' to the people who will act on them

Circle your answer

A   B   C   D

15 'Bounded rationality' means that:

A managers have to make rational decisions within the limitations of what information is available, digestable and understandable

B Managers have to make rational decisions based on complete and accurate information on all viable alternatives

C Decisions are 'made' for managers, determined by rational planning and policy-making

D Managers can only make decisions where they have authority to do so.

Circle your answer

A   B   C   D

CHAPTER 5

COMMUNICATION AND CO-ORDINATION

This chapter covers the following topics:

- The role of communication
- Communication processes
- Co-ordination and conflict

1. The role of communication

1.1 The most basic definition of communication is the transmission or exchange of information. It is a universal human activity, which may be directed at:

(a) initiating action - eg by request, instruction or persuasion;
(b) making known needs and requirements;
(c) exchanging information, ideas, attitudes and beliefs;
(d) establishing understanding - and perhaps also exerting influence or persuasion;
(e) establishing and maintaining relationships.

1.2 Communication therefore embraces a wide spectrum of activities in organisations, both in the way the organisation as an entity communicates or 'projects itself' to people who come into contact with it, and in the way that individuals within and around the organisation communicate with each other.

1.3 Among the more important roles of communication in an organisation are:

- providing information for *planning, co-ordination and control* activities of management. Managers need to be aware of what their departments *should* be achieving, and what they are and are not achieving. Information in organisations should initiate or support a decision or action

- encouraging the formulation, swapping and testing of *ideas*. Communication - in forms such as quality circles or brainstorming sessions - can contribute to innovation and the flexibility of the organisation in the face of change

- *co-ordination* of the activities of all the interdependent sub-systems of the organisation, so that the overall objectives of the organisation are met. This will also be important in the control of conflict. Co-ordinatory mechanisms such as committees and project teams depend on communication (see 3 below)

- fulfilling the needs of *employees* for information about their task, the standards expected of them, how their performance measures up to standard etc. Information is important for learning and development, because 'feedback' is necessary for the change or correction of behaviour. It has also been claimed to have benefits for employee job satisfaction and motivation: without performance information, the employee may be working without understanding or sense of purpose, without commitment and without the satisfaction of feeling that he is contributing to the achievements of the organisation.

1.4 According to a UK survey in 1986 by Vista Communications, however, few companies make any systematic efforts to find out the views of their own workers on the quality of communications within the firm. Most claimed that communications in the firm were good or very good, but based their appraisal only on feedback through line management. According to Vista, "that is like asking the salesman what he thinks of the product he is selling, rather than asking the consumer".

1.5 Systematic efforts can and should be made to:

- educate employees in the processes and techniques of communication
- help employees identify and overcome barriers to communication
- encourage communication through organisational structure, procedures, systems and culture, and
- evaluate the effectiveness of communication (including its *perceived* value to employees).

2. Communication processes

2.1 In order to communicate or manage communications effectively, you must understand how communication works and why it sometimes doesn't.

2.2 *The communication process*

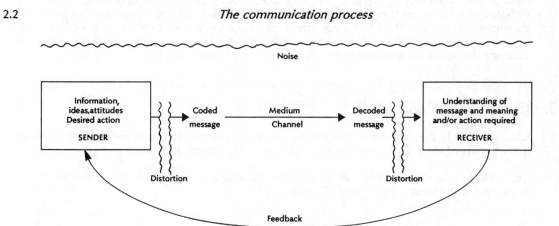

2.3 As illustrated in the above diagram, communication is a *two-way* process, rather than a simple send-receive relationship, because of *feedback*, an important and often neglected aspect of the process which indicates to the sender whether or not his message has been successfully received, understood and interpreted. Failure to seek or offer feedback, or ignoring feedback offered, is one of the most common problems in communication.

2.4 Barriers to, or breakdowns in, communication may be caused by:

'Technical' problems in the process itself	*Problems in the context of communication at work*
• Failure to communicate • Communicating too much (ie 'over load') • Sending the 'wrong' message (eg one that is irrelevant or meaningless) • Encoding or decoding the message wrongly (so that misunderstanding occurs) • Choosing an unsuitable medium or channel of communication • Failure to feed back	• Differences or conflict between objectives and/or individuals • Different 'vocabulary' of different disciplines • Subordinate's fear of transmitting 'bad news' to a superior • Giving more importance to communication from 'above' than from 'below' • Incorrect or incomplete information available within time constraints • Lack of opportunity and encouragement for subordinates to communicate 'upwards'

2.5 It is important to note that communication can be 'horizontal' (between people of the same level in the hierarchy) or 'vertical' in *both directions*. Too often in organisations there are elaborate provisions for downward communication - which is a good thing - but *not* for upward communication, other than in formal grievance procedures. The consequence of this is that downward communication will be made on the basis of possibly patronising and inaccurate assumptions about what subordinates want and need to know, and in what 'language'.

3. Co-ordination and conflict

3.1 Co-ordination is the process of integrating the work of the different individuals, sections and departments of the organisation towards effective achievement of its goals.

Co-ordination is vital so that the *timing* and *direction* of individual and group efforts are integrated in the most efficient and effective way.

3.2   In a working organisation there are many reasons why co-ordination may be difficult to achieve.

- Poor communications, formal and informal
- Inadequate planning and goal integration - lack of standardisation, schedules etc
- Differing timescales of work between departments such as R & D and operations
- Differences in leadership style between groups
- The uneasy balance of authority between 'line' and 'staff'
- Weak organisation structure and physical layout, eg without deliberate co-ordinating mechanisms such as matrix management, project teams, committees, co-ordinating positions etc
- Differences in 'culture' or type of work - eg problems of integrating 'innovation specialists' in a fast-change environment into the mainstream of the organisation
- Differences and conflicts between individuals, groups, disciplines etc.

3.3   Note that co-ordination is intimately linked to both *communication* and *conflict*. Conflict can be both a cause and a symptom of lack of communication and poor co-ordination. Similarly, poor communications can be both a cause and a symptom of conflict and a lack of co-ordination. Even more interestingly, one of the symptoms of conflict in an organisation is the proliferation of rules and norms, arbitration procedures etc - mechanisms for integration and co-ordination *misused* in the interests of empire building, rivalry and 'spoiling'.

3.4   Co-ordination is, essentially, about reconciling differences. This is commonly related to 'controlling conflict'. You should be aware, however, that differences can be expressed in various ways which can be beneficial rather than harmful to the organisation. Handy redefined the term 'conflict' to offer a useful way of thinking about its constructive and destructive effects.

   (a)   Organisations are political systems within which there is inevitable competition for scarce resources and unequal influence. This is the root of conflict.

   (b)   Differences are natural and inevitable, but may emerge as:

   - *argument* - constructive exchange of ideas with the positive intention of reaching agreement

   - *competition* - which can be 'open' and fruitful, or 'closed' (where one person or group can only do well at the expense of another) and harmful, degenerating into conflict; or

   - *conflict*, which if properly managed can be diverted into competition or argument.

QUESTIONS

1 Purely 'social' communication in a business is most likely to be limited in the interests of:

A formality
B employee satisfaction
C cost
D managerial credibility

Circle your answer

A   B   C   D

2 A fault in the communication procedure where the meaning of the message is lost 'in translation' from intention to language or from language to understanding is called:

A noise
B redundancy
C distortion
D feedback

Circle your answer

A   B   C   D

3 Egon Krezy, at the Paris office, needs to get an important message to his boss, who is in the London office for the day. He telephones. Only to find that refurbishment is in progress in the London office, and his boss can't hear him clearly over the hammering and drilling. Giving up, Egon sends a fax instead - but five minutes later gets a return fax saying: 'Can't read your handwriting. Please phone.' Egon phones his boss, who has found a quiet office somewhere. By this time Egon is exasperated, and soothes his nerves by telling his boss about it. He then relays the message.

Which types of 'noise' has Egon fallen foul of?

A Physical noise and psychological noise only

B Technical noise and psychological noise only

C Technical noise, physical noise and social noise only

D Physical noise, technical noise and psychological noise only

Circle your answer

A   B   C   D

4   Which of the following is most unequivocally an advantage of written (as opposed to oral) communication?

A   Concreteness and permanence
B   Opportunity for feedback
C   Susceptibility to duplication
D   Clarity of expression

Circle your answer

A   B   C   D

5   "Dimm", said the manager, "you've been scratching your head and frowning ever since I started the briefing half an hour ago. Have you got fleas or something?"

The communication problem suggested by this speech is *not:*

A   Dimm's failure to give feedback
B   the manager's failure to look for feedback
C   the manager's failure to interpret feedback
D   distortion of the manager's message

Circle your answer

A   B   C   D

6   Which of the following statements is/are true?

Statement
1.   The formal pattern of communication in an organisation is always supported by an informal one.
2.   The grapevine is active when the formal communication network is active.
3.   Staff executives tend to be more 'in the know' than line managers.
4.   Informal communication is harmful for the organisation.

A   Statements 1 and 3 only
B   Statements 2 and 4 only
C   Statements 1, 3 and 4 only
D   Statements 1, 2 and 3 only

Circle your answer

A   B   C   D

7   In a work group of five people at Pow Wow Ltd, a communication 'network' was observed to be operating. The group had a distinct leader, with other members taking on peripheral roles; members communicated with each other only through the leader. This communication pattern is called:

A   The circle
B   The 'Y'
C   The wheel
D   The all-channel

Circle your answer

A   B   C   D

8 The all-channel system of communication clearly achieves better results than other network formations in terms of:

A speed of problem solving
B quality of solutions to complex problems
C tolerance of pressure
D job satisfaction

Circle your answer

A   B   C   D

9 If a supervisor in the Sales department requests the help of the Personnel Director in a complex disciplinary matter, communication flow is said to be:

A Vertical
B Horizontal
C Lateral
D Diagonal

Circle your answer

A   B   C   D

10 If a task-force team required to look into a particular short-term problem were set up as a committee, what type of committee would it be?

A An ad hoc committee
B An executive committee
C A standing committee
D A joint committee

Circle your answer

A   B   C   D

11 Which of the following may not ultimately be an advantage of committees?

A Representation of different viewpoints
B Collective responsibility for decisions
C Combining activities
D Encouraging communication

Circle your answer

A   B   C   D

12 Problem-solving sessions involving 6-12 people who produce spontaneous 'freewheeling' ideas to solve a particular problem are:

A Networking
B T - groups
C Ad hoc committees
D Brainstorming

Circle your answer

A   B   C   D

13 Which of the following communication methods is designed to encourage upward communication?

A   House journal
B   Organisation manual
C   Team meetings
D   Team briefings

Circle your answer

A   B   C   D

14 Which of the following might inhibit upward communication?

Factor
1.   Organisational politics
2.   Class perceptions
3.   Employee aspirations
4.   Lack of trust

A   Factors 1 and 4 only
B   Factors 2, 3 and 4 only
C   Factors 1, 2 and 4 only
D   Factors 1, 2, 3 and 4

Circle your answer

A   B   C   D

Data for questions 15 - 16

Trubb, Latt, Tamil & Sons are having some problems with co-ordination. The project group which has researched, planned and designed the new computer system has just, finally, tried to introduce it into operational working in the production department. The operational department is not impressed. 'Never mind long-term benefits', they've been heard to say. 'What about tomorrow's productivity bonus? We're not wasting our time listening to *that* lot.' The following barriers to co-ordination have been identified by management.

Barrier
1.   Poor communication
2.   Different objectives
3.   Different timescales
4.   Confusion of authority

15 Which of these problems is most likely to be a fault of management, rather than a factor inherent in this type of situation?

A   Barrier 1
B   Barrier 2
C   Barrier 3
D   Barrier 4

Circle your answer

A   B   C   D

16 Which should and could have been attended to first?

A   Barrier 1
B   Barrier 2
C   Barrier 3
D   Barrier 4

Circle your answer

A   B   C   D

17 Which of the following is a positive indication of integration?

A   Proliferation of committees
B   Managerial adoption of purely consultative
    roles
C   Appeals to rules and arbitration
D   The existence of quality circles

Circle your answer

A   B   C   D

18 Productivity bargaining may be cited as an example of:

A   'zero-sum' competition
B   closed competition
C   open competition
D   conflict

Circle your answer

A   B   C   D

19 Which of the following 'teams' would not be considered a co-ordinating mechanism in the organisational structure?

A   A production committee
B   A project team
C   A corporate planning team
D   An autonomous work group

Circle your answer

A   B   C   D

20 Which of the following methods of improving co-ordination would you expect to be *least* effective?

A Delegating responsibility for co-ordination to the 'cross-over' point where different departments report to the same manager

B Preparing a formal budget which integrates the sub-goals of managers with each other, and with overall objectives

C Appointing liaison officers, eg progress chasers or product managers

D Encouraging informal exchange of information between managers of different departments

Circle your answer

A   B   C   D

21 Three of the following are 'environmental' or 'ecological' strategies for managing conflict. One is a 'regulation' strategy; which is it?

A Provision of arbitration to settle disputes

B Agreement of common objectives

C Reinforcing the 'team' nature of organisational life

D Sorting out territorial/role conflicts in the organisation structure

Circle your answer

A   B   C   D

22 The view that organisations are political coalitions of individuals and groups which have their own interests, requiring a mutual survival strategy involving the control of conflict through compromise, is called the:

A unitary ideology
B pluralist ideology
C radical ideology
D conflict view

Circle your answer

A   B   C   D

23 The Spa Narinder Works (bottlers of Indian mineral water) has some problems.

Problem

1. Team leaders withhold information from each other, or actively distort it, hoping that the other teams' performance will be impaired.

2. Two team-leaders have been heard shouting at each other: 'I've always hated the way you run your section!' 'Oh, *now* it come's out in the open!' etc.

3. Line managers refuse to accept the recommendations of staff experts.

4. The accounts department keeps imposing new procedures and requirements on operational departments.

Which of these symptoms of conflict will cause the Works Manager least worry?

A   Problem 1
B   Problem 2
C   Problem 3
D   Problem 4

Circle your answer

| A | B | C | D |

24 Other than integration/collaboration, the only managerial response to conflict which addresses the root cause of the conflict, rather than leaving it unchanged, is:

A   Denial/withdrawal
B   Suppression
C   Compromise
D   Dominance

Circle your answer

| A | B | C | D |

CHAPTER 6

PLANNING AND CONTROL

This chapter covers the following topics:

- Planning
- Objective setting and corporate planning
- Control

1. Planning

1.1 Planning is a decision-making process (see chapter 4). It is one of the most important management functions, being connected with:

- formulation of objectives for the organisation and its sub-units
- specification of means to attain those objectives, and
- monitoring results and providing feedback for further planning (which is where planning and controls are closely linked).

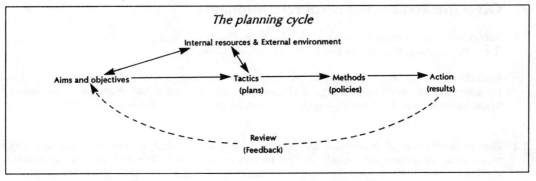

The planning cycle

Internal resources & External environment

Aims and objectives —— Tactics —— Methods —— Action
(plans) (policies) (results)

Review
(Feedback)

1.2 You should be able to see how closely planning and control are linked.

- Planning is the process of deciding what should be done, how, when and by whom

- Control is the process of checking whether plans are being achieved and, if not, planning corrective action or adjusting original plans

1.3 It should be clear that planning is an all-embracing activity of the organisation, from determination of its overall 'direction' ('what business are we in?'), right down to the nitty gritty of how in detail it fulfils its day-to-day operational tasks.

An organisation does not just have one plan to 'cover' all its activity, and one of the most important features of planning is its *hierarchical* nature. Plans vary from broad, long-term strategies, to medium-term tactics and policies, to short-term operational budgets and schedules.

1.4 Planning at different levels of management takes different forms and may take the form of:

- objectives   end goals to which activities should be aimed
- strategies   the 'means' to the organisation's ends: what to do and what resources to allocate etc
- policies   guidelines for decision-making
- procedures   sequences of actions prescribed for certain tasks
- rules   specific courses of action prescribed for a given situation
- programmes   co-ordinated groups of plans directed at particular objectives
- budgets   formal statements of expected results set out in numerical terms

1.5 The other important thing about planning is that it is concerned with the future, and therefore with uncertainty and risk. Planning involves making choices about what to do and how to do it: it is aimed at reducing uncertainty by providing guidelines for routine action and provision for the unexpected. However, forecasts and premises used in the planning process are not 'watertight', and unforeseen events are bound to occur. A compromise will need to be reached between the need for *flexibility*, (offered by short-term planning) and the need for *commitment* to plans once made (over the long-term if required).

2. Objective setting and corporate planning

2.1 'Objectives are needed in every area where performance and results directly and vitally affect the survival and prosperity of the business.' (*Peter Drucker*)

Objectives are the starting point of the corporate planning process. They are also fundamental to any kind of decision-making, and may be set for individual managers throughout the organisation hierarchy through a system of 'management by objectives', or MbO.

2.2 The *co-ordination* of individual and group objectives is vital to the organisation. Different managers, disciplines and levels in the hierarchy will have different visions, timescales and methods, and their efforts are not automatically directed towards a common goal. MbO attempts to solve this problem by a comprehensive approach to setting co-ordinated objectives, targets and plans for all levels of the organisation. Individual managers are often involved in the setting of their personal objectives, in order to secure greater commitment to their achievement, but a measure of control will be required in order to 'interlock' different objectives within the longer-term corporate plans.

2.3 A profit-making organisation might have many different objectives, to do with market standing, innovation, productivity, profitability etc. Although the *prime*, overall objective is best expressed *financially* as a quantified target, eg for return on capital employed (ROCE), or earnings per share (EPS), it should be said that organisations also have social and ethical obligations and objectives, to do with consumer safety, employee development, environmental protection etc.

'Not-for-profit' organisations have a non-financial main objective, with finance as a constraining factor or subsidiary objective (eg not to spend more than they receive).

2.4   *'Corporate planning* is a comprehensive, future-oriented, continuous process of management which is implemented within a formal framework.

● It is responsive to relevant changes in the external environment
● It is concerned with both strategic and operational planning and through the participation of relevant members of the organisation, develops plans and actions at the appropriate levels in the organisation
● It incorporates monitoring and control mechanisms and is concerned with both the short and the long term.'   *Argenti*

2.5   One variation of the simple planning cycle (1.1) to show the corporate planning process would be:

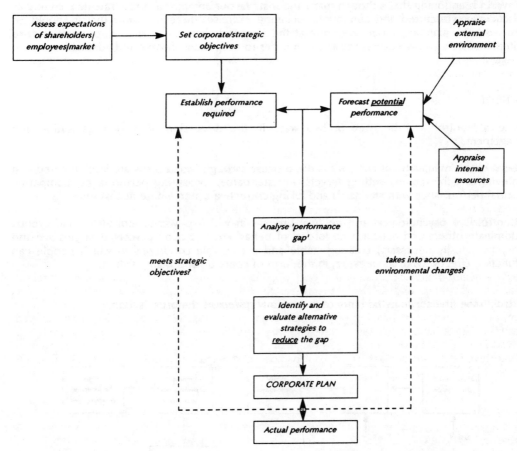

2.6 Appraisal of the internal potential and external environment of the organisation is important for the strategy identification and evaluation stages of the process. It is often known as SWOT analysis.

Internal	Strengths (Strategy: to exploit)	Weaknesses (Strategy: to minimise or eliminate)
External	Threats (Strategy: to counter and protect against)	Opportunities (strategy: to exploit)

2.7 It is worth mentioning that although many theorists favour an approach to strategic planning as a disciplined, structured and continuous planning exercise, there is a view that it should be more 'ad hoc'; planning should be done at the *corporate* level only when opportunities arise for implementing a new business strategy, in order to keep plans flexible and adaptable.

3. Control

3.1 The term 'control' can be used in two ways in the discussion of work organisation and management.

- Control (or 'management control') is the process through which plans are implemented and objectives achieved, by setting targets and standards, measuring performance, comparing actual performance with standards and taking corrective action where necessary.

- Control is a psychological and political process in which powerful individuals and groups dominate others and establish an 'order' of behaviour. It can be perceived as *positive* and psychologically necessary, creating stable and predictable conditions in which people can function effectively, or as *negative*, in the form of coercion and manipulation.

3.2 Control in the first sense is the basis of the *control system* of the organisation.

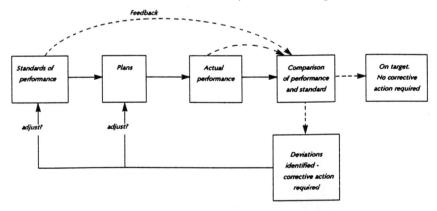

3.3 Control in the second sense involves strategies for the application of power and influence. Control can thus be effected through:

- organisation structure - constraining behaviour by job description
- recruitment and training - employing people who 'fit', and encouraging conformity to technical and cultural standards and methods
- reward and punishment - conditioning behaviour through positive or negative reinforcement
- policies and rules - constraining behaviour through guidance and prescription
- budgets - directing behaviour towards attainment of targets
- machinery - limiting behaviour to what the machinery requires or allows
- culture - guiding behaviour within a set of values, beliefs and norms.

QUESTIONS

1　Lou Kingerhead is a plant manager. He plans that "employees in Quality Control should be allowed 10 minutes at the end of their shift for clearing up their work bench".

This type of plan is:

A　a programme
B　a policy
C　a procedure
D　a rule

Circle your answer

A　　B　　C　　D

2　If Lou had expressed his plan as: "employees in Quality Control will pass their final job fifteen minutes before the end of their shift, submit their job sheets to the supervisor for signature, clear their work bench, and then sign off shift", this would be called:

A　a programme
B　a policy
C　a procedure
D　a rule

Circle your answer

A　　B　　C　　D

3　A policy is a statement about:

A　ends
B　means
C　conduct
D　results

Circle your answer

A　　B　　C　　D

4　Lee Pinderdark is a manager at Marr Plan Ltd. He hardly ever makes formal plans, preferring to deal with problems as (or if) they arise. The company has issued 'mission statements' and Lee himself has participated in the formulation of the corporate plan, with goals and objectives for each section. Lee has discretion to set operation targets for his unit. The company's Management Information System is effective. Unfortunately, Lee's unit isn't and he often has to deal with problems and complaints. He's good at firefighting - otherwise he would be in real trouble: the organisation always 'comes down hard' on deviation from plan.

The following are common reasons for managerial reluctance to plan. Which is Lee's main problem?

A   Lack of information about the environment

B   Lack of knowledge about organisation goals

C   Fear of failure

D   Resistance to imposition of control from above

Circle your answer

,   A   B   C   D

5   Which of the following is/are among the aims of budgets?

Aims
1.   To compel planning
2.   To communicate plans
3.   To authorise action
4.   To motivate employees

A   Aims 1 and 2 only
B   Aims 2 and 3 only
C   Aims 2 and 4 only
D   Aims 1, 2, 3 and 4

Circle your answer

A   B   C   D

6   Techniques of forecasting which predict changes in market demand, or demand for a company's products, are called:

A   econometric techniques
B   barometric techniques
C   network analysis
D   break-even analysis

Circle your answer

A   B   C   D

Data for questions 7 and 8

Bareham & Mynde Ltd has in its corporate manual the statement: "Management must balance the profit objective with pressures from non-shareholder groups in deciding the strategic targets of the business".

7 This embodies an approach to business objectives called:

A the stakeholder view
B the shareholder view
C the consensus theory
D consumerism

Circle your answer

A   B   C   D

8 In which of the following financial objectives is Bareham & Mynde's philosophy explicitly reflected?

A Growth in dividends to shareholders
B Maximum level of profit
C Maximum return on capital employed (ROCE)
D Satisficing level of profit

Circle your answer

A   B   C   D

9 In which of the following circumstances would a 'freewheeling opportunism' approach to corporate planning *not* be advantageous?

A A competitor unexpectedly drops out of the market

B There is a sudden steep rise in the price of a key commodity

C The organisation wants to create an intra-preneurial, innovative culture

D The organisation is a large conglomerate growing swiftly by acquisition

Circle your answer

A   B   C   D

Data for questions 10 - 12

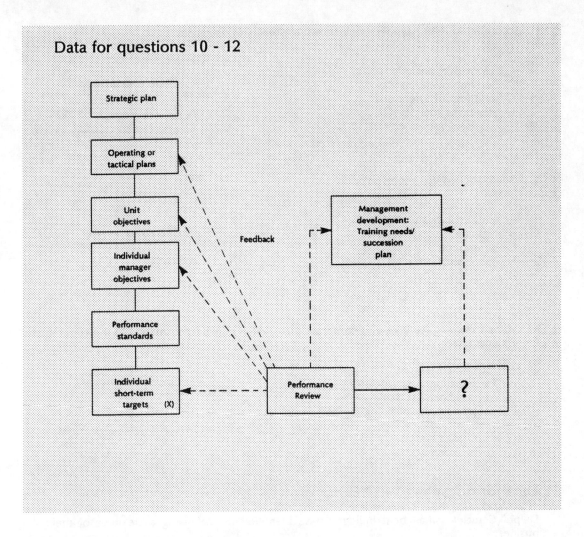

10 The diagram above, in its entirety, depicts a system of:

A   Corporate planning
B   Manpower planning
C   Management by objectives
D   SWOT analysis

Circle your answer

| A | B | C | D |

11 According to John Humble's well-known approach, (X) is called:

A key results analysis
B job improvement plan
C unit improvement plan
D key tasks analysis

Circle your answer

A   B   C   D

12 The unlabelled box represents:

A potential review
B training
C promotion
D job evaluation

Circle your answer

A   B   C   D

13 Of the following features of a corporate plan, which may be detrimental to the commitment of managers?

A Quantified targets
B Participation in target-setting
C Reward linked to achievement
D Long corporate planning periods

Circle your answer

A   B   C   D

Data for questions 14 - 16

Delphi Coracles (small boat builders) have identified the following as features of their business.

Features
1. The yard has just been refitted with more space and new machinery.
2. The area is being redeveloped as a coastal holiday resort.
3. The founder and senior executive, the charismatic Mr Delphi, is approaching retirement, with no obvious successor.

14 Feature 1 is:

A a strength
B a weakness
C an opportunity
D a threat

Circle your answer

A   B   C   D

15 Feature 2 is:

A   a strength
B   a weakness
C   an opportunity
D   a threat

Circle your answer

| A | B | C | D |

16 Feature 3 is:

A   a strength
B   a weakness
C   an opportunity
D   a threat

Circle your answer

| A | B | C | D |

17

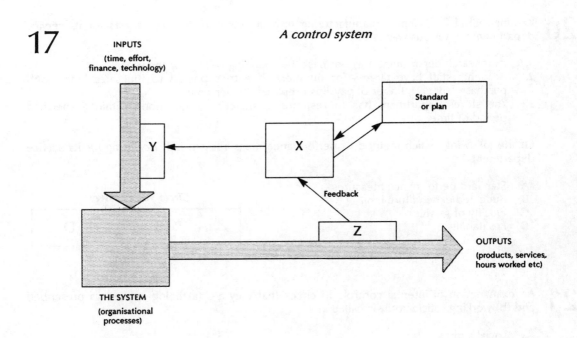

A control system

INPUTS
(time, effort,
finance, technology)

Standard
or plan

Y

X

Feedback

Z

OUTPUTS
(products, services,
hours worked etc)

THE SYSTEM
(organisational
processes)

The element marked X is the:

A   Effector
B   Activator
C   Sensor
D   Comparator

Circle your answer

| A | B | C | D |

18 Feedback which results in control action which causes actual results to maintain or increase their path of deviation from planned results is:

A positive feedback
B negative feedback
C feedforward control
D double-loop feedback

Circle your answer

| A | B | C | D |

19 Feedforward control compares planned results with:

A historical results
B actual results
C anticipated results
D ideal results

Circle your answer

| A | B | C | D |

20 Kaminen Glüd is a Finnish manufacturing firm. It sets performance targets for its service departments in various ways.

1. Its research department may not pass the spending ceiling for the year.
2. Accounts staff have targets for numbers of entries posted to the sales ledger and purchase ledger, number of payslips prepared etc per hour.
3. The stores department has to respond to materials requisitions within a specified period of time.

Of the following, which method of performance measurement is it *not* using for its service departments?

A Standard performance measures
B Budgeted expenditure limit
C Quality of service
D Profitability

Circle your answer

| A | B | C | D |

21 An examination of internal controls to check that they are (a) being applied as prescribed and (b) working satisfactorily is called a:

A social audit
B VFM audit
C systems audit
D efficiency audit

Circle your answer

| A | B | C | D |

22 Of the following, 'social control' is *not* directly operated through:

A   reference groups
B   work groups
C   organisational culture
D   rules and regulations

Circle your answer

A   B   C   D

23 Which of the following is an example of 'insidious' control?

A   Rules and regulations
B   Selective recruitment
C   Incentives
D   Machine pacing

Circle your answer

A   B   C   D

CHAPTER 7

MOTIVATION AND DISCIPLINE

This chapter covers the following topics:

- Motivation
- Job satisfaction
- Pay
- Discipline

1. Motivation

1.1 'Motivation' is a term used in different contexts to refer to:

- goals or outcomes that have become desirable for a particular individual, as in: 'he is motivated by money'
- the mental process of choosing a goal and deciding whether and how to achieve it, as in: 'he is motivated to work harder'
- the social process by which the behaviour of an individual is influenced by others, as in: 'the manager motivates his team'.

1.2 The social process of motivation is a function of management which has, since the Human Relations approach to management became current, taken the place of the classical function, 'commanding'. In other words, it is the process by which managers get things done through other people, and is close to 'leadership' in that sense.

1.3 Different approaches to motivation theory, however, concentrate on either the first or the second of the contexts listed above.

(a) *'Content'* theories of motivation focus on the 'package' of needs that individuals bring to the work situation and which dictate the goals of their behaviour - the satisfaction of those needs.

(b) *'Process'* theories of motivation focus on the calculation - conscious or unconscious - which each individual makes in order to determine on a cause of action or mode of behaviour. Such theories take a 'contingency' approach, by stressing the number of variables that influence the individual's decision in each case: there is no 'one best way' to motivate people.

1.4 Two influential content theories are those of:

- *Abraham Maslow*, who determined seven innate needs of all individuals, arranged them in a hierarchy, and suggested that an individual will be motivated to satisfy each category of needs, starting at the 'bottom', before going on to seek 'higher order' satisfaction.

Maslow's 'hierarchy of needs'

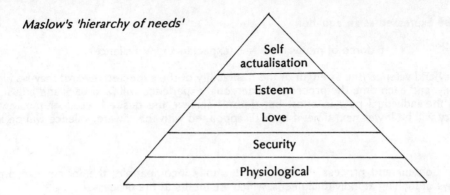

- *Frederick Herzberg*, who determined two basic need systems: the need to avoid unpleasantness and the need for personal growth. He identified factors which cause dissatisfaction at work - 'hygiene' factors - and suggested that these could be controlled to satisfy the first type of need. He also identified factors which cause satisfaction at work - motivator factors - and suggested that these alone satisfy the second type of need, and can positively motivate performance.

1.5 Process theories are generally variations on the *expectancy* model. If the motivation process is working as it were 'at full strength', it would look something like this.

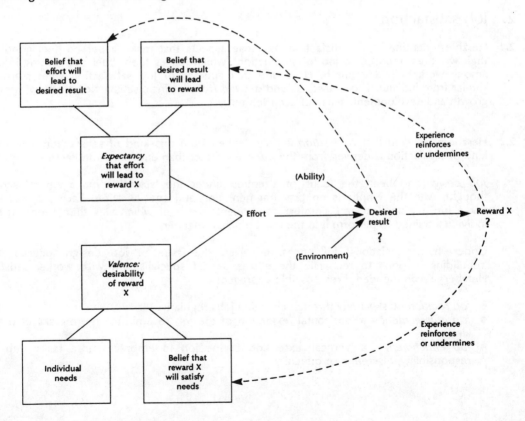

This can be expressed as an equation:

$$F \text{ (force of motivation)} = E \text{ (expectancy)} \times V \text{ (valence)}$$

Expectancy and valence (the strength of the desirability of the expected reward) may be high or low initially, and each time the process is undergone, experience will feed back and adjust their values. If the individual puts in effort but doesn't achieve the desired result or the rewards, expectancy will be lower next time: if he is disappointed with the reward, valence will be lower etc.

1.6 Note that content and process theories aren't wholly incompatible: the former can provide useful ways of looking at individual needs, which are inputs to the process.

1.7 The expectancy model neatly sidesteps the problem, faced by content theories, of the relative importance of

● intrinsic satisfactions and rewards - ie valued outcomes which are within the 'control' and perception of the individual himself. These are often referred to as *job satisfaction:* and

● extrinsic satisfactions and rewards - ie valued outcomes which are at the disposal of others, tangible rewards such as pay.

2. Job satisfaction

2.1 Herzberg identified 'job satisfaction' as those aspects that make a person 'feel good' about their work (as opposed to job 'dissatisfaction', which makes them 'feel bad'), using interviews among workers in Pittsburgh. He found that sources of job satisfaction were substantially similar from individual to individual, and derived from intrinsic satisfaction to do with personal growth and development, sense of achievement etc.

2.2 Herzberg believed that *motivation* is only derived from this kind of satisfaction, and that this kind of satisfaction is derived from the *job* itself, rather than environmental factors.

Job design had been the focus of attention under the 'scientific management' school of thought, with the emphasis on task fragmentation and specialisation. Each job was broken down into its smallest and simplest components, each of which was then allocated to one individual trained to perform it in the most efficient manner.

Under 'human relations' influences, however, the issue of job design focused on the 'rebuilding' of jobs to reconcile the efficiencies of specialisation with worker satisfaction. Herzberg recommended three possible approaches:

● *job rotation* - task variety through changing jobs regularly
● *job enlargement* - a 'horizontal' extention of the job to embrace more tasks of the same kind
● *job enrichment* - a 'vertical' extension of the job to embrace more tasks with added responsibility, discretion or difficulty

2.3 Following Herzberg, approaches to job satisfaction have concentrated on 'higher order' needs - for participation in decision-making, involvement in quality control, 'whole' jobs given to self-regulatory work teams (sometimes called 'composite autonomous group working'). However, this does not absolve management from attending to sources of *dis*satisfaction: work environment and conditions, style of leadership etc.

2.4 It is worth noting, too, that although 'satisfaction' theories of motivation state that 'happy bees make more honey', this is not the only view: no link between job satisfaction and motivation has been conclusively proven. Attendance, loyalty and goodwill may be increased, but this does not necessarily convert to more effective effort.

3. Pay

3.1 Pay has a central - but ambiguous - role in motivation theory.

- It is not explicitly included in any 'need' list - but is perceived as being potentially *instrumental* in satisfying all other needs. It is the prime means to many ends.

- It is only a 'hygiene' factor in Herzberg's theory - but the most important of them

3.2 An 'instrumental orientation' to work - ie working for pay and the satisfactions that pay enables the individual to obtain - undoubtedly co-exists with 'higher order' needs and expectations. The employee needs money to live. However, there is a trade-off between the *perceived value of money*, and the *deprivations* (eg long or antisocial hours, dangerous or unpleasant conditions) that the individual is prepared to accept.

3.3 The model of the worker as 'economic man' (Schein) who will adjust his effort for monetary incentive is therefore naive. Nevertheless, it remains the basis of *incentive* systems such as bonuses, profit-sharing, payment by results etc.

Equity (perceived fairness of pay in relation to the job and to the pay of others) is often more important than maximising income, once the individual has 'enough' pay to maintain a satisfactory lifestyle.

3.4 Payments systems then have to tread the awkward path between equity (objective rate for the job, preserved differentials etc) and incentive (reward for extra effort and attainment by particular individuals and groups).

The advantages of a rational, 'felt-fair' salary system often dictate the use of *job evaluation*, a variety of techniques for determining the worth of a job (in itself and in relation to other jobs) as a basis for salary structures. Incentives (monetary or otherwise) may then be added eg in the form of merit bands within each salary grade, or negotiated productivity bonuses.

4. Discipline

4.1 Discipline has the same end as motivation - ie to secure a range of desired behaviour from members of the organisation. Motivation may even be called a kind of 'self discipline' - because motivated individuals exercise choice to behave in the way that the organisation wishes.

Discipline, however, is more often related to '*negative*' motivation, ie the 'stick' rather than the 'carrot', an appeal to the individual's need to avoid punishment, sanctions or unpleasantness.

4.2 Disciplinary action at work is governed by a Code of Practice set out by ACAS (Advisory Conciliation and Arbitration Service), infringement of which may be the grounds of appeal to an Industrial Tribunal.

There is therefore some 'legal' pressure on management to apply discipline fairly and consistently, but discipline remains primarily a complex situation involving superior-subordinate relations, and will have to be treated with appropriate discretion.

QUESTIONS

1 Which of the following is *not* a process theory of motivation?

    A Expectancy theory
    B Path-goal theory
    C Two-factor theory
    D The motivation calculus

Circle your answer

| A | B | C | D |

2 Phil T Luker & Son offers its employees a reward package which includes salary and company car. It's factory is safe and clean and rather smart. It is a very successful company and holds regular staff meetings to report results to employees. The company is offering intrinsic rewards in the shape of:

    A the salary
    B the car
    C the factory
    D the meetings

Circle your answer

| A | B | C | D |

3 Maslow's need categorisation does *not* include:

    A 'physiological needs'
    B 'freedom of inquiry and expression needs'
    C 'need for affiliation'
    D 'safety needs'

Circle your answer

| A | B | C | D |

4 Of the following criticisms levelled at Maslow's hierarchy of needs theory, which is *not* a valid objection?

    A Progression up the hierarchy does not always work in practice

    B A need once satisfied doesn't always become less powerful

    C Needs can be satisfied by aspects of a person's life outside work

    D The hierarchy is only relevant to Western English-speaking cultures

Circle your answer

| A | B | C | D |

5 Which is the 'odd man out' of the following?

A Motivator factor
B Environmental factor
C Hygiene factor
D Maintenance factor

Circle your answer

| A | B | C | D |

---

6 Keepham (Hungary) Ltd offers its employees:

1. sensible company policies
2. good salaries and bonuses
3. considerate supervision
4. training programmes

Employees will, according to Herzberg, derive satisfaction from and be motivated to superior effort by:

A 1 only
B 4 only
C 2 and 4 only
D 3 and 4 only

Circle your answer

| A | B | C | D |

---

7 Willy Dewitt-Ornott is an employee in Sales who is 'up for promotion' to team leader. There is always a competition in the firm in January to try and boost post-Christmas sales. Everybody knows that the winner has for the last three years been made a team leader. Willy's quite certain that if he spends December planning a campaign, sends Christmas cards to all his 'leads' etc, he will be able to win: all his mates think so too. Willy knows that as team leader he will have more responsibility - which he would like. But he would also have to work much longer hours, and he has just started a family. In fact, he had promised his wife he would take two weeks holiday to help her organise Christmas: it is very important to both of them, since Willy 'lives' for the times he can spend at home. If an expectancy equation were used to assess Willy's motivation to work hard at January sales, based on the information given:

A valence would be high, expectancy high, motivation high

B valence would be high, expectancy low, motivation high

C valence would be around 0, expectancy high, motivation low

D valence would be around 0, expectancy high, motivation high

Circle your answer

| A | B | C | D |

8 Handy's 'E factors' would *not* include:

A expectancy
B effort
C energy
D expenditure

Circle your answer

A   B   C   D

9 Application of an expectancy approach to motivation in practice involves all but one of the following. Which is the exception?

A Clarifying intended results
B Giving feedback on actual results
C Immediacy of reward following results
D Consistency of reward for results

Circle your answer

A   B   C   D

10 According to the motivation calculus, if individuals are rewarded according to performance tied to standards (eg management by objectives) they will tend to:

A set higher standards for themselves

B set lower standards, the less important the reward is to them

C set lower standards, the more important the reward is to them

D set lower standards, the more they experience success

Circle your answer

A   B   C   D

11 Motivation through job satisfaction - ie Maslow's 'higher order needs' - became the focus of attention with the:

A scientific management school
B human relations school
C classical school
D neo-human relations school

Circle your answer

A   B   C   D

12 The management of Ascham Nyce-Leigh Ltd has been studying the behaviour of a group of workers (wirers and solderers) at its main plant. The group appears to have established a standard amount of production that it feels is 'fair'. Members of the group who produce above - or below - this norm are put under 'social pressure' to get back into line, and do - despite the company incentive scheme. One 'over-producing' employee is told: 'If they catch you, they'll just raise the rate and ask us to do more for the same money.'

Ascham Nyce-Leigh is entitled to assume that these workers are *not* motivated by:

A   job security
B   maximised earnings
C   satisfactory income
D   social needs

Circle your answer

A   B   C   D

13 Praise is a method of:

A   positive reinforcement
B   negative reinforcement
C   positive discipline
D   negative motivation

Circle your answer

A   B   C   D

14 A manager who subscribed to Douglas McGregor's 'Theory X' assumptions about his subordinates would recognise them in Edgar Schein's model of:

A   social man
B   rational-economic man
C   self-actualising man
D   complex man

Circle your answer

A   B   C   D

15 The approach to job design advocated by the scientific school of management was:

A   job rotation
B   job enlargement
C   micro-division of labour
D   autonomous group working

Circle your answer

A   B   C   D

16 Eva Moore-Drudgery used to pack chocolate bars into boxes of three dozen. Her job has been redesigned, so that she now packs them, applies a 'sell-by' date stamp, cellophanes the box, and applies a promotional sticker. This is:

A   job rotation
B   job description
C   job enrichment
D   job enlargement

Circle your answer

A   B   C   D

17 Which of the following *cannot* be claimed as an advantage of job enrichment?

A   It increases job satisfaction
B   It enhances quality of output
C   It replaces extrinsic rewards
D   It reduces supervisory costs

Circle your answer

A   B   C   D

18 Participation will *not* be effective as a motivator if it is:

A   limited in its scope
B   limited by the organisation culture
C   limited to certain employees
D   limited to trivial issues

Circle your answer

A   B   C   D

19 Employee satisfaction can be least effectively assessed through:

A   productivity levels
B   analysis of absenteeism
C   attitude surveys
D   analysis of labour turnover

Circle your answer

A   B   C   D

20 By which of the following factors may the effectiveness of pay as incentive to superior performance be limited?

Factors
1.   Taxation rates
2.   Equity of pay rates
3.   Regular salary review
4.   Work group norms

81

A   Factor 1 only
B   Factors 1 and 4 only
C   Factors 2 and 4 only
D   Factors 1, 2, 3, and 4

Circle your answer

A   B   C   D

21 Job evaluation puts a relative value on jobs primarily on the basis of:

A   equity
B   job content
C   negotiated pay scales
D   market rates

Circle your answer

A   B   C   D

22 Which of the following is *not* an advantage of job evaluation?

A   It determines a rate for the job irrespec-
    tive of the merits of the job holder

B   It gives differentials a demonstrably
    rational basis

C   It facilitates the setting of rates of pay

D   It involves the formulation of a job
    description

Circle your answer

A   B   C   D

23 Furr and Squeur (a Liverpool firm) uses a method of job evaluation in which a number of
factors are listed, which are thought to represent sought-after qualities, and the importance
given to each factor is decided by the allocation of a maximum points value. Each job is
then analysed factor by factor and given a score for each, up to the maximum. Jobs are then
ranked according to their total scores. This technique is called:

A   points rating
B   factor comparison
C   ranking
D   merit rating

Circle your answer

A   B   C   D

24 The purpose of disciplinary action which is less severe than is warranted by the offence is likely to be:

A   punitive
B   reformative
C   deterrent
D   permissive

Circle your answer

A   B   C   D

25 An example of what is technically termed 'constructive' or 'positive' discipline would be:

A   an administrative procedure incorporating tight internal controls and checks

B   an informal warning to an employee following a slight offence

C   an immediate, consistent and impersonal scheme of disciplinary action

D   offering incentives to employees who have a 'clean sheet' in a given period

Circle your answer

A   B   C   D

26 Streyton (Harrow) Ltd is having to justify itself to an Industrial Tribunal over a disciplinary action against an employee, a Mr Rock Arde, who had (allegedly) been persistently defiant and lax in his time-keeping. The supervisor failed to give an informal verbal warning when it first occurred, but issued an official written warning on a second offence. The offender was allowed to state his case; despite his protests, the supervisor insisted that the two of them discuss the matter alone, so as not to escalate the conflict. When Rock turned up to this interview he appeared to have no idea of the offence of which he was accused: the official warning had simply threatened him with 'further action should your recent conduct be repeated'.

At which of the following points did Streyton (Harrow) contravene the ACAS Code of Practice on disciplinary action?

Stage
1.   Informal warning
2.   Written warning
3.   Disciplinary interview

A   Stage 2 only
B   Stages 2 and 3 only
C   Stages 1, 2 and 3
D   At no stage

Circle your answer

A   B   C   D

CHAPTER 8

MANAGEMENT AND LEADERSHIP

> **This chapter covers the following topics:**
>
> - Management and leadership
> - Traits and styles
> - The contingency approach
> - Managerial use of time

1. Management and leadership

1.1 Many of the theories called 'leadership theories' in fact fail to make any distinction between 'management' and 'leadership' as one of the *functions* of 'management'. 'Leadership' as a concept has come to the fore fairly recently, with the increased expectations and power of employees (the 'followers'): earlier theories were content to talk about 'commanding' or 'directing', with little recognition of the need to motivate, inspire and persuade.

1.2 The functions of management have been variously listed, but fall into several main areas.

- Planning
- Organising
- Controlling
- Co-ordinating
- Commanding/motivating/developing people

1.3 In a *business* organisation, economic performance should be the overall function of a manager, and Drucker suggested that this entails:

- managing a business
- managing managers and
- managing workers and work

1.4 Leadership is variously defined, but generally comes down to: 'the process of influencing others to work willingly towards the organisation's goals and to the best of their capabilities - without having to resort to pure position power'.

> 'The essence of leadership is *followership*. In other words, it is the willingness of people to follow that makes a person a leader.'
>
> *(Koontz, O'Donnell, Weihrich)*

2. Traits and styles

2.1 Writers and researchers have for many years produced theories of leadership with a view to aiding organisations in the selection and training of leaders (or effective managers).

Two streams of thought emerged.

- *Trait theories*. The capacity to 'make others do what you want them to do' is an inherent characteristic. Leadership cannot be *taught*, only identified. Personal traits observed in successful leaders can be used as a basis for distinguishing 'leadership materials'. Such traits include intelligence, initiative, self-assurance and charisma.

> 'Research has produced such a variegated list of traits presumed to describe leadership, that for all practical purposes it describes nothing. Fifty years of study have failed to produce one personality trait or set of qualities that can be used to distinguish between leaders and non-leaders.'
>
> *Jennings*

- *Style theories*. 'Behaviouralist' researchers identified 'styles' in which leadership could be exercised. There are various classifications, based on a continuum or range of styles from autocratic to democratic.

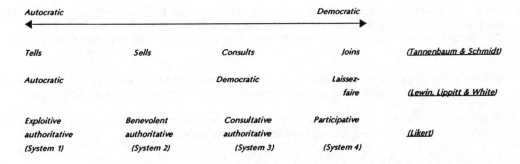

Another set of classifications is based on the concern for task/concern for human relations. This is expressed as a two-dimensional grid, since the two concerns are not considered incompatible.

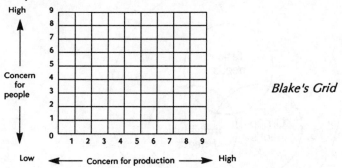

Blake's Grid

W J Reddin devised another version of the grid, adding a third dimension: *management effect-iveness*, which may be high or low, according to leadership style, for any pairing of task and people concern.

?? Neither of these approaches takes into account all the variables in the situation to be managed. Nor do they define 'leadership' in any very useful way. Style theories, however, still have some currency as ways of looking at a manager's attitudes and approach: the Tannenbaum/Schmidt continuum, for example, has been adapted for use in management training, and Blake's Grid has been used as a framework for performance assessment (despite the 'missing dimension' shown up by Reddin's 3D approach). The important point is that the usefulness in practice of such theories is strictly limited.

3. The contingency approach

3.1 The contingency approach identifies effective leadership not in a particular range of leader behaviour, but in the *appropriateness* of leader behaviour in the highly variable 'situation' in which leadership operates.

3.2 Fiedler pioneered the 'contingency approach'. He followed the 'concern-for-task/concern-for-people' framework, but suggested that the 'situation' of leadership is important. It is 'favourable' to the leader to the extent that it provides him with influence over his group members, and:

- where the situation is very favourable, or very unfavourable, the most effective leadership style is a highly structured, autocratic, task-centred, or '*psychologically distant*' style

- where the situation is only moderately favourable, the most effective style is a supportive, informal, people-centred, or '*psychologically close*' style.

3.3 John Adair formulated the *functional* or *action-centred* approach to leadership.

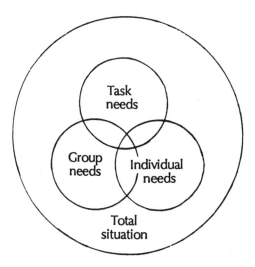

The total situation dictates the relative priority that must be given to each of the three sets of needs. Effective leadership consists of identifying and acting on that priority, to balance the three sets of needs in eight key leadership activities:

- defining the task
- planning
- briefing
- controlling
- evaluating
- motivating
- organising
- setting an example

3.4 The contingency approaches have some value for management training: they address more of the issues that a manager will face in practice as he tries to lead. Their usefulness, however, is limited by the fact that:

(a) study of a concept will not automatically change management style: values and norms will have to be changed first;

(b) the manager's personality may not be flexible enough to change styles according to the situation;

(c) a perceived inconsistency of style is unpopular with and stressful for subordinates.

4. Managerial use of time

4.1 In the past, the relationship between time and job performance was considered relevant only to manual workers or (through O & M) clerical workers. It is only recently that attention has been given to time management at higher and more 'discretionary' levels of activity.

4.2 The main factors affecting a managers' personal organisation and use of time can be depicted as follows.

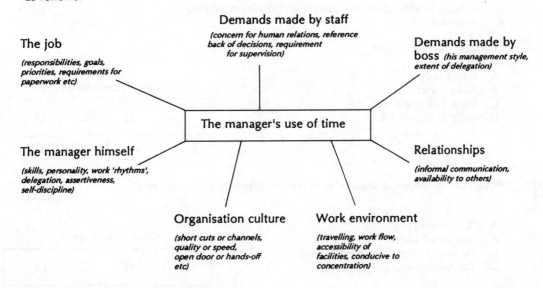

QUESTIONS

1 A 'leader' may be distinguished from a 'manager' by his lack of dependency on:

A person power
B position power
C physical power
D expert power

Circle your answer

| A | B | C | D |

---

2 Fayol's 'five functions of management' do not explicitly include:

A commanding
B co-ordinating
C communicating
D controlling

Circle your answer

| A | B | C | D |

---

3 Common leadership traits include:

Trait
1. assertiveness
2. interpersonal skills
3. skills in analysis/problem-solving and decision making
4. charisma

Managers can be *taught*:

A trait 3 only
B traits 1 and 3 only
C traits 1, 2 and 3 only
D traits 1, 2, 3 and 4

Circle your answer

| A | B | C | D |

---

4 Which of the following leadership 'style' models is the odd one out?

A The democratic style
B The 'joins' style
C Participative management (Likert)
D The laissez-faire style

Circle your answer

| A | B | C | D |

5 Otto Kratt is a team manager. He wants to change the working day to a flexi-time system. He knows this is an important change for the members of the team, so he calls a team meeting, and asks them what they think. Few group members want to go over to flexi-time, because the group will be working at less than full strength during the flexible times. Otto explains that this won't be critical, because the 'core' period will be as normal, and it will cover most of the day. He tells them about the personal convenience flexi-time offers. He invites further objections - and is able to counter most of them. 'I'll take your views into account' he says. Flexi-time is in operation a month later.

Otto's style may best be described as:

A 'tells'
B 'sells'
C 'consults'
D 'joins'

Circle your answer

A   B   C   D

6 Research has demonstrated that the consultative style of management is the most:

A popular among subordinates
B popular among leaders
C productivity-inducing
D hostility-provoking in groups

Circle your answer

A   B   C   D

7 Of the following ways of classifying leadership styles, the one which is *not* based on an authoritarian-democratic continuum is:

A theory X and Y
B the management grid
C Likert's systems 1 to 4
D the 'sells', 'tells', 'consults', 'joins' model

Circle your answer

A   B   C   D

8 On Blake's grid, a 1.9 management style is called:

A impoverished
B task management
C country club
D dampened pendulum

Circle your answer

A   B   C   D

9 Ed Oncho is the manager of an administrative department of a local authority. His team members complain that he doesn't give them any leadership. They keep coming up with ideas for changes and improvements, but he ignores them. He appears to have a 'why should I care?' attitude. The staff are frustrated and resentful at being forced to follow the rules and procedures laid down by the organisation. Ed seems to look no further than doing just that. 'Typical bureaucrat', they say.

According to Reddin's 3D model, in terms of concern for task, concern for people and effectiveness, Ed is:

A high, low, low
B low, low, high
C low, low, low
D high, low, high

Circle your answer

A   B   C   D

10 The management of Genguiss Cans Ltd runs a 'tight ship', with clocking-on timekeeping systems, close supervision and rules for everything. 'Well', says the general manager Koo Bligh, 'give 'em an inch and they'll take a mile.'

The management team seem to subscribe to:

A Theory X
B Theory Y
C Theory Z
D Theory J

Circle your answer

A   B   C   D

11

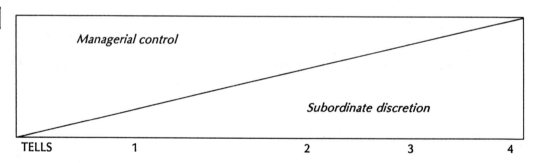

Points 1, 2, 3 and 4 represent management styles.

Point 4 represents:

A joins
B consults
C sells
D delegates

Circle your answer

A   B   C   D

12 Betty Willnot is a team leader in the R & D department of an electronics firm. She would really like to be a democratic leader. She's got every confidence in her subordinates - and so have they: they're all highly skilled, and enjoy a challenge. However, complex problem-solving is required, and research projects have long time-horizons. The department manager responds to this by exercising an autocratic style of management: 'That's how we do things here', he says.

Betty has read Handy's 'best fit' theory, and is trying to decide whether her situation is 'tight' or 'flexible'. Which factor(s) will be on the 'tight' rather than 'flexible' end of the continuum?

A   Subordinates and task only
B   Task and leader only
C   Subordinates, task and leader
D   None of the above

Circle your answer

A   B   C   D

13 The contingency approach which not only distinguishes between task, situation and people but also, with regard to people, between the needs of the individual and the group, is:

A   Handy's 'best fit' theory
B   Fiedler's contingency theory
C   Adair's 'action centred' leadership theory
D   Reddin's 3-dimensional theory

Circle your answer

A   B   C   D

Data for questions 14 - 15

Don Argew-Whimmey is a team leader.

Factors in Don's work situation
1. Don is liked and trusted by the group
2. The tasks of the group are not clearly defined
3. Don has authority to hand out rewards within the group

14 Of the above features of his work context, which would make the situation 'favourable' to Don, according to Fiedler?

A   Factor 1 only
B   Factors 1 and 2 only
C   Factors 1 and 3 only
D   Factors 1, 2 and 3

Circle your answer

A   B   C   D

15 Given that the situation is as described, Don should try to be:

A   psychologically distant
B   psychologically close
C   task oriented
D   autocratic

Circle your answer

A	B	C	D

16 The contingency approach to leadership is based on the identification of:

A   personal attributes which can be acquired
B   personal attributes which cannot be acquired
C   an optimum mode of leader behaviour
D   a framework for adaptive leader behaviour

Circle your answer

A	B	C	D

17 The purpose of leadership theories may be:

Purpose
1.   aiding management assessment
2.   aiding management training and development
3.   making managers into leaders
4.   changing management styles

For which of the above purposes will such theories be effective?

A   Purposes 1 and 2 only
B   Purposes 2 and 3 only
C   Purposes 2 and 4 only
D   Purposes 1, 2, 3 and 4

Circle your answer

A	B	C	D

18 Willy Krackett has a problem with personal time management. He takes on lots of his bosses' work and tries to fit it in with all his own work. The sheer size of the workload sometimes panics him - the number of reports to get through etc. He's popular with his staff, though, because he always finds time to talk to them and listen to their problems - which include boredom at work. Sometimes Willy 'just doesn't know where the day has gone'.

A colleague has recommended the following areas for improvement.

Areas
1. Delegation
2. Assertiveness
3. Communication
4. Goal planning

In which of these areas could Willy benefit?

A   Area 1 only
B   Areas 2 and 4 only
C   Areas 1, 2 and 4 only
D   Areas 1, 2, 3 and 4

Circle your answer

A   B   C   D

19 Which of the following factors is *not* a potential problem for time management?

A   An open door policy of supervision
B   A congenial work group
C   An office designed via method study
D   An emphasis on accuracy and quality

Circle your answer

A   B   C   D

20 Which of the following would be a feature of 'time management' rather than 'job management'?

A   Defining the manager's tasks
B   Prioritising the manager's tasks
C   Allocating required resources
D   Providing required training

Circle your answer

A   B   C   D

CHAPTER 9

TEAMWORK

This chapter covers the following topics:

- Groups
- Groups at work
- Team effectiveness

1. Groups

1.1 A *group* has been described (by Handy) as 'any collection of people who perceive themselves to be a group'.

1.2 Organisations are in this sense 'groups', but you should bear in mind that although the organisation as a whole may wish to project itself as a large group, with a single identity, unity and purpose, it will in fact be composed of many sub-groups - formal and informal - with such attributes of their own.

1.3 The smallest units of the organisation, which form the immediate social environment of the individual, have been called 'primary working groups'. These are units of typically about ten people, an optimum group size which balances the individuality needed for *generating* new ideas with the support and comradeship necessary for *developing* them.

1.4 Groups are not static, but *dynamic*. They mature and develop, and are subject to various 'forces' within and around the group itself. For example:

(a) collections of individuals *develop* into groups. A common pattern to this process has been identified by Tuckman as being:

- forming - ie coming together, and feeling each other out
- storming - conflict and creativity, prior to
- norming - the 'settling down' stage, which enables
- performing - becoming effective and 'getting on with it'

(b) groups prize loyalty and acceptance, which usually expresses itself in conformity to *norms* of behaviour and attitude which bind the group together. This type of solidarity may formalise itself in entrance qualifications, rules etc or may be an unspoken acceptance of ways of thinking and doing things. Groups are capable of exerting considerable social pressure on individuals to 'stay in line'.

- groups function through interactions between individual members and the blend of their skills and abilities.

> Belbin (Carnegie Institute of Technology, 1981) developed a useful model of the eight *roles* required - evenly spread - in an effective team.
>
> The *chairman* - presides and co-ordinates: balanced, disciplined
> The *shaper* - dominant, extrovert, a spur to action
> The *plant* - introverted but imaginative, a source of ideas
> The *monitor-evaluator* - analytically intelligent, dissects ideas and spots flaws
> The *resource-investigator* - popular, sociable, source of new contacts
> The *company worker* - practical organiser, turning ideas into tasks
> The *team worker* - concerned with team maintenance; supportive, diplomatic
> The *finisher* - chivvies the team to meet deadlines, attends to details.

- groups retain an identity despite changes of membership or personnel: there is a persistent 'survivability' of groups, despite their dynamic nature.

2. Groups at work

2.1 In considering the nature and 'use' of groups at work, it will be helpful to make a distinction between:

(a) what work groups can be organised to do (perform a task, make decisions, generate ideas etc); and

(b) the implication for management of the group dynamics discussed above, which may help or hinder the achievement of the group's task objectives.

2.2 In particular, the creation or encouragement of *cohesive* work teams is a double-edged sword for organisations.

- Cohesion fosters trust, loyalty and the submerging of personal differences and interests for the sake of the group. This may lead to greater readiness to put forward ideas, better evaluated decisions in the attempt to reach consensus and more co-operative effort. It will also satisfy the social and 'belonging' needs of individuals.

- Cohesion reinforces group attitudes and norms - which is *good* if these attitudes and norms contribute to organisational objectives, but a problem if they are indifferent or even contrary to the organisation's aims, culture and/or methods. Cohesion can provide a position of strength from which to behave in hostile or 'deviant' ways. Group norms frequently have the effect of restricting individual output to the level considered 'fair' by the group.

- Cohesion tends to be a product of group maintenance activity, the fostering of relationships etc. This may become an all-absorbing function of the group, diverting attention away from the task.

- Cohesion can lead to what I L Janis calls 'groupthink', where the cosy consensus of the group prevents consideration of alternatives, constructive criticism and conflict: the group can become dangerously blinkered to what is going on around it, and may confidently forge ahead in a completely wrong direction.

2.3 Another useful product of group dynamics is the effect of inter-group competition on competing groups. The perceived challenge or threat from 'outside' creates 'battle conditions' in the group: it is keyed up to performance, and diverts its energies predominantly to the task in hand.

3. Team effectiveness

3.1 An effective team is one which:

(a) achieves its allotted task *and*
(b) satisfies its members.

3.2 An effective team will therefore exhibit characteristics such as motivation, idea-sharing, consensus, low absenteeism and low labour turnover rate, as well as high output and productivity, good quality output, achievement of targets etc.

3.3 Handy suggests a useful contingency approach to group effectiveness. (In this context, as in others, the contingency approach says: 'It all depends'. There are a number of factors to be taken into account, in order to create an effective team. There is no 'one best way' to encourage teamwork.)

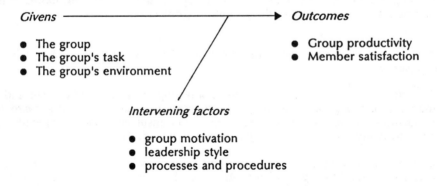

Givens → *Outcomes*

- The group
- The group's task
- The group's environment

- Group productivity
- Member satisfaction

Intervening factors

- group motivation
- leadership style
- processes and procedures

QUESTIONS

1 The most important attribute of a 'group', which distinguishes it from a 'crowd' is:

A leadership
B purpose
C conformity
D identity

Circle your answer

A   B   C   D

2 Which of the following is a 'primary working group'?

A A small work team
B A large department
C A trade union
D A business

Circle your answer

A   B   C   D

3 In which of the following situations will an individual's productivity be raised?

A He identifies closely with his work group
B He identifies closely with his trade union
C He identifies closely with his company
D None of the above situations, necessarily

Circle your answer

A   B   C   D

4 With regard to the relationship between membership of the group and the operation of group norms, which is the 'odd one out', of the following types of group?

A Primary working groups
B Reference groups
C Committees
D Social cliques

Circle your answer

A   B   C   D

5 The four stages of group formation, in order of occurrence are:

A Storming, norming, forming, performing
B Norming, forming, storming, performing
C Forming, storming, norming, performing
D Storming, forming, norming, performing

Circle your answer

A   B   C   D

6 At the Soli-Darretty Bros. factory, a project team has been put together by management to solve a problem with workflow on the factory floor. As we see this team, they are engaged in 'thrashing out' how they are going to approach the task, and who's going to do what; some of their first ideas have obviously not worked out. At the same time, they're starting to put forward some really innovative ideas: they get quite excited in brain storming sessions, and are uninhibited in putting forward their views and suggestions. 'Camps' are emerging, not only around different ideas, but around two individuals who seem to dominate the discussion and always seem to disagree.

This team is at the stage of:

A forming
B storming
C norming
D performing

Circle your answer

A   B   C   D

7 A response to group norms which involves 'toeing the line', without real commitment, is called:

A compliance
B internalisation
C counter-conformity
D identification

Circle your answer

A   B   C   D

8 A group member will be under less pressure to conform to group norms if:

A he lacks personal self confidence
B he values membership of the group
C the group employs 'badges' of membership
D the group doesn't employ sanctions

Circle your answer

A   B   C   D

9 Which of the following 'positive' features of a cohesive work group will invariably be advantageous for the organisation?

Features
1. Conformity to group norms
2. Solidarity or mutual support in the face of threat
3. Satisfaction of social and 'affiliation' needs
4. Increased confidence and willingness to take risks

A None of these features
B Features 1 and 3 only
C Features 2 and 4 only
D Features 2, 3 and 4 only

Circle your answer

A   B   C   D

10 'Groupthink', will be encouraged rather than prevented by:

A actively encouraging self-criticism
B paying more attention to group maintenance
C welcoming outside ideas and criticisms
D responding positively to conflicting evidence

Circle your answer

A   B   C   D

11 Which of the following is *not* a feature of a group which is engaged in competition with another group?

A Members close ranks and submerge their differences

B Leadership moves from democratic to autocratic, with group consent

C The 'climate' becomes sociable, supportive and group-oriented

D The group tends to become more structured and organised

Circle your answer

A   B   C   D

12 The Klaus Knit Group sells fashion knitwear, yarns and craft accessories throughout Europe. Its sales representatives are widely dispersed and so have little opportunity to form informal groups or relationships. The company wants to encourage 'teamhood' among the reps, though, so that they can pool their knowledge of changes in the different European markets and so that they present a consistent corporate image to customers everywhere. The company also feels that it should compensate for the isolated nature of the reps' role. The European Sales manager has found a book on teams, with chapters on:

1 Selection
2 Training
3 Leadership style
4 Culture

He only has time to read two chapters. From the scenario, which would you recommend as most relevant to his problem?

A Chapters 1 and 2
B Chapters 2 and 4
C Chapters 1 and 3
D Chapters 3 and 4

Circle your answer

A   B   C   D

13 Which of the following is not one of the 'givens' in a group leader's situation according to Charles Handy?

A   The group
B   The motivation of the group
C   The task
D   The environment

Circle your answer

A   B   C   D

14 Which of the following is *not* one of Handy's 'intervening factors', which influence group effectiveness?

A   Processes and procedures
B   Group motivation
C   Leadership style
D   Member satisfaction

Circle your answer

A   B   C   D

15 Alf Arwan and Juan Forol are arguing about the merits of using groups for problem-solving and decision-making. Alf thinks group-made decisions are:

1   more cautious
2   more swiftly made
3   more easily enforced, and
4   better evaluated.

Faced with the facts, Juan will have to admit that he's right about:

A   advantages 1 and 3 only
B   advantages 3 and 4 only
C   advantages 1, 2 and 3 only
D   advantages 1, 3 and 4 only

Circle your answer

A   B   C   D

16 Which of the following is most clearly a sign of an ineffective group?

A   Internal disagreement and criticism
B   Competition with other groups
C   Passive acceptance of work decisions
D   Achievement of individual targets

Circle your answer

A   B   C   D

17 If you were to assess the effectiveness of a work group, which of the following criteria should you use?

Criteria
1   Contribution to organisational objectives
2   Fulfilment of group task objectives
3   Satisfaction of members' development needs

A   Criteria 2 only
B   Criteria 1 and 2 only
C   Criteria 2 and 3 only
D   Criteria 1, 2, and 3

Circle your answer

A   B   C   D

18 The famous Hawthorne Studies were *not* carried out by:

A   Elton Mayo
B   Abraham Maslow
C   Roethlisberger and Dickson
D   The Western Electric Company

Circle your answer

A   B   C   D

19 The Hawthorne Studies did not, contrary to the researchers' expectations, demonstrate the importance of:

A   the effects of lighting on output
B   relationships between people
C   the informal organisation
D   attention paid to groups

Circle your answer

A   B   C   D

20 The Bank Wiring Room phase of the Hawthorne research discovered some important tendencies of informal groups. The group observed did *not*:

A   develop a keen sense of identity
B   restrict output levels to a group norm
C   apply social pressure to influence supervision style
D   follow company policy with regard to work practices

Circle your answer

A   B   C   D

CHAPTER 10

MANAGING CHANGE

This chapter covers the following topics:

- Change
- Overcoming resistance to change
- Organisational development
- Technology

1. Change

1.1 Change, in the context of organisation and management, could relate to:

- changes in the 'environment' of the organisation (changes in consumer trends, law, social behaviour and attitudes etc)
- changes in the products the organisation makes, or the services it provides
- changes in work methods, how the products are made and by whom
- changes in management and working relationships
- changes in organisation structure or size

1.2 Change *affects* individuals in several areas.

(a) There may be *physiological* changes in a person's life, both as the natural product of development, maturation and ageing, and as the result of external factors: a change in the pattern of shift-working, for example, may disrupt the body's cycle of eating, waking and sleeping.

(b) There may be *circumstantial* changes - change in location or work routines, for example - which involve 'letting go' of familiar things, and 'unlearning' old knowledge and ways.

(c) Change affects individuals *psychologically*.

 (i) It may create feelings of disorientation before new circumstances have been assimilated.

 (ii) Uncertainty and unfamiliarity may lead to insecurity. This is especially acute in changes at work, where the pressures for continuity (stay in employment, progress in your career) and/or fast acclimatisation (a short learning curve) may be very great.

 (iii) The secure basis of relationships may be up-rooted, and the business of forging new ones can be fraught with personal insecurity.

(iv)   Change affects the individual's self-image. He may be uncertain of being able to cope with new circumstances, for example, which may shake his sense of competence and of being in control of his life. The individual's 'role' may be changed, and he will have to adjust his sense of where he 'fits in'.

2.   Overcoming resistance to change

2.1   Resisting change means attempting the preserve the existing state of affairs - the *status quo* - against pressure to alter it. Not everybody will resist change. Many people - think of your own work organisation - long for change and have a wealth of ideas as to how it should be achieved. They might see it as 'progress' or 'improvement'.

2.2   Sources of resistance to change (according to Arthur Bedeian) include:

*   *self-interest:* ie if the status quo is perceived to be comfortable or advantageous to the individual or group, and the change is perceived to be threatening

*   *misunderstanding and distrust*. If the reasons for, or the nature and consequences of, the change have not been made clear, this aggravates uncertainty and suspicion

*   *contradictory assessments:* some individuals will not agree with the organisation's evaluation of the likely costs and benefits of changes and will consider them undesirable

*   *low tolerance of change itself:* low tolerance of ambiguity, uncertainty, fear of threat and challenge to the individual's self-image etc.

2.3   Strategies for overcoming resistance to change vary according to the circumstances in which change is taking place, the speed of change required, the nature of the change, the nature of the people affected and the power of the change agent.

Models for managing change include:

*   Lewin's 'forcefield' theory. The theory suggests that there is an equilibrium between opposing forces in the perception of those involved in change situations: *driving* forces (for change) and *restraining* forces (against change). People generally attempt to use driving forces - persuasion, threat etc - yet this often causes the restraining forces (eg resentment) to become stronger. Lewin suggested that a more effective way is to remove the restraining forces by identifying, discussing and tackling the *sources* of resistance.

*   Lewin/Schein's three-stage approach to changing human behaviour.

UNFREEZE ⟶	CHANGE ⟶	REFREEZE
existing	attitude/	new
behaviour	behaviour	behaviour

'Unfreeze' sells the need or reason for change, ie - gives individuals a *motive* for changing their attitudes, values or behaviour.

'Change' identifies what the new, desirable behaviour should be, communicates it and encourages individuals and groups to 'own' the new attitude or behaviour.

'Refreeze' implies consolidation or reinforcement of the new behaviour.

2.4 The above models suggest - and research confirms - that methods involving consultation and participation have a better chance of securing change. A checklist for this type of change management might be:

Tell	- the people: clearly, realistically, openly
Sell	- the pressures which make change necessary and advisable
	- the vision of successful, realistically-attainable change
Evolve	- the people's attitudes, ideas, capacity to learn the new ways
Involve	- the people where possible in planning and implementation

Bear in mind, though, that in some conditions, the autocratic or unilateral *imposition* of change may be effective in achieving the organisation's objectives.

3. Organisational development

3.1 Organisational development (OD) is an organisation-wide process designed to formulate and implement strategies for improving organisational effectiveness.

Bennis defines it as 'a complex educational strategy intended to change the beliefs, attitudes, values and structures of organisations so that they can better adapt to new technologies, markets and challenges and to the dizzying rate of change itself'.

This definition is useful because it emphasises that:

● OD is an *educative* and political process, and
● it is based on the belief that organisations must be *adaptive* to survive.

3.2 The OD programme is usually conducted or guided by an external 'third party' or 'change agent', who may have a wide range of roles from a highly directive/prescriptive role to a non-directive/consultative role. The success of the programme relies to a great extent on the quality of the relationship which develops between the employees, management team and 'third party'.

3.3 The techniques and approaches of OD are, since it is primarily a social/political process, rooted in the behavioural sciences (such as social psychology). They may aim to:

● change behaviour (by coaching, counselling and team building)
● change structures (by role analysis and job redesign)
● assess and solve problems (via diagnostic activities and process consultation)

4. Technology

4.1 Technology has been at the root of many sweeping changes in work and organisations in this century, in

- the way we work (eg new skills and materials in the electronic office or robotic factory)
- where we work (eg with home 'networking')
- whether we work (with the reduction in human intervention in some processes)
- our experience of work (reduced or enhanced skills and satisfactions?)

4.2 The technical and economic advantages of new technology for organisations are fairly obvious. The *fears* associated with it have an equally high profile, but you should be aware that there are two ways of looking at it from the worker's point of view.

(a) Process operators are victims of management's use of technology to create work that is unskilled - and unlikely to offer any learning opportunities - boring, repetitive, tightly controlled, lacking meaning, and socially isolating. Microelectronic extention of automation may alter the demand for operators' human skills, and may damage the quality of working life: it may replace the exercise of human mental capacity altogether.

(b) Process operators are skilled, knowledgeable decision makers, with responsibility, discretion and prosperous working conditions. Process automation eliminates dirt and hazard, and can offer a motivating work environment with task variety, meaning, learning opportunities and discretion. Electronic controls lack human flexibility and creativity: systems can enhance job skills and interest.

4.3 The principal fear is of *replacement* - ie the substitution of 'intelligent' machines for people. However, the effect of this is compensated for by:

(a) the generation of new products and services or simply maintaining competitiveness, encouraging or preserving work opportunities;

(b) the lapse of time between the arrival of a new device or system and its successful incorporation (during which time natural wastage may have reduced the workforce to absorb potential redundancies);

(c) the limitations of technology: as machines do more, people do not necessarily do less.

4.4 The outcome of technical change depends to a large extent on *managerial choices* about workplace layout, organisational culture and particularly the organisation of work around the new technology. Automated work *can* be organised so as to offer or retain interest and meaning for the worker, if the needs of the *social* system of the organisation are taken into account as well as those of the *technical* system.

QUESTIONS

1 Of the following four terms, the term which invariably means doing something completely new, which hasn't been done before, Is:

A change
B transformation
C growth
D innovation

Circle your answer

A	B	C	D

2 A change which does not directly affect an individual is likely to arouse in him:

A acceptance
B indifference
C passive resistance
D active resistance

Circle your answer

A	B	C	D

3 Ida Sednow is the manager of a department which is going over to a new shift system. There has been some resistance to the idea, and Ida is keen to change attitudes, not just secure compliance. Of the following, which will be the best way to do that?

A Pay the subordinates incentives to accept the changes

B Get team leaders to instruct others in the benefits of the change

C Present the change to the subordinates as a *fait accompli*

D Tell them it's 'just for a trial period' and hope they get used to it

Circle your answer

A	B	C	D

4 At the communication stage of introducing change, where full acceptance is desired, the best thing to emphasise will be:

A the expertise that has gone into the decision

B the authority of the change agent to enforce the change

C the problem or threat to which the
change is the response

D the desirability of 'peace' and
co-operation

Circle your answer

A   B   C   D

5 *Changes*

1. Repeal restrictions on Sunday trading

2. Relocation so that two previously
distinct teams share office

3. Introduction of word processing to the
typing pool

4. Formation of a personnel department
with functional authority throughout
the organisation

Sources of resistance

(i) Fear of the unknown

(ii) Attitudes or beliefs

(iii) Organisational politics

(iv) Loyalty to a group identity

Matching up the proposed changes (1-4) with the most likely source of resistance to them
(i-iv) you get:

A 1(i) . 2(iii) . 3(iv) . 4(ii)
B 1(iii) . 2(iv) . 3(i) . 4(ii)
C 1(ii) . 2(i) . 3(iii) . 4(iv)
D 1(ii) . 2(iv) . 3(i) . 4(iii)

Circle your answer

A   B   C   D

6 Organisational culture will clearly be a hindrance and source of resistance to the
implementation of change because:

A it is a force for continuity and cohesion
B it establishes values and attitudes
C it is a force for flexibility and innovation
D it is based on tradition and fosters
complacency

Circle your answer

A   B   C   D

7 Thoroughly Modern Milliners plc faced resistance to the frequent changes to jobs and work
methods necessitated by the development of the production technology of hatmaking.
Changes and transfers reduced efficiency ratings, and therefore caused loss of status and
earnings for staff. The company decided to try out three different approaches to introducing
the next lot of changes.

1. A 'non-participative' group was informed about the change, but not involved in the
decision-making

2   A 'representative' group was given a preliminary meeting or explanation of the change; group representatives were then trained in the new methods and asked to train fellow members themselves

3   A 'total participation' group also had the preliminary meeting, but then all took part in the design and standard-setting for the new job.

Which group would be expected to have recovered and even improved its efficiency rating most quickly, and without conflict?

A   The non-participative group
B   The representative group
C   The total participation group
D   None of the groups

Circle your answer

A   B   C   D

8   Consultation and participation are widely recommended for effective management of change - but are not the only methods of implementing change, in practice. Autocratic imposition of change *can* be effective, unless:

A   compliance is all that is required

B   employees have significant negative power

C   the balance of power is weighted in favour of the change agent

D   the prevailing culture is submissive to authority

Circle your answer

A   B   C   D

9   Ché Njova is a person who doesn't mind risk and uncertainty, and who feels passionately that organisations must adapt to environmental changes in order to survive. Given a choice of organisations, he will want to work in:

A   an organic system
B   a mechanistic system
C   a bureaucracy
D   a role culture

Circle your answer

A   B   C   D

10   If an organisation wants to grow, it might look at a variety of strategies. What it *won't* be interested in is:

A   merger
B   market extension
C   diversification
D   divestment

Circle your answer

A   B   C   D

11 Some aspects of a manager's job may be called 'entrepreneurial'. This would *not* apply to:

A profit maximisation
B innovation
C control
D risk-taking

Circle your answer

A   B   C   D

12 Frank Enstein wants to encourage creativity and innovation in his firm: they've almost saturated the market for their existing products, and they've got to 'grow or die'. Frank has jotted down some ideas. Which, in principle, would you *not* recommend?

A Increase spending on R & D, market research and pilot schemes

B Get departments/individuals to challenge each other's proposals

C Put innovation targets into the corporate plan and unit objectives

D Discuss with Personnel: recruitment, selection, promotion, training

Circle your answer

A   B   C   D

13 An organisation development programme is usually designed to follow a logical sequence. If you were running such a programme, which of the following would you want to consider first?

A Availability of resources to make the change
B Probable reactions to the change
C Nature of change to be implemented
D Need or desire for change in a particular area

Circle your answer

A   B   C   D

14 The variety of roles which may be taken by the 'change agent' or 'Third Party' in an OD programme may be illustrated as follows.

Authority of role

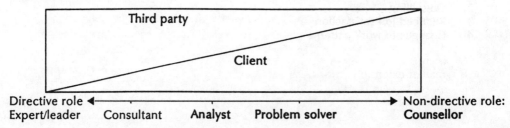

Directive role ← Expert/leader   Consultant   **Analyst**   **Problem solver** → Non-directive role: **Counsellor**

Third party

Client

The role of the analyst would be

A   to recommend proposed criteria
B   to identify options, add data
C   to probe, interpret, diagnose
D   to clarify, reflect, listen

Circle your answer

A   B   C   D

15 Which of the following features might be considered among the disadvantages of using an external consultant as the change agent?

Features
1   He brings an outsider's viewpoint to the organisation
2   His methods are based on wide experience of other organisations
3   He has no position in the organisation hierarchy
4   He is skilled in analytical, diagnostic and behavioural science techniques

A   Feature 3 only
B   Features 1 and 3 only
C   Features 1, 2 and 3 only
D   Features 1, 2, 3 and 4

Circle your answer

A   B   C   D

16 Tobias Histham is managing director of a small firm considering computerisation of its production processes and information processing. It is hoped that stock control will be improved, that management reports will be available faster and in more flexible formats, and that customer information will be held in a database for more efficient enquiry and transaction processing. Tobias can express the strategic purpose of his new technology as being:

A   reduction of operating costs
B   improved quality of service
C   improved control and integration
D   all of the above

Circle your answer

A   B   C   D

17 Of the following common fears associated with the introduction of new technology, which is necessarily justified in practice?

Fears
1   Redundancy
2   De-skilling
3   Reduced job satisfaction
4   Changes to work patterns

A   Fear 4 only
B   Fears 2 and 4 only
C   Fears 3 and 4 only
D   Fears 1, 2, 3 and 4

Circle your answer

A   B   C   D

18 Of the following operating conditions, the effect of technological change on the practice and style of management is likely to be felt more slowly where:

A   technical change itself is sweeping
B   there are low risks involved in technological breakdown
C   there is a high element of discretion in management decisions
D   the work is relatively predictable and involves little personal service

Circle your answer

A   B   C   D

19 Technological change will not alter:

A   the work environment of the organisation
B   the organisational/management structure
C   the status of the office in organisational life
D   the functions of management

Circle your answer

A   B   C   D

20 There is a theory which argues that work organisation is not wholly determined by technology but by organisational choices: any given technology can be operated by different work patterns and interrelationships and a 'best fit' should be found between technical demands and human needs. This theory is called:

A   human relations theory
B   socio-technical systems theory
C   ergonomics
D   scientific management

Circle your answer

A   B   C   D

111

CHAPTER 11

MANPOWER RESOURCING

This chapter covers the following topics:

- Manpower planning
- Recruitment
- Selection

1. Manpower planning

1.1 Labour is one of the resources of the organisation. In fact, organisations do not exist without people. Manpower planning is the process by which the organisation secures sufficient and suitable manpower to undertake its activities and fulfil its objectives. Systematically undertaken, it is a rational approach to the recruitment, retention, utilisation, improvement and disposal of the organisation's human resources.

Not all organisations *do* plan their manpower resourcing and utilisation in this way - especially small ones - but it is crucial that *large* organisations should do so.

1.2 The basis of manpower planning is demand and supply forecasting, and the development of strategies for closing the gap between likely demand and supply of appropriately skilled labour.

1.3 The process of manpower planning therefore embraces:

(a) forecasting the manpower requirements of the organisation

(b) acquiring manpower (recruitment, selection, transfer, promotion etc)

(c) retaining manpower and controlling its 'flow' through the organisation (conditions of employment, pay, welfare etc)

(d) developing manpower so that future requirements can be met from within (training, promotion etc)

(e) controlling manpower levels (natural wastage, level of recruitment, labour turnover, redundancies etc)

1.4 A systematic approach to manpower planning may be illustrated as follows.

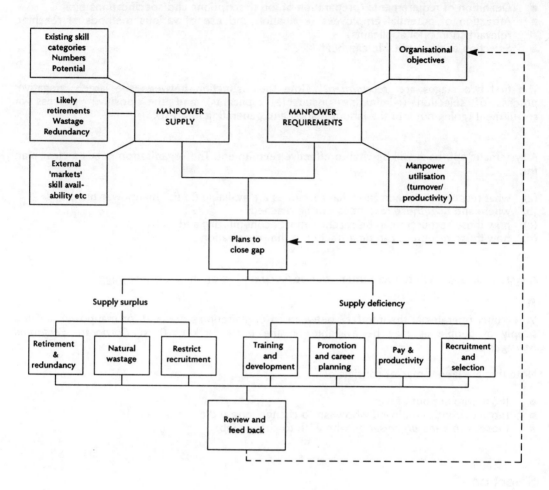

1.5 It should be recognised that while manpower planning is often perceived as a primarily quantitative or statistical exercise, it is based on judgements that are basically qualitative in character, with many uncertainties and assumptions involved. Trends in statistics - eg rates of labour turnover - are only the results of social processes.

2 Recruitment

2.1 The overall aim of the recruitment and selection process in an organisation is to obtain the quantity and quality of employees required by the manpower plan, with maximum efficiency.

The process can be broken down into three main stages.

- Definition of requirements (preparation of job descriptions and specifications etc)
- Attraction of potential employees (evaluation and use of various methods of reaching relevant sources of applicants)
- Selection of most suitable candidates.

2.2 The first two stages are *'recruitment'.* Note the distinction between the largely 'negative' process of selection (eliminating unsuitable applicants) and the 'positive' process of recruitment (going out into the labour market and generating interest).

2.3 A systematic approach will be vital to effective recruitment. The organisation needs a clear plan for:

(a) what resources it needs and what resources are available (ie the manpower plan);
(b) where and how those resources can be reached;
(c) how those resources can be reached most economically; and
(d) how those resources can be attracted to the organisation.

2.4 A systematic approach to recruitment can be illustrated as on the following page.

2.5 'A recruiter operates at the interface between an organisation's demand for manpower and the supply of people as may be available on the open market.' (Livy: *Corporate Personnel Management).*

Note that the labour market consists of:

- those who are out of work
- those currently employed who wish to change jobs and/or employers
- those *within the organisation* who wish to change jobs.

3   Selection

3.1 Selection involves measuring potentially suitable applicants against the organisation's specific requirements. Selection methods, including application forms, interviews and tests, should be designed with this in mind.

3.2 It should also be considered, however, that the selection process should not only find the best person for the job, but:

(a) give the applicant a chance to assess whether this is the best job for him;
(b) allow every applicant to feel that he has been treated fairly; and
(c) comply with detailed legislation on discrimination, advertising and employment.

3.3 Selection methods, despite attempts to exclude bias and subjectivity, are not scientific. Interviewing and the interpretation of the curriculum vitae, application form and references are most obviously subjective, although selector training and procedures can overcome some of the problems. Techniques which seem more scientific - personality or IQ tests, 'biodata feedback' (lifestyle/attitude questionnaires), graphology (study of handwriting) etc - are in fact little more valuable as predictors of future performance and success.

Research has been conducted into the reliability of various recruitment and selection procedures in predicting success. On a scale from 1 (meaning right every time) to 0 (no better than random chance), interviews scored only 0.2, IQ tests and biodata techniques 0.4. The overwhelming majority of companies, however, still rely on interviews and references.

3.4 Remember that selection is not the end of the manpower resourcing process: only the beginning. The organisation must retain, deploy and develop its new recruits.

Recruitment

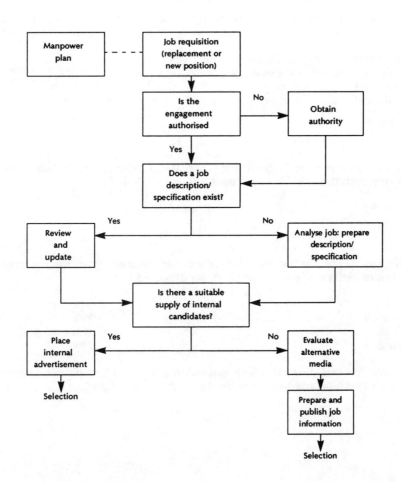

QUESTIONS

1 Which of the following aspects of the personnel management function should come within the manpower plan?

Aspects
1. Reduction of avoidable labour wastage
2. Policies for selection and declaration of redundancies
3. Programmes for reducing manpower costs
4. Identification of training needs

A Aspect 1 only
B Aspects 1 and 2 only
C Aspects 1, 2 and 4 only
D Aspects 1, 2, 3 and 4

Circle your answer

A	B	C	D

2 Manpower planning can be seen in terms of supply and demand forecasting. Which of the following is a factor in the anticipated demand for (rather than supply of) labour?

A Age structure of the workforce
B Proposed organisational expansion
C Skill profile of the workforce
D Trends in the labour market

Circle your answer

A	B	C	D

3 Stan Duppenby-Counthead (& Sons) has 1,000 staff in clerical grade 1, the lowest grade in the company, with the following age structure:

Under 20	600
20 - 30	300
Over 30	100

Based on last year's figures and this year's performance appraisals, wastage rates and promotion prospects in the next two years are expected to be:

	Wastage	*Promotion*
Under 20	30%	10%
20 - 30	10%	40%
Over 30	5%	20%

The demand forecast shows that with expansion at Head Office, given constant productivity levels, 1,200 clerical grade 1 staff will be required in 2 years' time.

The estimated number of recruits required in 2 years' time is:

A 215
B 415
C 585
D 615

Circle your answer

A   B   C   D

4 Which of the following will help rather than hinder the manpower planning process?

A Consumer fashion
B The importance of leadership in employee morale
C Improvements in information technology
D Unionisation

Circle your answer

A   B   C   D

5 In which of the following cases will the labour stability index

$$\left(\frac{\text{Number of employees with more than 1 year's service}}{\text{Number of employees one year ago}} \times 100\right)$$

be of more interest to the manpower planner than a simple wastage rate?

Cases
1 The organisation is undergoing a period of rapid expansion
2 The organisation is worried that it is losing experienced employees in significant numbers
3 A long-term forecast of promotion prospects is required

A Case 2 only
B Cases 2 and 3 only
C Cases 1 and 2 only
D Cases 1, 2 and 3

Circle your answer

A   B   C   D

6 Unless the organisation is *planning* to contract its workforce, the main disadvantage of 'natural' labour turnover is its:

A cost in financial terms
B effect on career prospects
C effect on the age structure of the workforce
D effect on morale

Circle your answer

A   B   C   D

117

7 A 'promotion programme' includes all of the following, *except*:

A job analysis
B manpower planning
C planning for training
D establishment of criteria for potential review

Circle your answer

A	B	C	D

8 Carrie R Planning Ltd has a job vacancy in one of its departments. Sonya Bykemate, the personnel manager, knows that there are people in the company who could do the job if they were promoted to it. There is also a reasonable pool of suitably skilled individuals available in the local area, who are easily reached through the employment agency used by the firm. Sonya might choose to recruit from outside rather than promote from within, on consideration of:

A reduction of risk
B motivation of the existing workforce
C socialisation of the new jobholder
D innovation and adaptability

Circle your answer

A	B	C	D

9 The selection process starts with the:

A content of the job advertisement
B medium chosen to advertise the vacancy
C application form
D interview

Circle your answer

A	B	C	D

10 Which of the following would be defined as a 'recruitment' rather than a 'selection' activity?

A Preparation of a job description
B Measurement of applicant against job description
C Interview
D Taking up references

Circle your answer

A	B	C	D

11 The Personnel Manager of Pullham Inn is recruiting a Head Chef. He has prepared a detailed statement of the physical and mental activities involved in the job, plus some notes to the effect that the handling of sous-chefs and pastry-chefs is a very delicate affair, and that the job requires a high tolerance of heat and pressure. This statement is expressed in behavioural terms, ie the actions, knowledge, judgement etc involved in the Head Chef's job. This statement is a:

A   job analysis
B   job description
C   job specification
D   personnel specification

Circle your answer

A   B   C   D

12 Job descriptions have advantages for all the following, *except:*

A   job evaluation
B   training needs analysis
C   recruitment
D   employee flexibility

Circle your answer

A   B   C   D

13 The following items appear on the job description of the Personnel Manager of Watt C Dew Ltd.

Items
1.   *Regular relationships:*
     Departmental managers
     Works Convenor
     Shop Stewards
     Local Job Centre officials *etc*

2.   *Principal responsibilities*
     Ensure the efficient recruitment of suitable and sufficient staff
     Implement the company's payment policy
     Provide adequate training programmes for staff induction and development *etc*

3.   *Attributes/qualifications required*
     Experience in personnel or line management in a relevant environment
     Professional qualifications, including membership of the IPM *etc*

4.   *Assessment*
     Leadership: Capable within own departmental responsibilities, but shows some reluctance in use of functional authority
     Decision-making: has consistently made sound decisions
     Technical-knowledge: shows good awareness of legislation, behavioural techniques *etc*

What *shouldn't* be on the job description?

A   Item 1
B   Item 2
C   Item 3
D   Item 4

Circle your answer

A   B   C   D

14 Professor Rodger's Seven Point Plan personnel specification does *not* explicitly include:

A   physical attributes
B   interests
C   motivation
D   background circumstances

Circle your answer

A   B   C   D

15 Mann & Glevilles Ltd has a job vacancy for a junior clerk/office helper at one of the offices. Of the following, the most suitable medium for their job advertisement would be:

A   the journal of an accountancy body
B   national newspapers
C   local newspapers
D   television

Circle your answer

A   B   C   D

16 Matt Black and Di Gloss run a small DIY shop. They're recruiting an assistant. Matt puts up an ad on the notice board of his Men's Club. It says: 'Person required to assist in DIY shop. Full time. Aged under 28. Contact ....' Two candidates turn up for interview the following day: a man and a woman (who's heard about the job by word of mouth, through Di). Matt interviews them both, asking work-related questions. He also asks the woman whether she has children and how much time she expects to spend dealing with family matters.

Under the Sex Discrimination Act 1975, Matt has laid himself open to allegations of:

A   one count of discrimination
B   two counts of discrimination
C   three counts of discrimination
D   no discrimination at all

Circle your answer

A   B   C   D

17 Under the Race Relations Act 1976, which of the following is a prohibited form of discrimination?

A   Auditioning black men only for the part of Othello

B   Specifying the race of models for an advertisement for reasons of authenticity

C   Offering training exclusively to a racial group which has so far been under-represented

D   Setting selection tests relevant to a particular cultural tradition

Circle your answer

A   B   C   D

18 A job selection interview has several aims. If you were conducting one, though, you should *not* be concerned with:

A   comparing the applicant against the job/personnel specification

B   getting as much information as possible about the applicant

C   giving the applicant information about the job and organisation

D   making the applicant feel he has been treated fairly

Circle your answer

A   B   C   D

19 The use of selection boards, or large panel interviews, has some advantages for selection process, mainly in its:

A   administrative aspects
B   formality
C   testing of human relations skills
D   variety and randomness of questions asked

Circle your answer

A   B   C   D

20 Amon Leigh-Hewman is interviewing a candidate for a vacancy in his firm. He asks a question about the candidate's views on a work-related issue. The candidate starts to answer, and sees to his horror that Amon is pursing his lips and shaking his head slightly to himself. 'Of course, that's what *some* people would say', continues the candidate, 'but I myself .....' Amon smiles. His next question is 'Don't you think that ...?'

Amon is getting a distorted view of the candidate because of:

A the halo effect
B contagious bias
C stereotyping
D logical error

Circle your answer

| A | B | C | D |

21 A selection test designed to measure abilities or skills already possessed by a candidate in a job-related area is called:

A an intelligence test
B an aptitude test
C a proficiency test
D a personality test

Circle your answer

| A | B | C | D |

22 Selection tests such as IQ tests and personality tests may not be effective in getting the right person for the job for several reasons. Which of the following criticisms is *false*, though?

A Test results can be influenced by practice and coaching rather than genuine ability

B Subjects are able (and tend) to deliberately falsify results

C Tests do not eliminate bias and subjectivity

D Tests are generally less accurate predictors of success than interviews

Circle your answer

| A | B | C | D |

23 'Ability', as diagnosed by interview and testing, is an indicator of:

A future performance
B current potential
C current motivation
D future success

Circle your answer

| A | B | C | D |

24 Which of the following circumstances for dismissal is not defined as redundancy, under the Employment Protection (Consolidation) Act 1978?

A The employer has ceased to carry on the business

B The employer has ceased to carry on the business in the place where the employee was employed

C The requirements of the business for employees to carry out work of a particular kind have ceased or diminished or are expected to

D The employee is not or is no longer capable or competent to carry out the work for which he is employed

Circle your answer

A B C D

Data for questions 25 and 26

Jobbs (Comforters) Ltd makes sundry woollen goods. Ray Troubel has worked there full time for three years. He has just been 'sacked' by the company, because - despite suitable warnings he has persisted in absenteeism and poor time-keeping. Tina Toyle has worked there six months and Jane Bubbal two years. They have both been given notice because of pregnancy - although they are both capable of carrying on their work adequately. Tom Hubble has reached the end of a fixed term contract, and the company is not renewing it on the same terms, having shut down Tom's area of the business, and selected him fairly for redundancy.

25 Who has been dismissed under UK law?

A Troubel only
B Troubel and Bubbal
C Troubel, Bubbal and Toyle only
D Hubble, Bubbal, Toyle and Troubel

Circle your answer

A B C D

26 Who will be entitled to compensation for unfair dismissal?

A Bubbal only
B Bubbal and Toyle only
C Bubbal, Toyle and Hubble only
D Hubble, Bubbal, Toyle and Troubel

Circle your answer

A B C D

123

CHAPTER 12

MANPOWER DEVELOPMENT

This chapter covers the following topics:

- Performance assessment
- Training
- Management development

1. Performance assessment

1.1 The general purpose of a staff assessment system is to improve the efficiency of the organisation, by ensuring that individuals are performing to the best of their ability and developing their potential. Within this overall aim, assessments are used in practice for:

- reward review
- performance review and
- potential review

1.2 *Performance* review is commonly used - but commonly misunderstood, and employed purely as a review of results in order to offer praise, criticism and remuneration (thus overlapping with reward review). It can have a much more proactive and constructive role in the fulfilment of organisational objectives (and the manpower plan in particular). And that is the assessment of current performance standards and results with a view to the future: planning and evaluating training and development programmes, identifying training needs, employee aptitudes, work problems and opportunities.

1.3 Whichever method of reaching and recording assessments is used, and whatever criteria they are based on, the attitude and role of assessor and assessed alike are crucial. The assessor, in particular, may adopt a role anywhere on a spectrum from 'judge' and 'critic' to 'counsellor' and 'helper', and at the latter end of this scale, appraisal will (organisational arrangements permitting) be a thoroughly *collaborative* process.

> "Why . . . are so few managers able to use the full capacities of their staff to increase productivity by expanding their contributions to their jobs? Surely it is largely because they concentrate on what is wrong, on solving problems and overcoming obstacles, rather than on where they want to go and the prospects of getting there through the fuller use of the individual talents of their staff."
>
> (Cuming, *Personnel Management: Theory and Practice*)

1.4   A typical system for assessment comprises:

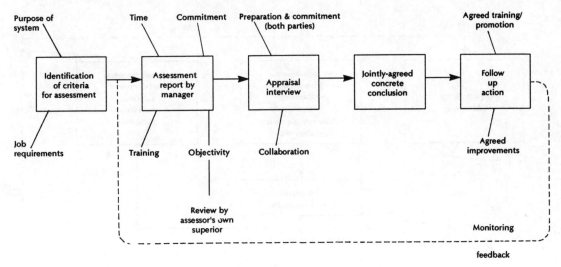

2.   Training

2.1   Training, like recruitment and selection, is an aspect of the management plan concerned with

- fitting people to the requirements of their jobs
- securing better occupational adjustment and
- in methodological terms, setting and achieving targets.

2.2   Like recruitment and selection, too, it is important that training be planned, implemented and evaluated in a systematic way. A rational training programme may be illustrated as on the following page.

2.3   There are so many decisions to be made about training - whether, in what, how, when, by whom - that evaluation, as you see from the diagram, is a complex business. It can focus on:

- training inputs (materials and methods used)
- trainee reactions to the experience
- trainee learning
- changes in job behaviour following training
- organisational change as a result of training or
- the impact of training on organisational goals (cost-benefit analysis).

Training

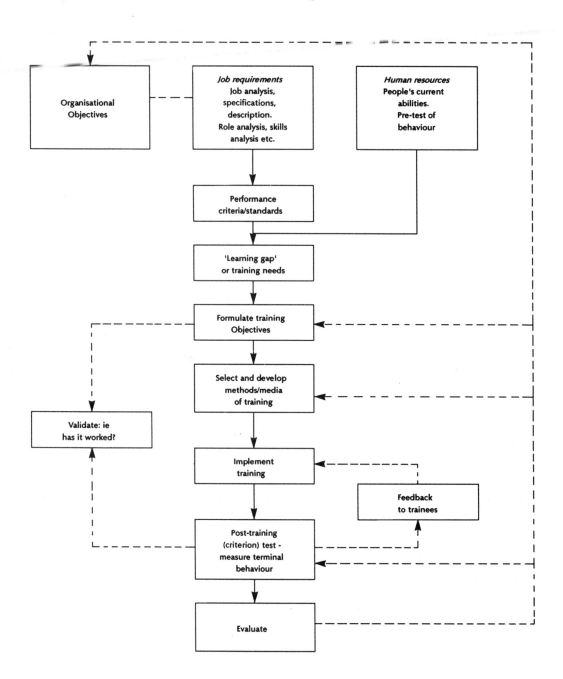

2.4 This indicates the potential impact of training on the organisation and the individual trainee. An impact as yet, according to recent reports, insufficiently acknowledged by British companies, since:

- British companies do not spend enough on training
- few employers think training is central to their corporate strategy, or directly linked to profitability
- most employers are complacent about the amount of training they provide
- there is little pressure on companies for on-going improvement of training provision.

Following reports by Constable, McCormick and Handy, the Management Charter Initiative (MCI) has set out to ensure that managers are (and can demonstrate that they are) properly trained.

3. Management development

3.1 Management development is a process whereby managers

- gain experience
- receive instruction and guidance from their superiors
- enhance their ability and potential through training and education
- plan their future and the opportunities open to them in the organisation

This is obviously a collaborative activity of the organisation and the individual manager.

3.2 It embraces both skill/ability development and career development, and its objectives therefore include not only improved performance capacity (from managers and those they manage) but also secured management succession (ie a pool of promotable individuals).

3.3 Approaches to management development fall into three main categories.

1. Management education - study for an MBA degree or Diploma in Management Studies, for example
2. Management training - largely off-the-job formal learning activities

3. 'Experiential learning' - 'learning by doing'.

The last of these categories has gained in popularity in recent years, with methods such as Management by Objectives claiming a higher degree of performance relevance and 'ownership' by the trainee. Constable and McCormick, however, in their influential report 'The Making of British Managers', suggest that there is still a place for a systematic education and training programme featuring study for professional qualifications and design of in-house training courses.

QUESTIONS

1 Which of the following is *not* an application of performance assessment?

A merit rating
B identification of training needs
C potential review
D job evaluation

Circle your answer

A   B   C   D

2 Howie Dewing is assessing the performance of his subordinates. According to the assessment system of the organisation, he has been given a list of characteristics and performance elements, with notes on how terms such as 'application' and 'integrity' are to be interpreted in the work context. He is required to comment on how the appraisee 'measures up' in terms of each factor.

This appraisal technique is called:

A overall assessment
B guided assessment
C grading
D behavioural incident analysis

Circle your answer

A   B   C   D

3
Appraisal techniques
1. Behavioural incident methods
2. Overall assessment
3. Results-oriented approach
4. Grading

Features
(i) Also known as rating scales
(ii) For example, Management by Objectives
(iii) Not based on trait analysis but observation of 'real-life' actions and reactions
(iv) Subject to managers' ability to express judgements clearly in writing

Which of the following matches the appraisal techniques (1-4) correctly with a feature of each (i-iv)?

A 1 (ii) ● 2 (iii) ● 3 (i) ● 4 (iv)
B 1 (iv) ● 2 (ii) ● 3 (iii) ● 4 (i)
C 1 (iii) ● 2 (iv) ● 3 (ii) ● 4 (i)
D 1 (iii) ● 2 (iv) ● 3 (i) ● 4 (ii)

Circle your answer

A   B   C   D

4 Changing from 'trait' appraisal to the use of results-oriented criteria for assessment of individuals and their work - ie specific targets and standards of performance agreed in advance by manager and subordinate - will have an effect on:

Aspects
1. the subordinate's role in appraisal
2. the assessor's role in appraisal
3. the subordinate's motivation
4. the effectiveness of the appraisal scheme

A   Aspect 4 only
B   Aspects 3 and 4 only
C   Aspects 1, 2 and 3 only
D   Aspects 1, 2, 3 and 4

Circle your answer

A   B   C   D

5 Tel Mistrate is conducting his appraisal interviews. His philosophy is simple. He tells the subordinate in question how he has been assessed - good and bad - and then gives him or her a chance to put questions, suggest improvement targets, explain shortcomings, identify problems. This approach is known as the:

A   'tell and sell' method
B   'tell and listen' method
C   'problem-solving' approach
D   peer rating method

Circle your answer

A   B   C   D

6 Appraisal is a complex human relations and political exercise. Apprais*er* and apprais*ee* alike need all the help they can get. Which of the following is *not* necessarily a helpful factor in an appraisal scheme?

A   The purpose of the system is positive, and clearly expressed

B   There is reasonable standardisation throughout the organisation

C   Time is allowed for appraisee preparation, appraiser training etc

D   There is an implied link between assessment and reward

Circle your answer

A   B   C   D

7 Peter Prince-Hipple is conducting potential reviews of all his staff, so that he can work out what training they need, and whether they're 'ripe' for promotion. The *least* relevant information he will need to gather for this purpose will be:

A performance in the job currently held

B strengths and weaknesses in existing skills and qualities

C goals, aspirations and attitudes of the appraisee

D opportunities available in the organisation

Circle your answer

A   B   C   D

8 If you were drawing up a checklist for the 'induction' process, for the use of departmental supervisors and managers, which of the following activities should you include?

Activities
1. Introducing the recruit to the people in the work place
2. Explaining the nature of the job, procedures, rules and responsibilities
3. Drawing up a list of learning priorities and objectives
4. Monitoring the progress of recruits' coaching/training/performance

A Activity 1 only
B Activities 1 and 2 only
C Activities 2 and 3 only
D Activities 1, 2, 3 and 4

Circle your answer

A   B   C   D

9 Formal learning activities which may *not* lead to qualifications, and which may be received at any time in a working career' are:

A education
B training
C development
D induction

Circle your answer

A   B   C   D

10 Phil E Stein & Sons is having problems with its training programme. Staff never seem to have learnt the 'right' things, ie things that are relevant to their jobs. Some of the staff don't seem to have learnt anything at all: they don't take to the methods used. The company hasn't been too worried so far, but the new personnel manager is passionate about training and has been horrified by some of the comments he has heard flying aound the senior management offices. Which of the following comments is likely to be his own view of the matter?

A   'Training is a matter for the personnel department'

B   'The important thing is to *have* a training programme'

C   'Training is both a cause and an effect of change'

D   'Training is all cost and no benefit'

Circle your answer

A	B	C	D

11 Three of the following pieces of information are required for the identification of training needs. Which isn't?

A   Job requirements
B   Entry behaviour
C   Cost of training
D   Learning gap

Circle your answer

A	B	C	D

12 You are required to draw up a training plan for that famous circus animal act, T. Chanoldo Gnu Tricks. Which is the most effective of the following ways of expressing its training objectives?

A   The course should improve key skills needed in the act

B   At the end of the course, team members should be able to apply those skills in the ring

C   At the end of the course, team members should have a better appreciation of animal characteristics

D   At the end of the course, team members should be able to distinguish between a gnu and a hartebeast

Circle your answer

A	B	C	D

131

13 In which of the following areas is there an advantage to formal training methods, as opposed to on-the-job experience or coaching?

    A   Safe environment for skills acquisition
    B   Relationship of learning to the job
    C   Application of learning to the job
    D   Continuity of work effort

Circle your answer

A	B	C	D

14 Which of the following are 'on-the-job' training methods?

Methods
1. Day-release
2. Job rotation
3. Coaching
4. Temporary promotion

    A   Method 3 only
    B   Methods 1 and 3 only
    C   Methods 2, 3 and 4 only
    D   Methods 1, 2, 3 and 4

Circle your answer

A	B	C	D

15 If you were a training manager - and a bit of a 'purist' as far as the teaching of skills, techniques and theories goes - and you had to choose between *on*-the-job and *off*-the-job training for your company, you might choose *on*-the-job training because of its:

    A   concentration on the learning process

    B   greater objectivity on the part of the trainer

    C   relevance to the custom and practice of the organisation

    D   application of skills in the work context

Circle your answer

A	B	C	D

16 Many group training methods are aimed primarily at exploring team-building, communication and interpersonal skills. Which of the following does *not* have this as its primary purpose?

    A   Role-playing
    B   Brainstorming
    C   Sensitivity training
    D   Leadership exercises

Circle your answer

A	B	C	D

17 Buttsworth Everypenny is the personnel officer of his firm. He has to justify the costs of his training programme to the company accountant. 'Quantifiable benefits, man,' says the latter, impatiently. 'Where are the quantifiable benefits?'

Which of the following benefits of his programme might Buttsworth hesitate to put forward?

A Increased speed of working
B Increased accuracy of working
C Increased satisfaction of employees
D Decreased accident rate

Circle your answer

A   B   C   D

18 In the process of the 'validation' of training, the question asked is:

A Did we do the right thing?
B Did we do it right?
C Was it worth doing?
D Did it achieve its objectives?

Circle your answer

A   B   C   D

19 Training can be evaluated in various ways. If you wanted a fairly straightforward and easily-measured criterion by which to judge the effectiveness of training, you would probably consider:

A learning objectives achieved
B behaviour change of trainees
C trainee views/reactions
D cost/benefit to the organisation

Circle your answer

A   B   C   D

20 Which of the following activities would be identified as 'development'?

Activities
1. Career planning for individual managers
2. Deputising while the boss is absent
3. Counselling and appraisal
4. Education and training

A Activity 1 only
B Activities 1 and 3 only
C Activities 2, 3 and 4 only
D Activities 1, 2, 3 and 4

Circle your answer

A   B   C   D

21 Management education and training may be more useful than 'on-the-job' development for:

A helping individual managers to perform at a satisfactory level

B helping functional managers to make the transition to general management

C improving the performance of work teams as a result of better leadership

D providing a pool of promotable managers

Circle your answer

A	B	C	D

22

Department:				Manager:	
Situation as at / /19 .				*On absence/leaving:*	*Ready?(✓)*
Post	*Jobholder*	*Age*	*Performance*		
				1: 2:	
				1: 2:	
				1: 2:	
				1: 2:	

This document is a:

A manpower plan
B retention plan
C succession plan
D training plan

Circle your answer

A	B	C	D

23 Climie Nupthelader is responsible for training and development in his company's head office. The young graduates currently on a two-year management programme have complained. Departmental heads don't seem to know what kind of training they're supposed to be providing. The graduates are given dull routine work they master in five days - but are kept at it for a month at a time. They are not told whether they're doing it well or badly. They're bored and fed up - despite the high salary paid to them while they're 'in training'.

The *first* element in the design of the training programme which Climie has got wrong (or ignored faults in) is:

A   training needs analysis
B   formulation of training objectives
C   instruction of training staff
D   provision of 'reinforcement'

Circle your answer

A   B   C   D

24 Study the following aspects of management, each of which has a different characteristic according to whether it is part of general or functional management.

Aspects	Characteristics	
Orientation	task-oriented	(1)
	goal-oriented	(2)
Role	facilitator	(3)
	organiser	(4)
Information	informal contacts	(5)
	formal channels	(6)
Goals	short-term	(7)
	long-term	(8)

Those aspects which apply to *general* management are:

A   1, 3, 5, 8
B   2, 4, 6, 7
C   3, 4, 5, 8
D   2, 3, 5, 8

Circle your answer

A   B   C   D

CHAPTER 13

THE WORK ENVIRONMENT

This chapter covers the following topics:

- The work environment
- Health and safety

1. The work environment

1.1 The physical environment of work includes:

- the external environment, ie. the *siting* of the office or factory and its surrounding area, and

- the internal environment: layout, decor, lighting, heating, ventilation etc.

1.2 A recent report from America investigated the relationship between the office environment and employee satisfaction and productivity. Among other findings, the report suggested that:

(a) office workers now feel that their productivity has 'peaked', and would not increase if the work environment were enhanced. Executives, however, persist in their belief that there is productivity potential to be realised;

(b) the office environment is still of importance to workers, despite the fact that it is no longer closely linked in their minds with increased productivity.

These findings fit in with Herzberg's view of working conditions as a 'hygiene' factor. A good working environment will not be able to motivate employees to enhanced performance (beyond the short-term effects of a fresh improvement, perhaps) but shortcomings will be important to them, as a source of dissatisfaction.

1.3 The physical environment's main effect on worker morale and/or productivity will therefore come from:

- *the health and safety of workers.* A hazardous or unhygienic environment is - humanly and legally - unacceptable, and will not give workers the physical support they need to put in consistent, sustained effort

- *its enabling of performance*. Certain conditions physically and psychologically enable the worker to perform tasks efficiently, without stress, fatigue and other forms of 'interference'. In addition, the planning and layout of space in the office or factory can contribute to the efficiency of work flow ie. the movement of people, documents and work-in-progress

- *its contribution to organisational culture*. The physical environment is an expression of the organisation's self-image to customers/clients *and* to employees. It can alter the way employees feel about their work and their organisation, (is it smart or 'shabby'? high-tech or antiquated? a sign of caring or indifference on the part of the organisation?). It can also affect the amount of social contact and interaction available to workers: consider the difference between cubicles and open plan offices, for example.

1.4 The work environment has undergone profound changes in recent decades, with the increased automation of production and information processing. New technology may have the affect of removing dirt and danger from the environment, but has also been said to isolate workers more, and to place new stresses on them: there may be fewer natural rest pauses and less task variety in automated work (eg. for the word processor, who spends more continuous time at the keyboard than the typist), and new health hazards (eg. from VDU radiation and glare). Technology also affects the rest of the work environment, with a need for support systems for heat control and ventilation, adjusted lighting, wire and cable management, noise shielding etc.

2. Health and safety

2.1 Health and safety at work may be considered important for three reasons.

(a) Primarily (one hopes) to protect employees from pain and suffering.

(b) To fulfil legal obligations.

(c) To control the (substantial) costs associated with absence through illness, accident, fire etc.

2.2 The purpose of a health and safety programme is therefore essentially *preventative* rather than 'reactive', although there should be contingency plans for when ill health, accident or fire *does* occur.

A systematic health and safety programme will work as illustrated on the following page.

2.3 It's important to remember that 'occupational health' addresses not only the control of toxic or otherwise dangerous substances and processes in the work environment (eg lead oxide, radiation or asbestos) but also the control of other influences on the employee's physical and mental wellbeing.

It therefore involves management choices about the design of jobs, work patterns and hours of work, and other aspects of employment which may cause fatigue or stress.

Health and safety programme

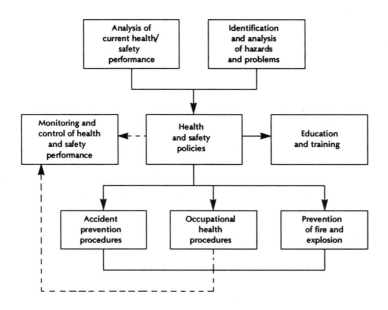

2.4 Stress has increasingly been recognised as a feature of modern working conditions, rapid change and the competitive ethos, and considerable research effort has been directed to:

(a) investigating the causes and symptoms of stress
(b) increasing awareness of stress in organisations and
(c) designing techniques and programmes for stress control

'Stress' is a term often loosely used to describe feelings of tension or exhaustion, usually associated with too much, or overly demanding, work. In fact, stress is the product of demands made on the individual's physical *and mental* energies: monotony, feelings of failure or insecurity etc are just as stressful to workers as 'work pressure'.

Stress can be *stimulating* as well as harmful: some people work best under pressure. Harmful stress or 'strain', however, manifests itself as low morale, withdrawal (reluctance to communicate, absenteeism or leaving) and/or nervous tension (causing irritability, preoccupation with details, and physical symptoms such as sleeplessness, headaches, skin disorders etc). This can adversely affect performance - which is why 'stress management' has become a major issue.

1

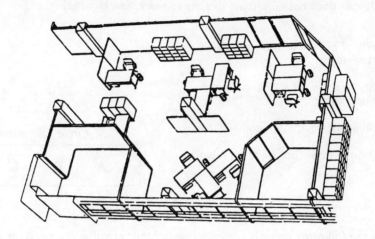

The above plan illustrates an office layout which would be described as:

A closed office
B open plan
C landscaped
D mixture of closed and open

Circle your answer

A   B   C   D

2 Here are some features of open plan offices that have advantages and disadvantages. Which one is an advantage only, without any 'minus' points?

A Lack of privacy
B Easier supervision of routine work
C Flexibility and economy of space utilisation
D Freer communication and contact

Circle your answer

A   B   C   D

3 Mr and Mrs Swett run a retail chain (Swett Shops). At their Head Office, staff have complained about the physical environment in which they have to work: it is not that it isn't safe, but it is very *stressful* to work in. Mr and Mrs Swett are surprised. They've had the office furniture designed specially to ensure a comfortable position. The decor is tasteful, in yellow, magnolia and green. Light is provided by bright bulb lighting. There is a continuous buzz of noise from printers and telephones and conversation, of course, but they hope to get some acoustic screens and hoods later on. What can be causing stress?

It's most likely to be the:

A furniture
B decor
C lighting
D noise

Circle your answer

A   B   C   D

4   Workplace layout does not contribute directly to *work flow* by offering:

A   proximity of people who need to be in contact regularly

B   flexibility to allow for staff growth and facility upgrading

C   accessibility of equipment and facilities

D   separation of non-work areas from work areas

Circle your answer

A	B	C	D

5   In which of the following areas is computer technology creating the need for adjustment of the office environment?

Areas
1. Heating and ventilation
2. Lighting
3. Furniture
4. Carpeting

A   Areas 1 and 2 only
B   Areas 2 and 3 only
C   Areas 1, 2 and 3
D   Areas 1, 2, 3 and 4

Circle your answer

A	B	C	D

6   Ergonomics is a sphere of scientific research which explores:

A   the best workplace layout to facilitate work flow

B   the design of machinery and furniture, to maximise comfort

C   the relationship between man and his working environment

D   the similarity of the control mechanism in man and machine

Circle your answer

A	B	C	D

7 Noise in the work place can be stressful, but is *least* damaging to concentration if it is in the form of:

A low volume, potentially meaningful sounds
B continuous, loud, random noise
C intermittent, loud, random noise
D unexplained variations in noise level

Circle your answer

A   B   C   D

8 Monotony has been identified as an 'interference' in worker performance. Which of the following is most likely to cause or aggravate monotony?

A Rest pauses
B Payment by results
C Social interaction
D Task fragmentation

Circle your answer

A   B   C   D

9 Breaks and 'rest pauses' in work are most effective in preventing the build-up of fatigue if they are:

Options
1. fixed/scheduled 'off-the-clock' breaks
2. naturally occurring in the 'pattern' of the job
3. infrequent but lengthy
4. short but frequent

A Options 1 and 4
B Options 2 and 4
C Options 1 and 3
D Options 2 and 3

Circle your answer

A   B   C   D

10 The main advantage of shiftworking for the organisation is:

A production efficiencies
B employee health
C economies on pay
D employee satisfaction

Circle your answer

A   B   C   D

11 Which of the following benefits can be claimed for flexitime?

Benefits
1. Reduced absenteeism
2. Reduced stress
3. Enhanced morale
4. Facilitated planning and scheduling

A Benefit 3 only
B Benefits 2 and 3 only
C Benefits 1, 2 and 3 only
D Benefits 1, 2, 3 and 4

Circle your answer

A   B   C   D

12 A person is less likely to suffer stress if he or she is:

A emotionally sensitive
B flexible and easily influenced
C competent in interpersonal relations
D acutely conscientious

Circle your answer

A   B   C   D

13 The activities of:

- identifying substances which are actually or potentially hazardous;
- identifying the effect of methods and processes of work on the human body and mind; and
- controlling the environment and substances, so as to minimise risk;

are all part of:

A ergonomics
B occupational health programmes
C safety programmes
D welfare services

Circle your answer

A   B   C   D

14 Which of the following costs of accidents would be significantly reduced if the organisation had successful accident prevention procedures?

Costs
1. Cost of providing first aid facilities and/or materials
2. Time lost by the injured employee and others
3. Insurance of employees against injury or death at work
4. Compensation payments and fines issuing from legal action by injured employees

A   Costs 2 and 4 only
B   Costs 2, 3 and 4 only
C   Costs 1, 2 and 4 only
D   Costs 1, 2, 3 and 4

Circle your answer

A   B   C   D

15 Grace Fuhl is going on an inspection tour of her Company's branch office in Norfolk. She is dismayed at the image it presents to visitors. Everything is shabby and untidy, with frayed carpets, peeling paint and files piled on the floor between desks. The staff have obviously got wind of her coming and tried to straighten things out: quite a bit of the mess has been hidden away on the back stairs, behind the fire door, and someone has rather obviously been mopping the floor, which is still wet as she walks in. There's consternation as people see her in the doorway. The supervisor is standing on a swivel chair trying to dust the top shelf of her bookcase. 'Welcome to the Diss Grace Fuhl office', she says.

How many common causes of injury or potential hazard can you identify in the scenario above?

A   2
B   3
C   5
D   6

Circle your answer

A   B   C   D

16 Which of the following is *not* the duty of an employer, under the Health and Safety at Work Act 1974 (and regulations under the Act)?

A   To allow safety representatives (appointed by a recognised trade union) access and inspection in order to check the effectiveness of safety measures

B   To establish a safety committee at the written request of two safety representatives

C   To comply with recommendations made by the safety representatives or safety committee not less than three months after consultation

D   To prepare and keep up to date a written statement of policy on health and safety

Circle your answer

A   B   C   D

17 Under UK law, responsibility for health and safety of people on work premises ultimately resides with:

A   the Health and Safety Executive
B   senior management
C   safety representatives
D   senior management, supervisory management and the employee

Circle your answer

| A | B | C | D |

18 Under UK law the employer is *not* considered responsible for an employee's injury where:

A   the employee 'consents' to the risk of injury because he is aware of the risk

B   the employee became inattentive or careless because of monotonous or stressful work

C   the injury occurred while the employee was not actually working (eg slipping while washing up a tea cup)

D   none of the above

Circle your answer

| A | B | C | D |

19 Under the Factories Act 1961, the occupier of a factory has an absolute duty to fence securely all prime movers (ie machines which provide power), all transmission machinery and every dangerous part of any machinery. The employer will *not* have complied with the Act if:

A   he fails to fence the dangerous machine because there is no practicable way of fencing it

B   he fails to keep the fence in place while the machine is not in motion

C   he fences a machine securely, but not so as prevent a determined and reckless employee from reaching through

D   he fails to fence a machine which would not normally be considered capable of causing injury

Circle your answer

| A | B | C | D |

20 Of the following arguments against the provision of welfare to employees, which contains most truth?

A   Welfare is provided by the State: there's nothing the organisation can do that wouldn't just be duplication

B   The non-work affairs of employees are not the employers' concern

C   Welfare is just charity: it's irrelevant to organisational objectives

D   Welfare is just a hygiene factor: it won't positively affect the performance of employees

Circle your answer

| A | B | C | D |

21 Under UK law, an employee is entitled to time off work with pay for all the following purposes - except one, and that is:

A   ante-natal care, for pregnant women

B   duties or training in the employee's capacity as a trade union official

C   public duties performed by employees who are Justices of the Peace or members of local authority bodies

D   duties under the Health and Safety at Work Act, in the employee's capacity as a union-appointed safety representative

Circle your answer

| A | B | C | D |

22 Collective bargaining is concerned with reaching agreement about two types of 'rules': *substantive* rules, and *procedural* rules. Which of the following are substantive rules?

Rules
1. Demarcation rules
2. Rules determining pay scales
3. Rules for what disputes should be referred to ACAS
4. Rules for what negotiating machinery should be set up

A   Rules 1 and 2 only
B   Rules 1 and 3 only
C   Rules 3 and 4 only
D   Rules 1, 2 and 3 only

Circle your answer

| A | B | C | D |

145

23 Japanese labour relations are often considered to be superior to those prevailing in most Western countries. The following are some of the possible reasons why this might be so. Which of them, according to current thinking, is *no longer* a major contributory factor?

    A   The use of quality circles

    B   Guaranteed lifetime employment

    C   Consultation and communication between management and workers

    D   The use of first-line supervisors, who have risen through the ranks rather than been appointed by management

Circle your answer

A   B   C   D

24 According to UK law, which of the following would be considered lawful trade dispute(s)?

Disputes
1. A dispute between workers and their own employers, wholly or mainly about work-related matters
2. An inter-union dispute about demarcation
3. A dispute between workers and employers other than their own
4. A dispute overseas (eg in support of South African workers)

    A   Dispute 1 only
    B   Disputes 1 and 2 only
    C   Disputes 1, 2 and 4 only
    D   Disputes 1, 2, 3 and 4

Circle your answer

A   B   C   D

CHAPTER 14

THEORIES OF ORGANISATION AND MANAGEMENT

This chapter covers the following topics:

- Theories of organisation and management
- Classical and human relations approaches
- Systems and contingency approaches

1. Theories of organisation and management

1.1 Theories about organisations tend not to be 'theories' at all, strictly speaking, but '*approaches*', offering ways of looking at issues such as organisational structure, management functions or motivation.

These approaches frequently form the basis of examination syllabuses, but it is worth getting into perspective their usefulness in practice.

None of these approaches can be used to predict with certainty what the 'behaviour' of an organisation, a manager or employee will be in any given situation. Nor can they guarantee that application of the principles they put forward will result in effectiveness and efficiency for the organisation.

1.2 They can, however, provide helpful and/or throught provoking ways of analysing organisational phenomena, and 'frameworks' within which practical problems and situations can be tackled.

Theories abouut organisation and management may also perform a useful function in encouraging managers to learn from the experience and knowledge of researchers and experts in other disciplines, eg the behavioural sciences or systems theory.

1.3 We have covered some of the well-known theories and research in other chapters of this book. The questions in this chapter are intended primarily to help you if you are expected to know about particular theories and 'names' for your study course or exams. They will test in some detail your knowledge of who said what, and why. If you haven't studied this area before, the questions may be tough - but the comments on the solutions are more substantial than usual, so you can get a 'flavour' of the various theories. The following paragraphs are designed to give you an overview of how approaches to organisation and management have developed over time.

2. Classical and human relations approaches

2.1 The main early theorists who put forward ways of understanding organisations were mainly early practising managers - such as Henri Fayol (1841 - 1925) and F W Taylor (1856 - 1915). They analysed their own experience in management to produce a set of what they saw as 'principles' applicable in a wide variety of situations.

The label given to this body of theory is the *'Classical'* or *'Scientific Management'* approach. It is essentially prescriptive ie it attempts to suggest what is good - or even best - for organisations.

2.2 The classical approach to management was primarily concerned with the structure and activities of the *formal* organisation. Effective organisation was seen to be mainly dependent on factors such as the division of work, the establishment of a rational hierarchy of authority, span of control and unity of command.

The practical application of Taylor's 'scientific management' approach was the use of work study techniques to break work down into its smallest and simplest component parts, and the selection and training of workers to perform a single task in the most efficient way.

2.3 The classical school contributed techniques for studying the nature of work and solving problems of how it could be organised more efficiently.

2.4 The great objection to the scientific management approach, however, was that:

> "We have failed to train students in the study of social situations; we have thought that first-class technical training was sufficient in a modern and mechanical age. As a consequence, we are technically competent as no other age in history has been; and we combine this with utter social incompetence." *Elton Mayo*

2.5 From this critical perception of scientific management, an alternative school of management thought developed which emphasised the importance of human attitudes, values and relationships for the efficient and effective functioning of work organisations.

This approach was pioneered mainly by social scientists - rather than practising managers - and was based on research into human behaviour, with the intention of describing and thereafter predicting behaviour in organisations. Like classical theory, it is essentially prescriptive in its approach.

2.6 The first social scientists concentrated mainly on relationships and the concept of Social Man, with an emphasis on the employee's social or 'belonging' needs. This was called the *Human Relations* movement, 'founded' by Elton Mayo (1880 - 1949).

These ideas were followed up by various social psychologists - eg Maslow, McGregor, Herzberg and Likert - but with a change of emphasis. People were still considered to be the crucial factor in determining organisational effectiveness, but were recognised to have more than merely physical and social needs. Attention shifted towards 'higher' psychological needs for growth and self-fulfilment. This was labelled the *neo-Human Relations* School.

148

2.7 The 'human' approach contributed an awareness of the influence of the human factor at work on organisational performance. Most, if not all, of its theorists attempted to offer guidelines to enable practising managers to take appropriate actions to motivate employees and therefore (theoretically) to obtain the benefits of high productivity.

However, human relations thinking is difficult to apply in practice, and tends to emphasise the importance of work to the workers without really addressing the economic issues of output and profits: there is still no clearly proven link between motivation/job satisfaction and productivity or the achievement of organisational goals.

3. Systems and contingency approaches

3.1 The *systems approach* to organisations was developed at the Tavistock Institute of Human Relations in the 1950s, although General System Theory, in which it has its scientific roots, was pioneered in the 1930s. The approach was based on the idea that a work organisation can be treated as an open system, which takes in 'inputs' (capital, labour, information, materials) from its environment and converts them into 'outputs' to the environment (information, products, satisfied customers) in a continuing cycle.

3.2 The 'system' analogy can be helpful in that it

- draws attention to the *dynamic* aspects of organisation
- creates an awareness of *sub-systems*, each with potentially conflicting goals to be integrated
- focuses on interrelationships between aspects of the organisation, and between the organisation and its *environment*.

3.3 A diagram of the organisation as a open system with sub-systems might appear as follows.

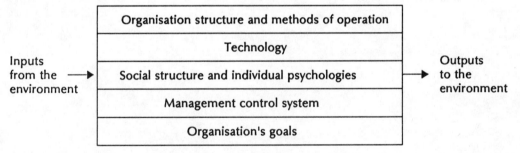

3.4 Trist and Bamforth developed a more complex approach which suggested that an organisation can be treated as an open socio-technical system. Any production system requires material technology (tasks, layout, equipment and tools etc) and social organisation (relationships between people): these two sub-systems are linked, and the system design must find a 'best fit' between the needs of both components.

This is called *'socio-technical systems'* theory.

3.5 Arising out of the open systems approach and its recognition of environmental influences, an essentially pragmatic view was developed which argued that *no* single theory can guarantee the organisation's effectiveness. Essentially, 'it all depends'.

This *'contingency approach'* aims to suggest the most appropriate organisational design and management style *in a given set of circumstances*. It rejects the universal 'one-best-way' approach, in favour of analysis of the internal factors and external environment of each organisation, and the design of organisational structure as a 'best fit' between the tasks, people and environment in the particular situation. As Buchanan and Huczynski put it: "With the coming of contingency theory, organisational design ceased to be 'off-the-shelf', but became tailored to the particular and specific needs of an organisation."

> "It is of great practical significance whether one kind of managerial 'style' or procedure for arriving at decisions, or one kind of organisational structure, is suitable for all organisations, or whether the managers in each organisation have to find that expedient that will best meet the particular circumstances of size, technology, competitive situation and so on."
> *Tom Lupton*

3.6 Awareness of the contingency approach will be of value in:

(a) encouraging managers to identify and define the particular circumstances of the situation they need to manage, and to devise and evaluate appropriate ways of handling them

(b) encouraging responsiveness and flexibility to changes in environmental factors through organisational structure and culture. Task performance and individual/group satisfaction are more important design criteria than having a single, unchanging type of organisational design. Within an organisation, there may be bureaucratic units, side by side with task-centred matrix units which can respond to particular pressures and environmental volatility.

QUESTIONS

1 Ivor Notion has a theory about his subordinates. He reckons they're mainly passive, but emotional and therefore unpredictable. If the firm is going to get any 'use' out of them at all, it'll have to control them: fortunately, they're easily manipulated. Offer them a bonus and they'll put forth the effort.

Ivor clearly subscribes to Edgar Schein's model of:

A complex man
B self-actualising man
C rational-economic man
D social man

Circle your answer

A   B   C   D

Data for questions 2 and 3

Look at the following lists, which are in random order

Term	Type of	Described by
Benevolent-authoritative	Power (1)	Trist (i)
Coercive	System (2)	Likert (ii)
Socio-technical	Culture (3)	Etzioni (iii)
Role	Leadership (4)	Harrison (iv)

You can use the arabic and roman numerals to answer questions 2 and 3.

2 'Coercive' is a type of what, as described by whom?

A (3) ● (iii)
B (1) ● (iii)
C (1) ● (ii)
D (4) ● (iv)

Circle your answer

A   B   C   D

3 'Benevolent-authoritative' is a type of what, as described by whom?

A (1) ● (iii)
B (3) ● (i)
C (2) ● (i)
D (4) ● (ii)

Circle your answer

A   B   C   D

151

4 "By the end of the . . . period, the worker had been reduced to the role of an impersonal cog in the machine of production. His work became more and more narrowly specialised until he had little appreciation for his contribution to the total production." *Hicks*

Even if you haven't come across Hicks' comment before, you can infer that the period of management theory that he's referring to is the 'period' of:

A systems theory
B socio-technical systems theory
C scientific management
D neo-human relations theory

Circle your answer

A	B	C	D

5 Which of the following writers is *not* a member of the school of thought to which the others belong?

A Fayol
B McGregor
C Blake
D Herzberg

Circle your answer

A	B	C	D

6 Study the following table of organisational characteristics.

	Theory 1	Theory 2	Theory 3
Length of employment	varies, but mainly short	lifetime	long
Career plan	specialised in chosen area	progression and exposure in many areas	less specialised than Theory 1
Personnel appraisal	appraisal based on performance	appraisal based on loyalty to firm	primarily loyalty
Promotion	rapid	slow	slow
Decision making	individual by managers	consensus by many, communication upward, as well as downward	consensus by many
Responsibility	individual (as a result of decision making)	collective (as a result of decision making)	individual
Degree of corporate concern for employee	focused on performance only	entire, all aspects of life, including housing, family and schooling	whole person and all aspects of life

Theories 1, 2 and 3 respectively are:

A   theories J, A and Z
B   theories A, J and Z
C   theories X, Y and J
D   theories X, A and Y

Circle your answer

A   B   C   D

7 Blake's grid is a chart representing:

A   the balance in a manager's leadership style between concern for the task and concern for staff

B   the success of a manager's performance, for the purposes of appraisal

C   a manager's position on the continuum between a 'tight' and 'loose' style of leadership

D   a matrix organisation structure combining functional and line authority

Circle your answer

A   B   C   D

8 In the Durham coalfields, in the early 1950s, the Coal Board had been trying to introduce new mechanical processes in order to increase productivity, but the innovation provoked severe industrial unrest. Eric Trist and his colleagues at the Tavistock Institute were called in to investigate. It turned out that the Coal Board had changed the work organisation in order to introduce new coal-cutting equipment. Trist's solution to the coal mining problem was to recommend a different form of work organisation. There are various ways of 'labelling' his new form, but they would *not* include:

A   a socio-technical system
B   composite autonomous group working
C   primary work groups
D   the conventional longwall method

Circle your answer

A   B   C   D

9 Joan Woodward conducted a survey of firms in Essex, and observed that: "It appeared that .... were the most important factor in determining organisational structure and in setting the tone of human relationships inside the firm."

The missing words are:

A   employee needs
B   control requirements
C   technical methods
D   leadership styles

Circle your answer

A   B   C   D

10 The contingency approach says, in essence, that there is no 'ideal' form of organisation: 'it all depends' on the situation and environment of the organisation. Which of the following writers was *not* primarily interested in the capacity of organisations to adapt to environmental change (eg changes in markets, changes in technology etc)?

A   Lawrence and Lorsch
B   Gantt and Gilbreth
C   Burns and Stalker
D   Peters and Waterman

Circle your answer

A   B   C   D

11 The scientific management approach has been criticised for its 'de-humanising' effects on work. Which of the following, however, might be a positive contribution of scientific management in terms of the quality of working life?

A   The systematic study and analysis of work

B   The analysis of work into its constituent parts

C   The separation of 'planning' and 'doing'

D   None of the above

Circle your answer

A   B   C   D

12 The world has ended. Somewhere in the ether, four organisation and management theorists have at last got together to discuss the nature of bureaucracy, and whether the tight job definitions, specialisation and prevalence of rules are a source of dissatisfaction to employees.

'Bureaucracy is, from a purely technical point of view, capable of attaining the highest degree of efficiency and is in this sense formally the most rational means of carrying out imperative control over human beings', says one.

'It is difficult to see how these [organisational] problems can be solved efficiently without restoring responsible autonomy to primary groups throughout the system and ensuring that each of these groups has a satisfying sub-whole as its work task, and some scope for flexibility in work-pace', mutters another.

'Dissatisfaction arises from environmental factors - satisfaction can only arise from the job', agrees the third.

Judging from the views expressed above, the party to the discussion who hasn't yet spoken is:

A   Frederic Herzberg
B   Max Weber
C   Eric Trist
D   Elton Mayo

Circle your answer

A   B   C   D

SECTION 2

MARKING SCHEDULES AND COMMENTS

1: MARKING SCHEDULE

Question	Correct answer	Marks for the correct answer	Question	Correct answer	Marks for the correct answer
1	D	1	14	B	1
2	A	1	15	A	1
3	A	1	16	C	1
4	C	1	17	D	1
5	D	1	18	A	1
6	B	1	19	C	1
7	A	1	20	D	1
8	B	1	21	D	1
9	C	1	22	B	1
10	D	1	23	C	1
11	D	1	24	D	1
12	B	1	25	A	1
13	A	1			

YOUR MARKS

Total marks available   25   Your total mark

GUIDELINES - If your mark was:

1 - 8
This topic is obviously causing you a lot of difficulty. You'll need to look again at the basic terminology and concepts.

14 - 19
You've got a good grasp of the basics, and the terminology under your belt. Well done.

9 - 13
Still a few gaps in your knowledge. Either that or you need to think the problems through more carefully.

20 - 25
There are at least three real teasers in this chapter, so well done indeed, if you've scored so highly!

COMMENTS

Question

1

This is a simple question of factual knowledge. Answer (A) *looks* as if it could be correct, but span of control refers to those *directly* subordinate to an individual - not to all those *below* him in the organisation chart. Answer (C) is a red herring; it is, in fact, a definition of the 'time span of discretion', a method of job evaluation devised by Elliott Jacques.

2

Quite tricky. An organisational chart is designed to show the *formal* structure and channels. It *can* also indicate problems, such as spans of control too large to handle, top-heavy structure, too great an emphasis placed on 'staff' activities etc. What it can in no circumstances do is show how 'power' is distributed - because power does not just derive from 'legal' authority, or a person's position in the formal hierarchy. The power of a charismatic shop steward, for example, or the power of an important group of workers, cannot be depicted.

3

Note that formal and informal organisations are *not* mutually exclusive. The informal organisation is the network of informal inter-personal and inter-group relationships within *every* organisation: the 'grapevine', the 'way of doing things', cliques, casual communication etc. It might help if you think of it as a lot of different informal 'organisations' existing within the formal one. It has its own objectives - although these *may* be brought into line with those of the formal organisation in some matters. Statement 3 requires some thought: a strong, close-knit informal organisation *can* improve morale and communication within the formal organisation, but can also divert energy and loyalty from it, and if the objectives of the informal organisation are not aligned with those of the formal, there is danger of serious conflict.

4

'Bureaucratic', 'role-culture' (Charles Handy) and 'mechanistic' (Burns and Stalker) all refer broadly to the same kind of formalised structure and culture. The 'odd man out' is the 'organismic' organisation, which thrives by task orientation, lateral communication and flexibility.

5

It is difficult to separate the structure from the task, personnel, management style etc. that create the conditions for innovation and motivation. You could on those grounds have given (B) or (C) as your answer - except that you would thereby have eliminated the only clear advantage of a bureaucratic structure, which is ease of control in a highly formal, specialised and defined environment. Innovation will be a problem for a 'mechanistic' organisation. Motivation often suffers where tasks are limited and defined, and little discretion given (although you might argue that a certain type of worker will value such an environment). Communication is highly formalised and vertical only: this

Question

will create a time-lag while information goes 'through channels', and will limit the range of exchanges that can take place. Lateral communication will probably be driven into the highly unreliable informal system, the 'grapevine'.

6 If you got this one wrong, it's up to you to decide whether knowledge of the central ideas of the main management theorists is important to your studies. Handy (*Understanding Organisations*) writes from the point of view of a contingency approach. Maslow and Mayo are generally known for the 'hierarchy of needs' theory and 'human relations' school of thought respectively: the information given about B Z Ness does not entitle us to make any connection with their ideas, which are relevant principally to motivation. The main exponent of the 'classical principles' on which B Z Ness is structured is Henri Fayol.

7 Rigidity of behaviour can create problems with clients and defensibility of individual actions (backed by the rule book) - but also creates reliability. Delegation may create narrow specialisms, sub-units of the organisation with their own goals and objectives - but achieves a necessary purpose as specialisation increases with organisational size. Rules may encourage a minimal or 'satisficing' level of behaviour, but also remove tensions from the superior-subordinate relationship. (B), (C) and (D) are 'functional' and 'dysfunctional' at the same time. Insensitivity to feedback (A), however, has been the basis for predictions of the death of bureaucracy: in a climate of fast change, no organisation can refuse to learn from its mistakes!

8 Economies of scale are by definition the effect of growth. They include the spreading of risks, greater availability of finance, buying economies (eg. bulk purchasing) and selling economies (eg. access to national markets). It is probable that the larger an organisation becomes, it will need to become more formalised to retain control: if it is growing from a very small size, a management structure may need to be established. The span of control *won't* necessarily increase (consequence 2): the organisation is more likely to get taller instead. The informal organisation (consequence 3) is an ever-present phenomenon.

9 This organisation has a narrow span of control and a 'tall' shape. We aren't entitled to infer anything at all about job satisfaction, which depends on many other factors. The choice is then between the work being systematic and routine, or complex. Where work is routine, repetitive and controlled by systems and procedures rather than supervisory attention, the span of control would tend to be much higher than three.

10 Glance back at the notes to this chapter, if you got this one wrong. Options (A) and (C) are associated with 'organismic' organisations. (B) is a red herring: don't confuse 'mechanistic' with 'mechanical'.

Question

11

The training manager has line authority over his subordinates in his own department. He has functional - 'expert' - authority over the training activities of all other departments. Note that while *staff* authority resides more in influence than power - ie. staff positions are service/advisory ones - *functional* authority is a formal recognition of expert power: the expert has formally delegated to him the authority to influence specific areas of the work of others.

12

The chart illustrates dual (product/functional) authority in the form of a matrix. The general manager's span of control is illustrated (seven), if not the other managers' (since we don't know how many staff are involved). The training manager is in a functional rather than staff position: staff management is usually indicated by a dotted line, to show the absence of direct 'legal' authority.

13

(B), (C) and (D) fairly clearly tend towards the retention of authority by a centralised decision-making body. A computerised MIS, on the other hand, may facilitate the spread of information for decision-making to 'lower' levels of the organisation and to geographically dispersed locations, as well as make information more easily obtainable by senior management: computers can aid *both* centralisation and decentralisation.

14

Answer (A) describes 'product' orientation. (C) and (D) describe 'sales' orientation. 'Market' orientation is based on meeting the requirements of the market - hence B is the right answer.

15

Short chains of command are more likely to help than hinder both crisis management and communication (C and D). They also help managers to develop (answer B), through regular and frequent contact with senior management. Management development is the term for the various ways in which managers can enhance their skills and abilities (by education, training, job experience and learning from other managers) and progress in their careers. Management *succession* (A) is a specific form of planning by the organisation, to identify who would be the best person to take over from each current manager, were he to leave or be absent. Management succession is likely to be the greatest problem here, because there are so few opportunities for promotion and 'upwardly mobile' career planning. There may be *lots* of candidates for each potential promotion - all going nowhere.

Question

16 If a manager has little time for supervision, he will not be able to handle a wide span of control (A). The span of control won't necessarily *be* narrower (B), however: the organisation may be badly structured! The manager will have to delegate more (C), (assuming that he has the authority to delegate, of course, as the question suggests. In practice, a manager might be spending a lot of time on non-supervisory work because he has lots of 'expert' work to do eg legal work, computer software writing etc that he *can't* delegate.)

19 Dedd (Boring) is acquiring a company with the intention of controlling a further stage in the value added chain from raw materials to providing a final product/service to the customer. This is vertical integration. The stage in question is one closer to the final consumer (ie forward). Horizontal integration occurs when a company buys a competitor in the same line of business, in order to gain market share. Diversification is a move into a different line of business.

20 (A), (B) and (C) are the obvious tools of cultural change: getting only the right 'sort' of people into the organisation, encouraging only desirable behaviour and attitudes, and 'selling' the values of the organisation. The way in which the product is *perceived* by employees may then change (eg if they are encouraged by the culture to be very proud of it, loyal to it etc), but the specifications of the product itself are determined by other market and production factors.

However, it is worth adding that the product *can* affect the culture indirectly. If - for reasons of market positioning, say - the product is improved, goes 'up-market' etc, it will contribute to a culture where 'our product is best', where employees identify with the quality image of the product etc.

21 When a limited company is formed - public (3) or private (4) - the Registrar of Companies issues a Certificate of Incorporation, which gives the company a separate legal personality. This means that it can do the legal things that are available to an ordinary person, eg it can own property, employ people and be involved in legal action. Sole traders (1) and partnerships (2) do not have this: the business will be a separate *accounting* entity - ie accounts are prepared for the business as distinct from the individuals - but not a separate *'legal personality'. Anyone making a legal contract with a sole trader or partners does so with them as individuals, and does not make a contract with the trader's business.*

Question

22

Private enterprises are business organisations which are owned and operated by certain clearly identified individuals who are also entitled to the rewards of the undertaking. They include sole traders (A), partnerships (C), private limited companies, public limited companies (D) and holding companies (private or public limited companies which control other companies by virtue of holding 51% or more of their voting shares). A professional body (B) is not in this category, but would fall into the category of not-for-profit (NFP) organisations, which exist to confer benefits or promote objectives which may, or may not, involve commercial activities.

23

The first successful 'co-op' was founded in 1844 by Rochdale textile workers to buy foodstuffs at wholesale prices and sell them to members at market prices: the profits or 'surpluses' were then divided among members in proportion to the value of their purchases. Co-operative trading is today applied to retail, wholesaling, farming and agriculture. In the UK, co-operatives are limited liability companies, under the Industrial and Provident Societies Acts (A). The principles of co-operative trading include distribution of surplus by 'dividend (B), democratic control (one man one vote) (D), open membership and political and religious neutrality - so (C) is the 'odd one out', and the answer here.

24

You had to work quite hard, here, thinking about not only health and safety, but about the different 'environments' of organisations. The acronym 'PEST' - political, economic, social, technical - is a useful one to learn, to remind you of what 'the environment' means.

The *political* environment (1) includes governmental influence (eg through fiscal and economic policy) and legislation. Health and safety will thus be affected by legislation in the UK such as the Health and Safety at Work Act (and regulations under the Act), Factories Act 1961, Fire Precautions Act 1971 etc which make detailed provisions for measures to be taken.

The *economic* environment (2) consists of investors, suppliers, competitors, customers, government economic policy - and also *labour*, ie the availability of a (skilled) pool of labour at the 'right' price. An organisation should ensure that its attitude and provisions towards health and safety are such as will attract rather than repel labour - especially where the pool of suitable labour is scarce.

The *social* environment (3) consists of the customs, attitudes, beliefs and education of society as a whole, and accepted 'rules' of considerate and 'moral' personal and organisational behaviour. Society is increasingly aware of the conduct of organisations, and can put pressure on them (through consumerism, choice of product etc) to be socially responsible - which includes providing a safe and healthy environment for workers.

The *technological* environment (4) consists of 'ways of getting things done' - methods of working, as well as scientific inventions and developments, microprocessing applications etc. New technology, and the work organisation around it, can affect health and safety, creating or removing hazards from machinery or toxic materials (eg radiation), altering the incidence of stress, fatigue etc.

Question

25

Social responsibility covers a wide range of behaviour, including the formation or maintenance of safety and quality standards, the provision of 'humane' conditions of work to employees, protection of the environment, investment in social projects, not trading with South Africa etc. Some of this is covered by legislation and regulation. Members of professional bodies are accountable to those bodies for adherence to codes of conduct (D). Organisations may make employees accountable for their adherence to or breach of the organisation's own ethical code or guidelines (B). Option (C) may have made you pause: self-interest equated with profit-maximisation might have the opposite effect from imposing responsibility. But it is in the long-term interests of the organisation to preserve its image of being socially responsible, in an era when ethics and environment are very much the focus of attention and may influence the spending patterns not just of clients/customers/consumers, but also of potential investors in the business.

(A) is the answer because, although you could argue that social responsibility will *influence* the way in which an organisation seeks to extend its product range, the need for new products *per se* is unlikely to *make* managers take a socially responsible attitude. Organisations are usually under pressures that make a "we'll only do it if society really needs it" approach unlikely.

2: MARKING SCHEDULE

Question	Correct answer	Marks for the correct answer	Question	Correct answer	Marks for the correct answer
1	D	1	13	B	1
2	C	1	14	B	1
3	B	1	15	C	1
4	C	1	16	D	1
5	B	1	17	B	1
6	C	1	18	A	1
7	B	1	19	C	1
8	D	1	20	C	1
9	B	1	21	D	1
10	D	1	22	B	1
11	A	1	23	D	1
12	C	1	24	A	1

YOUR MARKS

Total marks available   **24**   Your total mark   [ ]

GUIDELINES - If your mark was:

0 - 8
Shame on you! You need to go over basics. More probably, you need to think a bit harder about your answers!

9 - 13
You've got the basics, but you need to widen your coverage a bit. If the interpretative questions were a problem, you may need to think through a few areas, too.

14 - 19
If marketing isn't your main subject, this is a pretty good result. Well done. If you're doing a whole exam on it, you may like to do a *bit* more revision.

20 - 24
OK. You know your stuff. There are a couple of really searching questions here, so well done indeed.

164

COMMENTS

Question

1

This question serves to illustrate that marketing embraces many more activities than selling. Not all of these activities will necessarily be carried out by the marketing *department* of an organisation, but they are all aimed at 'satisfying customer requirements profitably' in various ways.

2

The C5 (A) was an unfortunate example of the consequences of *production* orientation, where the investment in development and manufacture was not justified by the size of the market for the product. The Concorde (B) may be said to be symptomatic of *product* orientation, where product, design and quality is high, but not necessarily economical or supported by customer demand. Double-glazing (D) is most often subject to a *selling* orientation, with a hard-sell approach to the consumer. The personal stereo (such as Sony's 'Walkman') has developed out of several market trends (eg widespread favour for popular music and jogging), together with technological changes (eg miniaturisation) and related product advances (eg in digital recording, audio teaching techniques etc)

3

The factory and price rises are examples of things that the consumer may not *want*, but are not to his detriment: Fairley Greene will not be marketing something that will be contrary to society's best interests. (The issue of the environment is justifiably sensitive, but the implications of the factory proposals are that it will be sensitively handled. The price rises *might* have been an ethical issue if the products were essential and unavailable elsewhere.) The extension of the soft-drink range is clearly something both desired by *and* good for the consumer. Only the pill bottle raises serious questions: some buyers might consider such a product attractive, but the increased safety risk (eg to small children) would render it socially undesirable.

4

Capital goods (C) are most commonly identified with *industrial* markets: they include plant, land, machinery, vehicles etc. Services (D) are provided both in consumer and industrial markets. Non-durable products (or 'fast moving consumer goods') (A) include foodstuffs, fuels etc. Durable goods (B) include furniture, cars, clothing etc.

5

The plans *directly* affect place (channels of distribution) and promotion (sales force management and advertising), so (B) is the answer. Note: they might later, indirectly, affect price and product, since all the elements are interdependent. Feedback through agents, or change in consumer perception of the brand due to the advertising campaign, may cause product reappraisal; increased expenditure, or branding as 'trade specialist' may necessitate or enable price changes etc.

Question

6 These are all classic characteristics of a mature product. The 'brand loyalty' objective is a particular 'give-away'; market expansion, market penetration and operational efficiency objectives tend to be features of introduction, growth and decline respectively. High cash in-flow is likewise distinctive. Product modification may have hinted at 'growth' - but is equally a feature of maturity in the attempt to extend to duration of the stage, or to recreate the market or whole life cycle.

7 'Market fragmentation' (A) is the splintering of markets - because of various factors such as product developments or lifestyle changes - into a variety of consumer groups with different preferences: it is a reason why market segmentation needs to be carried out. 'Product positioning' (C) is a marketing activity which uses the identified segments as targets: the product and promotional mix emphasise relevant product attributes and differences, and address the specific people who make up the segment. 'Quota sampling' (D) is a technique used in market research.

8 Straightforward. 'Undifferentiated' strategies (D) imply lack of market segmentation analysis, and no attempt to differentiate or position products according to specific segment requirements.

9 Market penetration (B) implies a strategy of increasing market share within existing markets/ segments.

10 Market segmentation (C) may be a suitable *prelude* to diversification, but the latter (D) is the expansion of a company's activities into new (or related) areas.

11

Market growth rate \ Market share	High	Low
High	★	?
Low	Cash Cow	Dog

Question

12　If the market share of the question mark doesn't increase, it will be a dog, so (C) is wrong.

13

Price Quality	High	Medium	Low
High	Premuim	Penetration	Super value for money
Medium	Over-pricing	Average price-quality	Value for money
Low	Hit and run	Shoddy goods	Cheap goods

14　Mail order, direct response advertising and direct mail are the terms for what Old Crocks are doing here. They are the three main methods of direct marketing, which is a form of direct supply, since goods pass straight from the manufacturer/supplier to the customer.

The main types of distribution channel

Question

15 Merchant supply (A) applies mainly to *industrial* goods. Direct supply (B) is not the answer, because there are retailers involved, and although direct corporate customers *could* in principle buy in bulk and demand discounts, they are unlikely to be in the market for pottery goods. Long channels (D) also expose the supplier to bulk-buying power of the purchaser (here, the wholesaler) but minimise the number of accounts and the risk of payment default. So (C) is the answer.

16 (A) refers to the length of the channel, not the number of channels. Intensive distribution (B) means obtaining space in as many sales outlets as possible: a chocolate bar or coffee brand is commonly marketed in this way. Exclusive distribution (C) means granting rights to a certain dealer in a certain territory: consumers will not expect 'readily availability' eg of a BMW car. Selective distribution (D) means granting rights to certain dealers only - eg car dealers - as the question indicates.

17 The terms 'above-the-line' and 'below-the-line' have their origins in past UK tax regulations. 'Above-the-line' now denotes mass media advertising from which the agency receives a commission on the value of media time/space purchases, while 'below-the-line' denotes non-commissioned media and promotional activities. Only the sponsorship carries no agency commission and is therefore 'below the line'.

18 This is tricky, because we left out *the* most obvious candidate: the performance-related trade/industry incentive, eg bonuses for dealers/agents/distributors who beat targets or each other in selling the product. Sponsorship (C) and point-of-sale display (B) *might* occasionally be used. Consumer incentives (D), as the name implies, are directed more at consumer markets, and consist of eg free samples, 'bonus' packs, giveaways, competitions etc. (A) is very common: you may have seen 'Trade Only' exhibitions advertised.

19 'Reach' (A) is expressed as 'cost per thousand reached' - so that's not the problem. Audience recall suggests that message repetition (B) isn't the problem either. The campaign has impact (D) on consumer attitudes, because market share is growing. 'Wastage' (C) means that the advertiser is paying for the message to be transmitted to people to whom it is irrelevant - in this case, clearly, non-drinkers.

Question

20 & 21

There is no precise scientific validity in the graph, but it does suggest the relative usefulness of different elements of the promotional mix at different stages of the 'sale' process.

W is publicity: awareness enhancing, but not much more.

X is sales promotion: it can be fairly effective, once the product has come to the market's attention, right up to action - through incentives to buy.

Y is advertising - the most effective medium for bringing the product's existence to the market's attention.

Z is personal selling, with its direct persuasive element for 'conversion' ie eliciting action: expensive for the awareness stage.

22

Price (B) is a separate area in which misleading statements should not be made. A trade description includes any indication of results of testing (A - the British Standards Institution mark), composition (C), history (D) and other aspects.

23

(A), (B) and (C) are *aspects of* (D), marketing research.

24

The choice between (A) and (B) makes an important distinction. A *market* forecast assesses environmental factors which will affect demand: the economy, total market volume and potential etc. You might have thought twice about (C) - but it's a red herring: the marketing mix for the product will have been determined before a sales forecast is possible.

3: MARKING SCHEDULE

Question	Correct answer	Marks for the correct answer	Question	Correct answer	Marks for the correct answer
1	D	1	13	A	1
2	D	1	14	B	1
3	A	1	15	C	1
4	B	1	16	C	1
5	D	1	17	B	1
6	B	1	18	C	1
7	C	1	19	B	1
8	B	1	20	D	1
9	A	1	21	D	1
10	B	1	22	A	1
11	D	1	23	A	1
12	C	1	24	B	1

YOUR MARKS

Total marks available   24   Your total mark   [ ]

GUIDELINES - If your mark was:

0 - 8   You can't have been concentrating. There are at least this many 'general knowledge' questions.

9 - 14   OK. This may not be an important area for you. Look back at the notes and get some of the terminology questions fixed in your mind, though.

15 - 20   Pretty good. This is all *fairly* straightforward stuff, though, so if production majors in your exam syllabus, have another quick look.

21 - 24   We're impressed.

COMMENTS

Question

1

Process (B) and mass production (C) are types of flow (A) production, where a product is made in a continuous flow. Batch production isn't continuous, as its name implies, so (D) is the odd one.

2

This may have taken a while to work out, but if you know your terms it's a straightforward matter of fact.

3

The scenario is typical of a capital-intensive organisation (1), where there is a large capital investment in machinery, plant and equipment in relation to the workforce. The labour-intensive organisation (2) (eg retail, service industries or craft-technology manufacturers) is the opposite. (3) was straightforward - and you were given (4) for free! Only (2) didn't 'fit'.

4

Greater flexibility in manufacturing systems and the need to produce a wider range of products result in the need for shorter production runs. Fewer units will be made of each product, but many more different products will be made.

There is a danger that making many more different products could result in larger stockholding (A) and higher production costs (C), but quicker response times to customer orders and the greater production efficiency of capital-intensive production means that stockholdings should get *lower* and unit costs should be kept under control. Although capital-intensive systems mean less labour, the workforce must be highly skilled, and so training requirements are likely to increase, not be reduced (D).

5

The key to Just In Time production is the ability to rely on suppliers to deliver materials or components on time and to a high quality standard. This means that stocks can be kept low, but there will be no production hold-ups caused by late stock deliveries or rejected/scrapped items in production. This argues for using just one or two tried and trusted suppliers, not a large number of them. This is why (A) is wrong and (D) is correct. Quality control is an important element in JIT.

The requirement to minimise stockholding stems from the increasing variety of products that manufacturers are finding that they have to make, with product design and greater market segmentation being the trend that businesses are now following. (C) is therefore incorrect.

JIT can operate with either centralised or decentralised management. (B) was a red herring.

Question

6

As you should know from Chapter 1, (C), a 'mechanistic system' (Burns and Stalker), is nothing to do with technology. (D) was a complete red herring. The question was designed to make the important distinction between 'automation' and 'mechanisation'. Mechanisation would appear as:

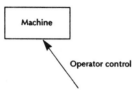

7

(C) will be done by the manufacturing function itself. Of course, the *requirements* for materials and components will have to be known by the production planning department, in order for them to be able to prepare job cards and materials requirements plans. The actual withdrawal or requisition from stock, however, will not happen until the items are needed, ie where the job starts.

8

Tricky distinctions. 'Quality assurance' (A) and 'value analysis' (D) both go beyond the manufacture of the product, and include considerations of the product specifications themselves. Inspection (C) is 'narrower' than quality control, involving identification of faulty output rather than control of the manufacturing process.

9

(A) would simply be too costly, given that the tolerance for error is reasonably high, and more than 3% reduction in the percentage of defectives already uneconomical.

Question

10 The AQL is the maximum percentage of defectives that can be allowed, before the quality-control-related costs outweigh the benefits to be gained from improved quality. We're told that this is 5% (B).

11 This sorts out some terminology. A supplier's quality assurance scheme (A) involves a guarantee of the standard of goods supplied. 'Vendor rating' (B) is a method whereby each supplier is rated according to on-going performance. 'Tolerances' (D) are the variations which are allowed before an item is deemed to have failed to meet its specifications: a wide one will let in greater defects. A high inspection sample (C) will reduce the risk of defective items reaching the manufacturer.

12 This question brings out some of the potential problems with QCs. If they are made up of production workers (A), they may be inhibited by pre-designed specifications. If they are made up of design workers (B), the operations 'angle' may be ignored. A quality circle is a *voluntary* grouping, requiring participative attitudes, so (D) is not a good idea - even if resistant individuals most *need* to be 'switched on' to quality. Training (C) will enhance the QC's contribution enormously, and should embrace not just quality testing methods etc, but also communication techniques.

13 *Quantity*, quality (B), price (C) and delivery (D) are the four elements. 'Delivery' might sound like the 'odd one out', but refers to essentials such as the lead time between order placement and delivery, reliability etc. 'Quantity' is the size and timing of orders.

14 X is maximum stock level. Z is 'buffer' or minimum stock level. O is zero stock.

15 Maximum stock level (X) is the maximum amount of stock which is necessary and can be held cost-effectively: it is a balance between the cost of delays in production caused by *insufficient* stock holding (involving a consideration of (A)), and the costs of high stockholding: tied up capital, storage space (B), deterioration (D), insurance etc. (C) would be a consideration in setting optimum re-order level, because the lead-time must be taken into account if the goods are to be ordered early enough to avoid stock dropping to unacceptable levels. It will not affect the maximum amount of stock Rhi Sauces can or wishes to hold.

Question

16 The distance between the vertical dotted lines represents the lead time between reorder point (where the diagonal lines cross Y) and delivery. It is shortest for N, who has therefore responded most speedily to Rhi's order. (In practice, and in 'just in time' manufacturing in particular, the purchaser may actually *prefer* supplier M, who gets him the supplies before buffer level is reached, but not very much before, thus cutting down on the length of time capital and space are tied up in the supplies before they're ready to be utilised.

17 OK, (D) is pretty clearly a red herring. Pure research (A) is investigation to gain new scientific or technical knowledge: applied research (B) is the same activity directed to a specific practical end; and development (C) is the use of scientific or technical knowledge to produce new or improved products or processes with a view to commercial exploitation. In this case, a product hasn't yet been invented and so we are at the applied research stage (B), not yet at product development.

18 If you got this right, you might think it simple - but many organisations do just this (C), because of the risks and uncertainties involved. Separate budgeting (A) will be important because research projects are likely to have longer time-scales and less clear-cut progress indicators than development projects. Cultural tolerance (D) is another ambivalent area - but encouragement of innovation requires it (especially since technical experts have a high market value and tend to find controls and appraisals inhibiting).

19 (A) is constrained by market expectations, or 'brand' identification. (C) is very price-sensitive, so low-cost production will be important. (D) will be constrained by market sensitivity and competitor action. However, the *imperative* constraints of statutory regulations applies to the use of safe (fire-resistant) materials in furniture (B).

20 Work study (A) is a generic term for techniques *including* method study and work measurement. Method study (B) is the recording and examination of existing and proposed ways of work. Job evaluation (C) is appraisal of a job for the purpose of setting reward levels or gradings. It's work measurement (D) that is designed to establish timings.

21 If you thought that was easy, well done! If the purpose of the activity (D) is not worthwhile (or if it has *no* purpose), then all other questions are meaningless. The approved order is: (1) purpose, (2) place, (3) sequence (ie when), (4) person and (5) means.

Question

22 Value analysis (3) is an approach to cost reduction (2), which is the task of *reducing* the current or planned level of costs (eg to £2.39 per aerial). Budgetary control (4), whereby actual costs are compared to budgeted or standard costs and variance reported, is a form of cost control system (1): the aim of both is to keep costs to the planned level, as in this scenario.

23 This is the essence of the difference between value analysis and conventional cost reduction techniques.

24 Cost value (A) is the cost of production and selling.
Use value (C) is the purpose the product fulfils.
Esteem value (D) is the prestige and aesthetic appeal the customer sees in the product.
The value defined in the question is (B).

All are terms which apply to value analysis studies.

4: MARKING SCHEDULE

Question	Correct answer	Marks for the correct answer	Question	Correct answer	Marks for the correct answer
1	C	1	9	C	1
2	B	1	10	D	1
3	B	1	11	B	1
4	D	1	12	B	1
5	C	1	13	C	1
6	A	1	14	D	1
7	A	1	15	A	1
8	C	1			

YOUR MARKS

Total marks available   **15**   Your total mark

GUIDELINES - If your mark was:

0 - 4
You're having difficulty with some basic concepts here. Have a thorough review of this area of your study material.

9 - 12
You can probably tackle most of the questions on this area that might get thrown at you. If it was only detailed terminology questions you got wrong - rather than interpretive ones - well done.

5 - 8
You have probably got most of the basics under your belt. Review the relationships between authority, responsibility, power and delegation; that's the most important area.

13 - 15
You have even got some detailed terms at your fingertips. Now apply them to other topics and your work situation: they are not just 'mark-winners' but tools of the trade!

COMMENTS

Question

1

This is where we start sorting out types of authority and the environments in which they flourish. In a bureaucracy such as (C), authority is bestowed via the division of the organisation into jurisdictional areas: the official in charge is backed by rules and procedures. This is rational-legal authority. A scientific research team (B) *may* require a leader with pure 'positional' authority simply to control potential conflict between the members who may be from different disciplines - but 'expert' authority (ie inspiring respect through know-how) is the most likely basis for leadership. The family firm (D) often functions through 'traditional' or 'patriarchal' authority, where authority is bestowed by virtue of hereditary entitlement. (A) is an interesting case, potentially involving 'charismatic', 'expert' (in industrial relations) or even physical power: trade union leaders in any case derive their authority 'bottom-up' on the basis of election, rather than 'top-down' legal authority.

2

Responsibility (A) is the *duty* to perform an action.
Power (D) is the *ability* to perform an action - and in particular to influence others.
Influence (C) is the process by which a person directs or modifies the behaviour of another person.

3

Expert power resides in *acknowledged* expertise. The Chief Accountant hasn't got it - because he is incompetent. The Personnel Manager hasn't got it - because her area of expertise is not acknowledged. The mixer, on the other hand, clearly commands his colleagues' respect - without 'position' power to back him up - because 'he knows his stuff'. So (B) is the answer.

4

Resource power (A) is illustrated eg by the manager, who controls pay. Charismatic power (B) is illustrated by Mr Warnaby-Bosse. Negative power (C) is illustrated by the work-to-rule and sabotage: it is the use of disruption to *prevent* action. Physical power (D) is *not* directly related to behaviour such as sabotage but to the use of physical presence or force to obtain submission: it is not involved here.

5

The shop floor workers exercise negative power (A) (see comment 4 above). The manager exercises position power (B): he is 'responsible for operations' and for the mixer's redundancy. Neither exercises expert power (D) in the scenario. Resource power (C) resides in the manager by virtue of this control of pay and indeed of livelihood. It *also* resides in the workers' ability to withdraw their labour.

Question

6 The withholding and distortion of information (3) is a tactic of political activity which has degenerated into conflict, where the needs and objectives of the organisation are secondary to the need to 'win'. Such 'spoiling' behaviour can only be harmful. Internal *competition* (2) - as distinguished from conflict - can be a valuable source of team cohesion, commitment and 'intrapreneurialism': research into inter-group competition has shown increased loyalty and orientation towards task achievement among competing groups. Dissent (1) may have made you think twice, but again it has a useful function in preventing complacency and the dangers of blinkered, unquestioned decisions. It can keep new ideas emerging and being tested, can bring problems out into the open and classify issues via the polarisation of views.

7 It is possible to have authority but not 'power': power (B) is not necessarily transferable. The most important point of this question is that responsibility (C) and the accountability that accompany it (D) are *not* delegated. The superior makes the subordinate responsible and accountable to him for the authority he has delegated (A), but he remains responsible and accountable for it to his own boss. No 'passing the buck'.

8 Fairly straightforward. (A) is crucial. (B) sounds more surprising - but it is just as important to address 'inclination' (or willingness) as ability, in securing performance. The important point is the distinction between (D) - making the subordinate *accountable* - and (C), which is not true delegation at all. As long as a decision is within the scope of the authority delegated to the subordinate, he should not be expected to refer it back: if the superior does not trust him to make the decision, he should not have delegated at all!

9 A manager should not delegate a decision where tact and confidentiality are required (1) or where the quality of the decision is important and he has reason to doubt the competence of his subordinates to contribute to it (3). He *should* delegate where the quality of decision is important and the expertise of the subordinates will enhance it (2) and where quality is less important than acceptance of the decision (4).

10 Justifiably low confidence in subordinates (2) is clearly enough of a discouragement to delegate (and rightly so). As is an organisational culture which discourages trust and depicts delegation as 'shirking responsibility' (3). An organisation culture which emphasises management by exception and management specialisation is as clearly an encouragement to delegation, which puts (4) out of the picture. (1) is tricky, though: the capability of the subordinates may give the manager confidence to delegate, but might also make him feel threatened by redundancy or fear of political rivalry. Managers may be unwilling to admit that subordinates have developed to the extent that they could perform the manager's job.

Question

11 Straightforward terminology. (A) is in fact the principle that once policies and corporate plans are established, required decisions are predetermined and follow naturally. (C) is an approach to objective-setting at all levels of management, and for managers to direct and control their performance in relation to their individual objectives. (D) describes a situation where decisions can be made on the basis of predetermined categories and rules and even by computer, because they are routine and/or quantitative in nature.

12 Programmed decisions (A) are those for which decision rules can be predetermined - for example, many operational decisions, which can be computerised or entrusted to junior levels of the organisation. Part of the reason for this is that they are quantitative (C) in nature: quantifiable problems are those which can be resolved by mathematical techniques, ie where the decision option offering the 'best numbers' will be selected. Scientific decision (D) are likewise based on the belief that complete information and quantitative techniques will lead to the ideal solution. Non-programmed decisions (B) are those where *judgement* is required, eg commonly where qualitative factors such as risk and human intervention affect the decision.

13 Ivor identified and analysed the problem (A and B): he figures out what was wrong with the management reports and where the problem lay - with the technological capabilities of the system. He also remembered to evaluate alternative solutions (D): the reason why his list of alternative solutions was limited and 'off-target' was because at no stage did he consider the resources available - in terms of finance, and more particularly in terms of staff skills, abilities and inclinations.

14 (D) incidentally illustrates an advantage and a disadvantage of the Western 'rational' model of decision-making. (C) may have given you pause: it is commonly thought that the Japanese approach works through 'consensus'. True - but consensus through a conflict resolution process, not 'on the facts' alone.

5: MARKING SCHEDULE

Question	Correct answer	Marks for the correct answer	Question	Correct answer	Marks for the correct answer
1	C	1	13	C	1
2	C	1	14	D	1
3	D	1	15	A	1
4	C	1	16	B	1
5	A	1	17	D	1
6	D	1	18	C	1
7	C	1	19	D	1
8	B	1	20	D	1
9	D	1	21	A	1
10	A	1	22	B	1
11	B	1	23	B	1
12	D	1	24	C	1

YOUR MARKS

Total marks available   24   Your total mark

GUIDELINES - If your mark was:

0 - 7
If the ones you got right were basic terminology, you will need to look back at the notes to this chapter at least, for some meat on the bones.

8 - 13
Was it terminology or interpretation you had trouble with? Review the relevant comments.

14 - 17
Well, there were quite a few straightforward ones. If it was only the 'technical' terms that you missed, and if you don't think you will need them for your exam, fair enough.

18 - 25
Bravo! (Having got this far, it may be worth reviewing 'the ones that got away' - just for the satisfaction...)

COMMENTS

Question

1

Many organisations are ambivalent about 'social' communication which has no direct business-oriented or productive purpose. Indications are that employee satisfaction (B) is *enhanced* by the opportunity to develop social relationships and networks at work. Managerial credibility (D) *need* not be damaged by social communication with workers - indeed employees may trust and respect a manager more if he shows that he remembers who they are, and treats them as human individuals: social communication may contribute to making a manager a 'leader'. Similarly, formality (A) is not necessarily a desirable feature of business organisations: successful organisational cultures are often characterised by first-name terms, informal dress rules and a general lack of status-consciousness. The problem with social communication (C) is that it takes up time that could be more productively spent. This is an 'opportunity cost' - although in the long term, arguably, there could be costs associated with *lack* of such communication, eg the absenteeism, turnover or poor motivation of alienated, 'de-humanised' workers seeking satisfaction of their social needs elsewhere.

2

Noise (A) is the *other* main type of communication problem, ie distractions and interferences in the environment in which communication takes place, affecting the clarity, accuracy or even 'arrival' of the message. Redundancy (B) is a useful principle to apply to communication - though not the right one for this question: if you use more than one channel of communication, a message can fail to get through by one (eg because of noise) but succeed by another. Feedback (D) is the response which indicates to the sender that his message has (or has not) been received, properly interpreted and understood. Shame on you, if you put (D), because feedback is very important - and explained in the notes to this chapter!

3

Physical noise is sound, pure and simple, preventing the message from getting through - such as refurbishment noise. Technical noise is any failure in the channel of communication during transmission - such as bad handwriting: a breakdown of the fax machine would have been technical noise as well. Social noise is a failure of communication created by differences in personality, perception etc of the sender and receiver: it doesn't feature in the scenario. Psychological noise refers to interference caused by emotion or attitude in the sender or recipient - such as Egon's irrelevant expressions of emotion holding up his message. (D) is therefore the correct option.

Question

4

Concreteness (A) can be an advantage eg for use as legal evidence or confirmation and recall - but can also be a disadvantage where circumstances change or errors are discovered; there is a lead time required to alter or correct the message. Opportunity for feedback (B) is not conspicuously an advantage of written communication: again, there is a time lag in transmission, receipt, preparation and return. Oral communication offers 'real time' feedback, ie response in time to influence events. Clarity of expression (D) will not necessarily be any greater via a written media than an oral one - although the *opportunity* is offered eg by the facility to use diagrams. Tone of voice, facial expression etc, which may help to clarify underlying meanings, will not be available. (C) is a modest claim, but a real advantage: written messages can be sent out in identical form to numerous recipients, for labour-saving and consistency.

5

Dimm *has* been giving feedback so (A) is not the problem: you need to be aware of the range of signals feedback embraces. The manager has ignored the possibility for half an hour that feedback is being given (B) and has misunderstood its message (C). The meaning of the briefing has clearly not got across to Dimm, as it has been distorted: perhaps the manager is using inappropriate vocabulary, faulty logic, irrelevant information etc.

6

You may have been surprised by (2), but research shows that the grapevine does not in fact simply fill the gap created by ineffective formal communication systems: it thrives on information 'fed' into it through formal channels, and co-exists even with healthy organisational communication (1). (3) is also a finding of Davis' famous research into informal communication: staff executives are more mobile and get involved with more different functions in their work. Only (4) is untrue: the grapevine *can* be harmful if it creates hostility or fear, or prompts action on the basis of inaccurate rumours and speculations. On the other hand, it is acknowledged that an informal system has widespread acceptance and works extremely fast, so that if accurate and useful information is fed into it, it is a valuable support for the formal system.

7

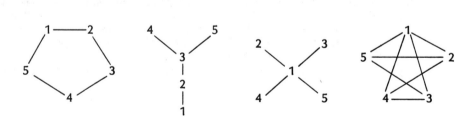

Only the wheel (C) has the centralised leadership characteristics specified.

182

Question

8   All-channel networks solve complex problems well (B), because of the participative approach. However, they are slower than the wheel system where simple problems are concerned, and tend to disintegrate under pressure (eg time pressure to get results) into a wheel system. (A) and (C) are out, therefore. Job satisfaction (D) is a trickier area: there are conflicting views on whether the circle - active, error-prone and leaderless - provides the high job satisfaction first found by researchers, or whether the higher quality performance of the all-channel gives greater satisfaction. The *leader* of the wheel is agreed to have the highest satisfaction, while 'fairly high' enjoyment is available to *all* members of the all-channel network - depending on the size and makeup of the group and therefore the extent of participation.

9   Diagonal is how it would actually look on the organisational chart, if you think about it: communication upwards, but not straight 'up the line' because the personnel director is (a) in a different department and (b) a staff or functional specialist whose role cuts across the 'line of authority': strictly speaking, he has no direct authority over the sales supervisor. This is a straightforward question, really, but illustrates the complexity of the formal communication structure of an organisation.

10   These are some of the simple classifications you ought to be able to use with confidence. An ad hoc committee (A) is a fact-finding or special committee which achieves its specified purpose, reports and then disbands - like a taskforce team. An executive committee (B) has powers to govern or administer. A standing committee (C) is formed for a particular purpose, but on a permanent basis, with routine business to perform at regular meetings. A joint committee (D) is not - as it may sound - simply an interdisciplinary team: it is a body formed to co-ordinate the activities of two or more committees.

11   Of course, 'it all depends'. You could, conceivably, argue that *none* of the options, in certain circumstances, would be an advantage - but then you would have a thorough grasp of contingency theory and the ambivalence surrounding the use of committees. Generally speaking, (A) is useful in gaining acceptance for decisions without having to 'sell' them later, and in discouraging complacency and 'groupthink' by bringing disagreement into the open. Like (D), it could be said that it lengthens the decision-making process and may waste time - but the Japanese, for example, *prefer* that decisions take longer and *win* consensus for implementation. (C) and (D) are clearly advantageous for co-ordination and the quality of decisions. (B) is a very double-edged sword. Since no individual is held responsible for consequences, there may be greater creativity and risk-taking, which may be important where innovation is required. On the other hand, it may also encourage compromise, lack of accountability for bad decisions, and a lack of 'conscience'. This is why (B) is correct.

Question

12

Some more useful terms. Brainstorming sessions (D) commonly take the form of conferences, relying on the members' ability to feed each others' ideas. Ideas are not *evaluated* at the meeting, so there is less inhibition or fear of being 'shot down'. Networking (A) is a collection of people, usually with a shared interest, who tend to keep in touch to exchange informal information. T-groups (B) are training groups (pure red herring), although brainstorming *may* be one of the exercises they are set, to develop creativity and participative skills. Ad hoc committees (C) may also use brainstorming as a problem solving technique, but are essentially different in function: the words 'to solve a particular problem' might just have rung bells, though.

13

The house journal (A) may - and arguably should - allow contributions from lower levels of the organisation but in practice it is largely an organ for downward information flow: it may 'fall into the hands' of non-members of the organisation, and indeed is often used for PR purposes, so it is not the place for suggestions for improvement, dissent, grievance etc. The organisation manual (B) is the 'handbook' for guidance of members of the organisation with regard to its structure, history, market, rules and policies etc. It's a bit like a written briefing. Which brings us to the nub of the question: the distinction between team meetings (C) and briefing groups (B) such as were pioneered by the Industrial Society. A briefing is not intended for upward communication - although questions may be permitted. Team meetings are a more effective forum for feedback up the line.

14

Organisational politics (1) might inhibit upward communication in different ways: through the belief that 'knowledge is power', for example. Class perception (2) is a common barrier in the UK between 'workers' and 'management'. Lack of trust (4) is a *very* important barrier. An individual will not give his superior information that is confidential if he does not trust his discretion; he will not convey negative business information if he cannot trust the superior to respond objectively and without prejudice to the messenger; he will not make helpful suggestions if he cannot trust the superior to take them seriously, follow them up as promised etc. You may have thought twice - remembering the trust-control dilemma of delegation - about the *direction* of flow inhibited, but that's all. (3) is perhaps least expected. You would think an aspiring employee would be keen to show up well, provide 'input', keep in his superior's eye. True, but aspiration puts pressure on the individual to provide only positive and safe information. According to a well-known study by Read, the more a subordinate wants promotion, the *less* likely he will be to transmit important but unfavourable information.

15

(1) and (3) are only to be expected. The project group represents a very different culture from the production department. It is likely to be used to working without tight time constraints, with large and flexible resource allocation, and with long-term objectives. The objectives of the operational department are likely to be short-term and productivity based (especially if they are paid on a productivity basis): they will naturally resist disruption to schedules and efficiency ratings. They are unlikely to share the long term view and may feel that they have not got time to learn new methods

Question

and get the system up-and-running. (4) is inherent in any situation where functional/staff authority is involved, and especially where there is the perceived gulf between 'boffins' and 'producers'. Poor communication (1) is not explicitly a problem in the scenario and is not necessarily a feature of the situation: difficulties of 'vocabulary' between the systems people and production staff could have been overcome if they were identified.

16 Corporate planning and objective-setting for the organisation as a whole would have minimised other difficulties by targeting effort towards common or compatible goals and achievements and directing attention beyond - and through- such intervening barriers as timescales, functional authority and lack of communication. The systems analysts, for example, might be trained to deal with the human aspects of innovation, if their objectives include gaining co-operation of operational departments.

17 Derek Pugh identifies proliferation of committees (A) and the use of 'red tape' (C) as signs of *inadequate* integration: (A) because it 'fudges' integration issues and (C) because it indicates a desperate attempt to enforce integration. Proliferation of rules and use of arbitration, appeals to higher authority etc are also recognised symptoms of conflict. (B) looks like integration of a sort: trust, participation etc. But the exercise of a *purely* consultative relationship with others is a mechanism for avoiding responsibility and authority. This is *not* a healthy sign. Quality circles (D) are, by definition, voluntary groups of individuals from different disciplines concerned to discuss their viewpoints on and suggestions for quality assurance. This is a positively integrating mechanism.

18 Open competition (C) exists where all participants can increase their gains: productivity deals are intended to result in the increased productivity desired by management, the profits of which can then be passed on as increased pay for workers.

Closed or zero-sum competition (A and B) are synonymous, and exist where one party's gain is another's loss eg in competition between departments for finite resources. Competition of this destructive kind degenerates into 'conflict' (D). Open competition is considered constructive, encouraging performance, without the pressures of fearing that one side must 'beat' the other, or 'lose'.

19 OK. You may have thought the answer obvious. But the incorrect options needed some thought. A production committee (A) is often used to co-ordinate the efforts of all the different functions involved in production and the 'staff' experts who have functional authority over aspects of its activity eg quality control, production planning and control, work study, finance and personnel.

Question

A project team (B) is often interdisciplinary, and carries elements of matrix management. Its role is often progress chasing, or innovation, and it often has a membership that fluctuates according to the needs of the project. Essentially, it is task-orientated and broad-based, and as such is a valuable co-ordinating mechanism. A corporate planning team (C) will co-ordinate the planning and objective setting activities of the organisation, which in turn will aid co-ordination overall. The autonomous work group (D) may have needed a second glance. Its special feature is that it is given a 'whole job' rather than fragmented tasks, and is given discretion to allocate and schedule its own activities: it has an integrated approach to work *internally*, but its very autonomy as a group may isolate it from the organisation as a whole. Cohesive work groups have been shown to work against organisation objectives as well as for them.

20 (A) is a structural mechanism whereby there is a co-ordinating level of management responsible for the integration of the activities of different groups or departments. This would also prevent conflicts from escalating all the way up to the most senior level. (B) builds co-ordination into the basic system of planning and control of the organisation: essential, especially where managers can be brought to agree the budget and its provisions for integration of sub-objectives. (C) is also useful, if the necessary authority is given to the 'integration officer' in his various guises: this would usually be achieved through a matrix management structure. (D) should certainly not be discouraged, but it is certainly the least positive of the options given: a 'shot in the dark', in the absence of any formal system or procedures for integration. (PS. If you can remember the *incorrect* options for this question, you will find them very useful: this is a fertile area for exam questions and organisation problems....)

21 'Environmental' strategies (B, C and D) aim to create conditions conducive to co-operative working. 'Regulation' strategies are directed at controlling conflict (often by making it so much part of the formal organisation system that it is perpetuated): hence (A). Other regulation strategies would include establishing rules of conduct, separating conflicting individuals and meetings to hammer out differences.

22 The pluralist ideology (B) is related to the 'evolutionary' view of conflict: the legitimate pursuit of competing interests can balance and preserve social and organisation arrangements as a basis for evolutionary change. The radical ideology (C) is related to the conflict view (D): a primarily Marxist perspective. Organisations are arenas for conflict on individual and group levels, as members battle for control and economic resources: conflict does not aim for mutual survival, but revolutionary change. The unitary ideology (A) is related to the 'happy family' view of organisation, based on the belief that all members of the organisation, despite their different roles, have common objectives and values which unite their interests and efforts. It is important to recognise that 'conflict' can be inevitable or avoidable, good or bad - depending how you look at it.

Question

23 1, 3 and 4 are classic symptoms and tactics of conflict, aimed at increasing the power of the managers/departments in question and 'spoiling' the efforts of rivals. 2, however, is a symptom of *constructive* conflict, the effect of which is to clarify issues, bring emotions into the open, release long-repressed hostilities and generally 'energise' the situation. These two team leaders are more likely to resolve their conflicts than the others mentioned.

24 These categorisations were identified by John Hunt, but you didn't need to think of them as technical terms in order to address this question. Denial (A) is 'sweeping under the carpet', hoping the conflict will 'blow over'. Suppression (B) is 'smoothing over' in order to preserve working relationships. Dominance (D) is the application of power or influence to 'settle' the conflict. All of these responses can be effective in certain circumstances, but all have the flaw of leaving the conflict unaltered. Conflict which doesn't 'blow over' may 'blow up' out of all proportion; some cracks can't be papered over; dominance leaves the lingering resentment of a 'win-lose' situation. Compromise (C) is bargaining, negotiating and conciliating. It is not unilateral action on the part of the manager. The conflict situation will change because the process of compromise changes attitudes to it: an element of acceptance is built in. Of course, this strategy has its own problems: positions may be deliberately polarised to *compensate* for anticipated compromise; compromise itself may be seen to weaken the value of the outcome. Only integration/collaboration is truly effective. But not easy.

6: MARKING SCHEDULE

Question	Correct answer	Marks for the correct answer	Question	Correct answer	Marks for the correct answer
1	D	1	13	D	1
2	C	1	14	A	1
3	C	1	15	C	1
4	C	1	16	B	1
5	D	1	17	D	1
6	B	1	18	A	1
7	A	1	19	C	1
8	D	1	20	D	1
9	D	1	21	C	1
10	C	1	22	D	1
11	B	1	23	B	1
12	A	1			

YOUR MARKS

Total marks available   23   Your total mark

GUIDELINES - If your mark was:

0 - 8
You really need to to go back and look at some fundamentals. If pushed for time just pick the basic planning and control issues: MbO and corporate planning are probably lower priority for you.

9 - 14
Even allowing for a few high-level and technical questions, which may be beyond your scope, you could have scored a little better: review the notes and comments.

15 - 19
Good work. But if all the errors you did make were in a particular area, you'll need to ask yourself if it's an area you can really afford to ignore - eg if it's really not in your syllabus.

20 - 23
You have a very thorough grasp indeed, covering the qualitative and quantitative sides of the subject.

COMMENTS

Question

1 and 2

Programmes (A) are co-ordinated groups of plans which have a clear objective and a separate identity within the general planning structure: eg an expansion programme, or relocation programme.

Policies (B) are guidelines allowing discretion to individual decision-makers within defined limits: no such discretion is apparent here.

Procedures (C) are chronological sequences of actions required to perform a task (or rules). This is the nature of the plan in question 2.

Rules (D) are single prescribed courses of action, allowing no deviation or discretion: this distinguishes them from policies and procedures, and is the nature of Lou's plan in question 1.

3

Objectives are about ends (A); *plans* or *strategies* are about means to attain those ends (B). A statement of results (D) achieved is *feedback* to the control system. A *policy* is a statement of intent, of what the organisation will and will not do in pursuit of its objectives (C). Policies direct managers to act in a particular way: they are not actions in themselves, nor are they objectives or plans, though they are often confused with them. They cut down the amount of 'fresh' consideration that has to be given to recurring, routine matters. Marks and Spencer has a *policy* of only selling goods under its own brand name; an organisation may formulate health and safety policies as a guide to accident prevention, compensation etc; a newspaper will have an 'editorial policy' on the type of material it will include.

4

Fairly straightforward - but it is worth your thinking about factors that get in the way of planning in practice. The existence of an effective MIS implies that (A) is not the problem here - but it can be for managers who need to know about market size and needs, new legislation, the strength of competition or state of the economy etc in order to make useful plans for the future. Knowledge of organisational goals (B) is similarly not a problem here, with a communicated mission and participation in corporate planning - but could be: planning can be perceived as a waste of time if resulting activity is thought likely to duplicate or conflict with that of other departments, or if performed 'in a vacuum', without a sense of purpose and contribution. (D) is also not a problem for Lee, who has participated in corporate planning and has discretion in his unit - but is a common source of 'political' resistance to targets. We learn, however, that the organisation punishes failure to meet targets, and this is a common cause of resentment of the planning process, as the yardstick by which 'failure' can be clearly identified. Since Lee is bound in any case to have low expectations of his team - from experience- he is likely to feel that target-setting will expose him to punishment (C).

Question

5

(2) is most obviously among the purposes of a budget. The other three options may not have occurred to you, however. (1) is regarded by some writers as the *most* important feature of budgeting: forcing managers to look ahead, set targets, anticipate problems etc. (3) may be a predominant role of government budgets and not-for-profit budgets, which offer authorisations and ceilings for management actions, spending etc. (4) may be even more unexpected, because of the much-quoted 'human problems' of budgeting, but by setting a specific level of attainment as a target, a budget helps employees to assess what they need to do, how much effort it will cost them and what purpose that effort fulfils. It is thus important to the 'motivation calculus' (which you'll meet again in chapter 7). A 'desired standards' budget - rather than a 'minimum expectation' budget - may in addition offer a challenge, which will have a motivatory effect where employees seek intrinsic satisfaction (sense of achievement etc) and where organisational culture reinforces heroic effort and 'winning' as important values.

6

Planning and control involve forecasting, subjective or statistical. You may not need to know about 'quantitative techniques' for your management studies, in which case this is a tricky one. Even so, an educated guess might have been in order: 'barometric' techniques (B) predict market changes, just as a barometer predicts changes in the weather. It depends on identification of key 'indicators' of change, and prediction of the time between change in the indicator and change in market demand. Econometrics (A) is the study of economic variables and their interrelationships, using computer models. Network analysis (C) embraces a number of techniques (eg Critical Path Method and PERT - Programme Evaluation and Review technique) for the planning and control of complex projects. Break-even analysis (D) shows how costs and profits vary with the volume of production, break-even point being where neither a loss nor a profit is being made.

7

The shareholder view (B) is that the main corporate objective is to obtain a satisfactory return on the shareholders' capital, and that all other objectives must be subordinated to that aim. The consensus theory (C) is that objectives emerge as a consensus of the differing needs of stakeholders, but that (in contrast to the stakeholder view) they are not all selected or controlled by management. Consumerism (D) relates to the influence of *one* of the stakeholder groups (ie the consumers) on objectives: it is a social movement seeking to increase the rights and powers of buyers (in relation to sellers) so that they can defend their interests.

8

Only (D) reflects an approach which balances the demands of managers, shareholders, employees, government and public opinion. In other words, the company will seek a level of profit *acceptable* to management and shareholders, but consistent with, for example, expenditure on pay and benefits, and financial support for the community (eg Sainsburys' 'Good Neighbour Scheme'). The other options imply a shareholder view.

Question

9

(A) and (B) both represent sudden changes - the first an opportunity and the second a threat - to which the organisation will need to be able to respond swiftly: a formal corporate plan may take too long to prepare and document. Freewheeling opportunism also tends to encourage more flexible and creative attitudes among lower-level managers (C). The conglomerate (D), however, will be in danger of disintegration and fragmentation if it does not provide for disciplined planning, even though its opportunities for takeovers might emerge suddenly, calling for a quick decision.

10

This is tricky, by virtue of the fact that *elements* of (A), (B) and (D) are present in the diagram. The link between corporate planning and management by objectives (MbO) is clearly intimate, but the emphasis on individual manager targets, appraisal and development indicate that this is not primarily a corporate planning diagram. Manpower planning also contains common elements with MbO: performance review against targets will be part of the assessment of current manpower resources, and training/ development/succession plans will be part of the overall manpower plan. SWOT analysis will be carried out in order to formulate the strategic plan at the starting point of the diagram. The diagram in its entirety, however, depicts the full range of MbO.

11

Humble pioneered the approach to MbO in the UK. (D) and (A) are earlier stages of the process: individual objectives are formulated with regard to key tasks and results - ie critical tasks and targets in the manager's job. The unit improvement plan (C) (setting out objectives for improvements, performance standards and timescale) is broken down into a series of short-term targets for individual managers, in accordance with key results and performance standards. This is the 'job improvement plan' (B).

12

Potential review (A) is an essential part of Humble's model, which complements performance review. It is concerned with the manager's anticipated ability to succeed in his next job, and feeds back into the management training, development and succession systems. (B) and (C) may be later *consequences* of (A). (D) has nothing to do with it: job evaluation is an examination of the job (not the job holder) specifically with a view to determining salary structures.

13

(B) and (C) are demonstrated in the experience of companies and in motivation theory. Commitment is also enhanced if clear targets are set, against which performance can be objectively measured (A). Long planning horizons (D) create problems in various ways. It is difficult to communicate them to lower levels of management in such a way that they are not soon forgotten. Long-term plans are also perceived to be prone to inflexibility: they are likely to go out of date rather quickly in rapidly-changing environments or where unforeseen events occur, and so lose credibility. Long-term plans tend to be general - because of the flexibility problem - and so of limited value at operational levels, and tend to be the province of senior management, which may cause political resistance.

Question

14 to 16

These questions should be straightforward - but indicate the range of areas on which SWOT analysis can be carried out: here, management succession, plant and equipment, social/market. If you had to think twice about 2, the environmental change can be anticipated to create a new demand for boats. (The name of the company wasn't *just* a joke....)

17

You may not have come across these terms for control system mechanisms before - but if you knew the control cycle, you could derive the answer from the meaning of the words. Z is the sensor (C): it senses or measures output, ie actual results, and feeds back to X, which is the comparator (D). It compares actual results with the standard or plan. Corrective control action is then put into effect by Y - the effector (A) or activator (B), which alters inputs to the system.

18

Negative feedback (B) attempts to change the direction or movement of the system *back* towards its planned course. Feedforward control (C) is anticipating results - based on current progress - and taking control action if it looks as if they will deviate from plan. Double-loop feedback (D) is reported to more senior management and is concerned with overall task control: control action may include adjustment to the *plan*, as well as to the course of action that is found to be deviant. The answer is therefore (A). An example of it would be where feedback indicates that production, or sales, are higher than the organisation has budgeted for: management would wish to maintain or increase this deviation from plan.

19

Feed*back* control compares planned results with historical (A) actual (B) results - ie what has in fact happened. There may be a 'control delay' between deviation from plan and reporting/action. This is eliminated by feed*forward* control, which anticipates results according to current trends while the system is still in process and can be changed if a deviation is foreseen.

20

Straightforward - although standard setting and performance measurement in service departments is not always easy in practice! 2 is an example of (A): routine work is susceptible to standard timings. 1 is an example of (B). 3 is, less obviously, an example of (C). (D) *would* apply if, for example, the printing department were designated a profit centre. It would charge other departments for its services at a 'commercial' rate.

Question

21 An internal audit department may be asked by management to look into any aspect of the organisation. (A) is a type of audit which is applied to the influence of the organisation on its various 'stakeholders': eg staff incentives, welfare, retirement provisions etc, or pricing policy, product quality and safety, advertising integrity etc. (B) is an audit which looks at the 3Es in the organisation systems: effectiveness, efficiency and economy. (D) similarly looks at efficiency. (C), the answer here, is still the most prominent type of audit in internal audit work, although VFM audits have been 'catching on' more in recent years .

22 Social control is applied through interpersonal and group processes. (A) is the term for groups with which a person identifies himself and which have a significant influence on his behaviour by providing him with models and 'norms' eg Bros fans, Pepsi drinkers etc. (B) and (C) also develop 'norms' of behaviour to which the individual must 'buy in or get out', through peer pressure. (D) does not involve social influence: it would be classed as 'bureaucratic control'.

23 Insidious controls are these which are not *experienced* and recognisable as controls. (A), (C) and (D) are overt, obvious controls: the employee knows to what extent his behaviour is being influenced. Recruitment (B) is a method of control which is not experienced as such by the individuals selected.

7: MARKING SCHEDULE

Question	Correct answer	Marks for the correct answer	Question	Correct answer	Marks for the correct answer
1	C	1	14	B	1
2	D	1	15	C	1
3	C	1	16	D	1
4	C	1	17	C	1
5	A	1	18	D	1
6	B	1	19	A	1
7	C	1	20	D	1
8	A	1	21	B	1
9	C	1	22	C	1
10	C	1	23	A	1
11	D	1	24	B	1
12	B	1	25	A	1
13	A	1	26	B	1

YOUR MARKS

Total marks available   26   Your total mark

GUIDELINES - If your mark was:

0 - 6 This is an important topic, so a low score here is potentially dangerous. You need to do some more: start with Maslow, Herzberg and expectancy theory, which are vital.

7 - 13 If you fell down on job evaluation this may not be too critical - but most of the other questions are mainstream, in an important topic area. Revise.

14 - 20 Not bad at all - but for peace of mind, make sure you understand why you got things wrong, especially in the motivation and discipline area.

21 - 26 You're well on top of the essential principles in this area. Did your errors fall in a particular topic area that is important to you? It's worth checking.

COMMENTS

Question

1 Motivation is one of those topics where it really helps to have under your belt some of the names and basic ideas of the main theorists. Otherwise, it is very difficult to think about motivation in other than the vaguest possible terms. (A) and (B) are similar approaches, based on the idea that behaviour (eg productivity) is, for the worker, a path to valued goals; whether or not to behave as required is a decision made according to the individual's needs, valued outcomes and the perception that the desired behaviour is the path to their fulfilment. (D) is an expectancy model put forward by Charles Handy. As you might infer from the name, it too is based on the calculation of likelihood of outcome, desirability of outcome, and action required for outcome. (C) is the name for Herzberg's theory of hygiene/motivator factors: it is a *content* theory.

2 (A), (B) and (C) relate to tangible rewards and working conditions, which are 'extrinsic' satisfactions. The meetings (D) provide feedback which allows employees to feel pride in the organisation's success, a sense of involvement etc, which is what 'intrinsic' satisfactions are all about: their source is within the experience of work itself and not in its 'by-products', bestowed by the organisation to encourage work effort.

3 Maslow's categories of needs are a famous model, and can provide a useful way of thinking about motivation - but not if you get them mixed up with bits of other people's theories! (C) belongs to David McClelland's categorisation of three needs: for achievement, power and affiliation. Maslow's term for the same type of need (for relationships, a sense of belonging etc) is 'love' needs. (B) may have caused some problems. The *hierarchy* embraces five types, but Maslow actually identified *seven* innate needs including (B) and the need for knowledge and understanding: these last two are channels through which we find ways of satisfying all other needs.

4 (A), (B) and (D) are commonly identified problems with the use of Maslow's hierarchy to predict behaviour. Altruism, for example, where a person puts his own safety and comfort at risk for the sake of others, is an example of (A) in practice. (B) is most obviously true at the 'upper' end of the hierarchy: satisfaction of an esteem need, for example tends to *stimulate* further such needs rather than 'get them out of the way'. The 'ethno-centricity' of the hierarchy has been confirmed by cross-cultural research: it fits America and Britain, but no other group of countries. (C) is an invalid objection because Maslow never intended his views to be applied specifically to the work context.

Question

5

(B), (C) and (D) are all terms for the same thing: Herzberg's category of factors that must be controlled if they are not to cause dissatisfaction, but cannot elicit positive satisfaction beyond the short-term. They are essentially preventative, therefore - hence 'maintenance' and 'hygiene' - and come from the environment rather than the job itself. (A) is the term Herzberg used for the *other* sort of factor, ie those aspects which lead to satisfaction.

6

1, 2 and 3 are all 'hygiene' factors. 4 represents growth in the job and personal development, and as such is the only 'motivator' factor.

7

Expectancy would be high - close to 1 on a probability scale of 0 (no chance) to 1 (certainty) - because there is a clear link between effort towards January sales and promotion to team leader: that rules out (B). Valence will be neither high (a positive number) nor low (a negative number), because of the pressures in both directions: Willy would 'like' the responsibility but wouldn't like the hours - and there would be a particular sacrifice involved at Christmas: that rules out (A) as well. When either valence or expectancy is 0 in the equation, $F = E \times V$, motivation (F) will also be 0: motivation will be low, ruling out (D). Notice that if Willy had actively disliked the idea of promotion, V would have been a *negative* number, and he would have been *de*-motivated.

8

We threw this one in because the idea of 'E factors' is so useful in thinking about motivation. So if you hadn't come across the term, never mind getting the answer wrong - but take it on board now. In Handy's calculus, expectancy (A) occupies the same place it does in expectancy theory. *'E' factors*, however, are something different. They are Handy's term for what 'being motivated' means in practice. Other theories identify it as putting in *effort* (B), but Handy suggests that motivated individuals put forth a number of other performance-related factors which (coincidentally) seem to begin with 'e': energy (C), expenditure (D), enthusiasm, emotion, excitement, endurance etc.

9

Without (A), (B) and (D), it will be impossible for the individual to complete his motivation 'calculus'. Intended results help him to work out what the reward will be and how much 'e' was justified and will be justified in future - ie will influence 'expectancy'. The same is true of the organisation's consistency in following results with promised rewards: if it doesn't always do so, expectancy will be low. (C) is *not* necessarily required, however. Handy suggests that psychological maturity lengthens the time span the individual will tolerate between result and 'pay-off': some people have a very high tolerance for 'delayed gratification', and build it into their calculation of whether or not it is worth expending extra 'e' on a task. A student may, for example, work sacrificially hard now, if he thinks it will help him to gain qualifications which will benefit his career in three years' time.

Question

10 This is another effect of the expectancy equation which can be useful for management to know. The likelihood of the individual having his needs met by the course of behaviour considered here depends on *success:* he won't be rewarded without it. So the more important the rewards, the higher will be his desire to achieve, and fear of failure: he will lower his standards, if possible, to increase the likelihood of success and therefore the expectancy that effort will be instrumental in satisfying his needs (C). (D) is an interesting side-issue: in fact, the experience of continual success has been shown to increase the level of aspiration and also the desirability of the goal (or 'valence'): it is felt to be 'worthwhile'.

11 One for the more advanced student, perhaps, although reference to Maslow may have given a clue. Scientific management (A) and the classical school (C) are both early approaches to management theory. Their exponents, eg Taylor and Fayol, concentrated on pay and discipline in securing effort from workers: physiological and safety needs, in Maslow's terms. The human relations approach (B) followed them, with the work of Elton Mayo, who was predominantly interested in social or affiliation needs - the role of the work group etc. Following the Second World War, the emphasis switched to social psychology, which drew attention to man's capacity for self-awareness and self-fulfilment: this was the work of Maslow, Herzberg and later researchers of the 'neo-human relations school' (D).

12 Straightforward - but an important point about the limitations of pay as a motivator. You may have recognised the scenario from the famous Hawthorne Studies (Bank Wiring Room phase). Group restriction of output is consistent with earning enough to live on (C) but not so much as to incur group disapproval by 'rate busting' (D) or overproducing and damaging long-term prospects (A). Lack of interest in the incentive scheme indicates that maximising earnings (B) is not the primary goal.

13 'Reinforcement' is a useful term drawn from learning theory: it refers to the way in which experience of reward and punishment can confirm or deter behaviour. Positive reinforcement (A) is reward - including praise. Negative reinforcement and motivation (B and D) are punishment. Positive discipline (C) is a technical term for forms of discipline which leave the individual no choice *but* to behave in the appropriate way - eg safety guards on machinery.

14 Theory X is the belief that the average human being is passive and easily led, needs to be controlled and coerced, and will respond best to economic incentives. This is (B) in Schein's famous model (in *Organisational Psychology*). (A) looks for self-fulfilment in social relationships. (C) is influenced by a wider range of motivations, and is capable of maturity, autonomy and commitment. (D) represents Schein's own view of people: they are driven by different and variable motives and will respond to no single motivational strategy.

Question

15 Taylor, pioneer of scientific management, advocated specialisation and fragmentation of work; in other words, (C). (A), (B) and (D) are ways of alternating or widening 'jobs' as a reaction against the 'de-humanising' effect of specialisation. (D) in particular involves rebuilding a whole job out of its component parts and giving responsibility for its organisation and completion to a work group.

16 The answer is in the notes to this chapter (see 2.2). Eva's new tasks are of the same skill level and responsibility as her original task, so her job has been enlarged rather than enriched. Students often confuse the two, so take the time to get it straight in your mind if you got this wrong. (B) is not, of course, a job design technique at all, but a written description of the elements of a job as a result of job analysis.

17 (A), (B) and (D) have been found in practice to be benefits of job enrichment. We deliberately left increased motivation and productivity out of it, because these are still controversial areas: beware extravagant claims. What job enrichment *cannot* do is offer management a cheap way of motivating employees (C): even those who want enriched jobs will expect to be rewarded with more than job satisfaction for their new responsibilities, eg more pay.

18 A tricky one. Participation *should* be limited in its scope or 'terms of reference' (A): it should be clear whether information, advice or decision is being sought, otherwise it will be suspected that participation is not 'genuine', when the employees' input does not influence the decision. It should also be limited to cultures conducive to its practical implementation (B), otherwise it will appear an 'inauthentic' attempt to pay lip service to the concept. It should be limited to employees (C) who have the ability and information to contribute - otherwise failure to implement (or failure *through* implementation) will demoralise participants. Where the issue or task is trivial (D) and realised to be such, however, it is reckoned that little interest will be aroused and, again, the genuiness of management or motives will be suspect.

19 Satisfied workers tend to be loyal and stay with the organisation, so labour turnover (the rate at which people leave the organisation) is a popular indicator (D). Absenteeism (B) may be caused by physical or emotional stress, but is also an indication of 'withdrawal' which is a response to dissatisfaction. Attitude surveys (C) are widely used - especially in the USA - to obtain information about how employees regard their work, their boss etc. The assumption that satisfaction *per se* leads to increased productivity lies behind (A) - and it is a false assumption. Satisfaction may be very low, but employees successfully coerced into high productivity, for example.

Question

20 Most people work 'for the money' - yet pay is very limited as an incentive (which is why it is a 'hygiene' factor). High taxation rates (1) may make the extra money seem not worth the extra effort and deprivation. Equity (2) implies a rate for the job or 'fair compensation' rather than incentive related to individual performance: Herzberg and others have suggested, moreover, that differentials (or *imagined* differentials) will always be a source of dissatisfaction. Regular salary review (3) makes 'incentives' seem like 'entitlements': again, this robs pay of its connection with extra effort, and can be a source of dissatisfaction where the rise does not meet expectation. Work group norms (4) tend to set output restrictions, through suspicion that high output and earnings will make management alter standards and incentive rates to reduce future earnings: the desire to conform to the group outweighs the money urge.

21 The incorrect options are the most important thing about this question. It is important to remember that job content alone will not determine the value of a job, although it is the main focus of job evaluation. Social custom and expectations (A), obligations to unions (C) and supply and demand (D) will affect pay levels. (*Note*. Job evaluation looks at job content (B) - to determine the *relative* value of jobs, not their worth in money terms).

22 If you thought (A) was the answer, you were thinking along the right lines, because this is *also* a disadvantage - ie lack of incentive. However, it is an advantage in preventing wage 'drift' from being built into the structure: a newcomer to the job will not be unfairly paid his predecessor's merit bonus, and the job will not have to be re-evaluated with every change of personnel or performance fluctuation. (B) is clearly an advantage eg if the organisation has to defend itself against allegations of unfairness or discrimination. (D) is a beneficial by-product: job descriptions also aid in recruitment and selection, the planning of training and development and management's understanding of the organisation (eg in an O M study). Answer (C) is right because job evaluation *doesn't* make any recommendation about *levels* of pay: market rates, equity, negotiated settlements, organisational resources and culture will influence the actual rates paid for the job-evaluated grades or rankings.

23 This is (A), the most popular method of formal job evaluation. (B) also starts with factors, but then takes key benchmark jobs, whose salary is 'felt fair', breaks down the total monetary value of each of them according to the relative importance of each factor in the job and so derives a pay scale for each factor; factor values are then added together in their relative proportions for other jobs. (C) is a much simpler method whereby 'whole jobs' are (subjectively) ranked in order of importance to the organisation and then separated into 'bands' or grades: very unscientific. (D) is not job evaluation at all: it's an assessment of an individual, according to desirable qualities eg initiative, punctuality, output etc for the purposes of bonus-setting, promotion planning etc.

Question

24 Punitive (A) is to punish: the punishment should usually 'fit the crime'. Deterrant (C) is to warn and discourage the offender and others from repeating the offence: the action is often *more* severe than the office warrants, to 'make an example' of the offender. 'Letting them get away with it' (D) is not properly the purpose of any disciplinary action. Where the intention is to point out the nature of the offence trusting that the offender will not repeat it, (B), lenient action is likely to be sufficient, and less likely to *create* problems by causing resentment. It would be appropriate, for example if an employee did not realise that personal use of office stationery was, technically, theft.

25 Constructive' or 'positive' discipline is a technical term for discipline which gives the employee no *choice* but to act in the manner desired by the organisation. (A) would mean, for example, that no task could be badly or fraudulently performed or forgotten. Another example would be automatic shutdown of a machine when its safety guard was lifted. (B), (C) and (D) are all 'positive' in a non-technical sense, but are nevertheless 'negative discipline' in that they are designed to make employees *choose* to behave in a desirable way.

26 Informal verbal warnings are not covered by the Code of Practice: that rules out (C). Streyton Harrow contravened the code at the written warning stage by failing to inform the offender of the nature of his alleged misconduct. They should also have allowed the offender to be accompanied by a colleague or employee representative at the disciplinary interview: trying to be 'discreet' is *not* to be taken to extremes. (B) is therefore the answer.

8: MARKING SCHEDULE

Question	Correct answer	Marks for the correct answer	Question	Correct answer	Marks for the correct answer
1	B	1	11	D	1
2	C	1	12	D	1
3	D	1	13	C	1
4	D	1	14	C	1
5	B	1	15	B	1
6	A	1	16	D	1
7	B	1	17	A	1
8	C	1	18	D	1
9	B	1	19	C	1
10	A	1	20	B	1

YOUR MARKS

Total marks available   20   Your total mark

GUIDELINES - If your mark was:

0 - 7
We recommend that you pick one style theory (eg sells-tells etc), Blake's grid, and one contingency approach: whichever appeals to you. Learn them.

13 - 16
Very respectable. If it was a particular theory (or two) that you were weak on, check whether it's in your syllabus: if so, revise. If it isn't, you can be perfectly satisfied with this score.

8 - 12
You are scraping by. This is a topic where it really does help to know some theories, though, so it's worth another going over.

17 - 20
Impressive indeed. You were probably only unfamiliar with one of the theories. Questions 3 and 17 are the most interesting of all, in some ways, though, so if you got those wrong, have a look at the comments.

COMMENTS

Question

1

The only valuable definitions of leadership, as distinguished from management, stress its capacity to secure from others *more* than mere compliance to the 'legal' requirements imposed by organisational authority. A leader is therefore someone who doesn't have to depend on position power alone (B).

2

Fayol's well-known five functions of management are planning, organising, commanding (A), co-ordinating (B) and controlling (D).

3

This is, admittedly, a controversial area. However, traits theories of leadership - largely discredited - still linger in selection and training processes, as guidelines for the skills, abilities and attributes thought desirable by the organisation. The important thing to realise is that leadership is *not* a case of 'born, not made': some people may have *natural* 'leadership qualities', but the practical application of them can be taught. 1, 2 and 3 are common subjects of courses, workshops and techniques, using role play, case studies, practice etc. 4 is the controversial one. 'Charisma' is traditionally surrounded by 'mystique', but it has been suggested (eg by House: *A theory of charismatic leadership*) that it can be acquired and developed through training in specific behaviour for: role modelling (setting an example); image creation (giving off 'success' signals); confidence-building; goal articulation (adding moral overtones to objectives); and motive arousal (inspiring).

4

(A), (B) and (C) are all democratic or participative. Decisions are reached on the basis of consensus or agreement, with input from subordinates supported by the leader. (D) is different in emphasis. 'Laissez-faire' implies little or no direction or involvement on the part of the leader; he simply 'lets them get on with it'. In experiments, this style was found to be less popular and less productive than more positive 'democratic' style.

5

Otto's style is not based on pure autocratic imposition of the decision (A), nor on group consensus (D). It *looks* like consultation (C), because he invites group input, and says he will take their views into account in making his decision. However, a pitfall with the 'consults' - limited participation - style is that it can be a 'front' for what is actually a 'sells' style (B). That is what Otto is doing. He has made up his mind in advance, and invites participation only as a means of persuading his subordinates to accept his decision.

202

Question

6

This contains some surprising elements. The 'consults' style was indeed most preferred by subordinates (A). It was in fact the *least* prone to hostility and discontent (D). The most frequently-used styles (B) were, however, 'tells' and 'sells'. And although *motivation* was strongest in the democratic group, the amount of work actually done was greater (C) where a more autocratic style was used.

7

Straightforward. Look back at the notes to this chapter if you need to. Theories X and Y (Douglas McGregor), by the way, are not *strictly* 'leadership styles', but the assumptions managers make about their subordinates which issue in a given leadership style. Theory X assumes the need for direction, control and coercion. Theory Y assumes the possibility of participation, integration of personal and organisational goals, voluntary commitment etc.

8

(A) is 1.1 (low concern for task and people)
(B) is 9.1 (high concern for task, low for people)
(D) is 5.5 - also called 'middle of the road'
(C) is the answer. Try and remember which comes first - task or people - if you find the grid useful. It's easy to get (B) and (C) the wrong way round.

9

Reddin's model is very interesting. It indicates, for example, that a manager who would be a 1.1 on the managerial grid (and in Blake's terms, therefore ineffective) *may* still be effective in fulfilling his task objectives, because he is a bureaucrat or rule-follower (and can not, in a sense, 'go wrong'). That is Ed Oncho: (B).

The options, as classified by Reddin, would be:

	Concern for task	Concern for human relations	Effectiveness	Style
(A)	low	low	high	Bureaucrat
(B)	high	low	low	Autocrat
(C)	low	low	low	Active deserter
(D)	high	low	high	Benelovent autocrat: good persuader

Question

10 Theory X (A) is the theory that the average human being will avoid work if he can, prefers to be directed and needs to be controlled and coerced into putting forward adequate effort for the organisation. Behaviour based on these assumptions commonly includes that of the scenario.

Theory Y (B) is the theory that man will exercise self-direction and self-control in the service of objectives to which he is committed: he is not naturally passive or resistant to organisational objectives: MbO, consultative supervision and 'loose' controls would be features of this approach. William Ouchi compared the American way of managing (which he called Theory A) with the model of successful Japanese management techniques (Theory J - (D)). He formulated his own Theory Z (C) to suggest how the key elements of the Japanese way - consensus decision-making and a spirit of trust - can be applied to Western management and organisation.

11 This is the form of Tannenbaum and Schmidt's continuum used for training. It's a matter of common sense, though. Where the subordinate has complete discretion, authority has been delegated to him to perform the task or make the decision (D). (C) is 1, (B) is 2 and (A) is 3, to complete the continuum.

12 In Handy's 'best fit' theory, the *flexible* end of the spectrum includes:

Leader - preference for democratic style, confidence in subordinates
Subordinates - high confidence, like challenge
Task - long timescale, complex problem-solving

None of the elements is therefore 'right' (D). Note that the 'leader' is Betty herself - not *her* boss, who is part of the *'environment'*. (The environment, incidentally, would be a constraint on Betty's choice of style here: the organisation culture and political pressure from her own (autocratic) manager will hinder her democratic preference. Environment is not, however, part of the 'best fit' equation, although the context in which it occurs.)

13 Straighforward. See the notes on this chapter. (D) is not a contingency approach at all, but a 'style' approach.

14 Fiedler suggested that the situation is most favourable when:

- the leader is liked and trusted by the group (1)
- the leader has authority and power over the group (3)
- the tasks are clearly defined (*not* 2)

Question

15 Fiedler suggested that when the situation is very favourable, the leader will be able to concentrate on the task rather than on group maintenance. When the situation is very unfavourable, he will *need* to be task-oriented and autocratic, or 'psychologically distant': psychologically distant managers (PDMs) are high-producing, because they emphasise control and discipline, concentrate on task performance and are competent - though reserved - in interpersonal relationships. If the situation is only moderately favourable, as in Don's case here, the manager will need to develop the team's relationships and be a psychologically close manager or PCM (C). This is detailed stuff - but it is in the notes to this chapter.

16 A very important concept. (A) and (B) suggest trait theory in its various manifestations. (C) suggests style theories. (D) is contingency theory: the word 'adaptive' should have told you.

17 Not an entirely 'objective' testing question - but worth it, to get you thinking about the potential usefulness of leadership theories. They can be used to highlight shortcomings in a manager's approach (1): eg Blake's grid will expose disproportionate concern for the task rather than for people. They can be used in training and development (2): the 'tells-sells - consults - joins' continuum is used in development programmes to get managers to recognise that style is flexible. Adair's functional approach is particularly useful as a framework for leadership training based on precept and practice in his eight key activities (see the notes), considered in the light of interrelated variables of task, group, individual and whole situation. That is as much as can be claimed, however. Theories may not make 'better leaders' (3) - because management style and action is not the only thing that determines success, and in any case the theories tend not to distinguish between management and 'leadership'. Part of the problem is the failure of (4): just studying a concept will not necessarily change a manager's attitude or behaviour. Even if he *wants* to adapt his style as indicated, he may be unable to do so, because his personality is too inflexible, he is not a good enough 'actor', organisational norms and politics do not permit it, or his subordinates resist what they regard as unpredictability or 'fickleness'.

18 Fairly clear. Willy needs to delegate (1): he is overloaded, and his subordinates are bored. He needs assertiveness (2) to say 'no', where appropriate, to his subordinates and even to his boss. He needs to practise goal-planning (4) to break down the size of the workload which demoralises him, and to prioritise and schedule his tasks so that he knows just 'where the day is going' and which elements of his day he will have to cut down (probably the talking). You may have paused at (3), with the thought that Willy's communication skills and inclinations are if anything *too* good: he communicates too much. However, learning to read faster, write more concise reports, sort out essential from non-essential communications etc also come into this area. Bear it in mind!

Question

19

(A) and (B) are clearly invitations to the disorganised to waste time in non-essential talk. (D) will inevitably take more time than an allowance of shortcuts, a tolerance of small errors etc. All these things are good and desirable in other ways but potential problems for time management. (C), on the other hand, is likely to improve work flows, cut down on unnecessary travelling, ensure accessibility of common facilities and proximity of people who need regular contract. Physical layout should not be forgotten as an element in time-efficient working.

20

Job management is making sure the manager is equipped to do his job and that his job is designed so as to be conducive to effective performance: (A), (C) and (D) are all about providing such 'resources' (information, knowhow, finance and labour etc).

Time management is the process of allocating time to tasks in the most effective manner - primarily by prioritising (B) and scheduling.

9: MARKING SCHEDULE

Question	Correct answer	Marks for the correct answer	Question	Correct answer	Marks for the correct answer
1	D	1	11	C	1
2	A	1	12	B	1
3	D	1	13	B	1
4	B	1	14	D	1
5	C	1	15	B	1
6	B	1	16	C	1
7	A	1	17	D	1
8	D	1	18	B	1
9	A	1	19	A	1
10	B	1	20	D	1

YOUR MARKS

Total marks available [20] , Your total mark [   ]

GUIDELINES - If your mark was:

0 - 5 Learn the factors in group leadership, if your got those questions wrong. That'll give you something to be getting on with. Worth more work.

6 - 10 Not too bad. Learn the factors in group leadership and effectiveness and have a look at the Hawthorne research as well if you got questions 18-20 wrong.

11 - 15 You're well-grounded in this topic now. Well done. Maybe it's the group psychology that's eluded you: check your syllabus, just in case......

16 - 20 Very well done. You can face just about anything in this area. If you got questions 13, 14 or 18-20 wrong, though, they might be worth another look.

COMMENTS

Question

1

Handy (in *Understanding Organisations*) describes a group as 'any collection of people who perceive themselves to be a group'. The sense of identity (D) is most important: there are acknowledged boundaries to a group - formal or informal - which define who is 'in' and who is 'out', 'us' and 'them'. (A), (B) and (C) are very often attributes of groups as well, but a group will not *always* have a leader, or an expressed purpose or direction. Conformity, as a common expression of loyalty to, and acceptance within, a group, grows out of the sense of identity: it can also be found in individuals or random collections of people, in the sense of conformity to social convention, fashion etc.

2

The primary working group is the smallest unit of the organisation structure, and therefore the immediate social environment of the individual worker. (A) therefore fits the bill, while the others don't.

3

This question raises an interesting point. Why do many organisations use or encourage cohesive work groups? They offer opportunities for pooled knowledge and skills, encourage the exchange of ideas, and satisfy workers' needs for friendship and belonging. The reason why (A) isn't the answer to this question, however, is that identification with a work group will only raise an individual's productivity if the group 'norm' is higher than his own standard. The more he identifies with the group, the more he will conform to the 'norm' - and it has been demonstrated that groups actually restrict productivity in many cases. Coch and French reckoned that the most productive member of a work group is more frequently the 'social outcast' than the one with the most ability. If the worker identifies with a trade union (B), his energy may be diverted to non-work goals, which may even run *contrary* to the organisation's interests. If he identifies with the company (C), he may still not be more productive, through caring for quality rather than output level.

4

A *reference group* (B) is a group with which an individual closely identifies himself and which has a significant influence on his behaviour, by providing him with 'models' and 'norms'. But he doesn't need to be a member of the group itself in order for these norms to influence him: any group to which he *aspires* to belong is also a reference group. (A), (C) and (D) have norms which operate as a result and 'badge' of membership of the group itself.

Question

5
and
6

Forming is the first stage when the group is coming together. Individuals are 'feeling each other out', and there is usually a wariness about introducing new ideas, appearing radical etc. Objectives and leadership are still unclear.

Storming is the second stage, where conflict is more or less open. Objectives, norms and procedures are challenged and changed. Greater risks are taken, with enthusiasm, brainstorming, identification of individuals with 'causes'. Political conflicts emerge as leadership becomes an issue. (This is the scenario of question 6).

Norming is the settling-down period, where agreement is reached on roles, procedures and customs. Enthusiasm and brainstorming are reduced, in favour of consensus, method and adherence to group norms.

Performing is where attention is directed away from the difficulties of growth and development and the group sets to work to execute its task.

7

Internalisation (B) and identification (D) imply full acceptance of the norm, or 'ownership' of the attitude in question. Counter-conformity (C) is rejection of the norm and/or the group itself. Compliance (A) is the answer here, and is an important concept for team leaders and managers wanting to secure conformity to a rule, norm or instruction: it implies a change in *behaviour*, but not in *attitude*. It is harder to change attitudes (and secure internalisation) than behaviour. A manager may be content to get the action he desires without commitment, but there are likely to be problems arising from the suppression of disagreement and lack of positive commitment in the long run.

8

Fairly obvious. Norms are reinforced where the individual lacks support for independent attitudes or behaviour (A) and values membership of the group (B), especially where the group emphasises its solidarity and the sense of belonging and acceptance (C). Norms are also reinforced where the individual wishes to avoid the negative sanctions at its disposal: ostracising the 'deviant' member, ridicule, reprimand and, ultimately, expulsion. A group which refrains from such methods will gain less conformity (D), since non-conforming members will not lose any of the security or benefits of group membership.

Question

9 You may have had to think carefully about this. Good. Because there's a lot said about 'how to create cohesive work teams' without considering whether the organisation would invariably *want* to do so! Conformity to norms (1) may be desirable where the group sets a high standard of production/quality etc but not if its goals are non-work oriented or even contrary to the organisation's objectives - eg deliberately restricted output. Solidarity (2) is likewise helpful in injecting an element of competition to enhance performance, and in compensating for difficulties or dangers in the work - but it can also provide a position of strength where the organisation itself is considered the 'enemy' or threat. Satisfaction of social needs (3) is an important function of groups for employee satisfaction and morale: it may prevent labour turnover or absenteeism from employees seeking such satisfaction elsewhere - but it can also become all-absorbing, diverting attention and energy away from the task. Increased confidence and risk-taking (4) can be valuable where innovation is required by the organisation - but can lead to trouble in cohesive groups which fall victim to 'group think', the tendency to feel invulnerable, filter out criticism and divergent views, and forge ahead - blind to risk - in a completely wrong direction.

Creating a cohesive group is not in itself enough to guarantee effective performance!

10 Straightforward - and useful to know. Bear it in mind when you're in a team somewhere. (B), although positive in itself, is one of the prime causes of 'group think', preventing the group from receiving input from non-members and fostering the desire for unanimity, consensus and solidarity to 'guard' the blinkered decisions made. (A), (C) and (D) are essential strategies for prevention. ('Group think' is discussed in the notes to this chapter, if you want to refresh your memory.)

11 (A), (B) and (D) *are* features of competing groups - and they can be very useful to the organisation. Cohesion and effective performance are often assumed to be the result of communication, trust and co-operation, but it should be remembered that in the face of a perceived 'enemy' or 'threat', group cohesiveness and productivity can be enhanced. (C) is in fact the opposite of what happens: the climate changes from informal and sociable to work- and task-oriented; individual needs are subordinated to achievement.

12 (1) will be largely irrelevant here, although in groups where there is regular physical proximity, compatibility of group members and what they can bring to group functioning are crucial. The same goes for (3): there is no implication that leadership style is an issue, or even that the reps have any kind of constant leader - although in 'steady' groups who work together under a team leader, it will be the role of that leader to foster *esprit de corps*, to encourage all-round contribution etc. (2) and (4) will be vital in Klaus Knit's situation, though. The company wants a consistent image portrayed, so train-ing of the reps in shared sales techniques and shared knowledge of the group as a whole will be valuable: it will also be a mechanism for bringing the sales team together on a regular basis, as a whole or in regional units, for social contact with a business purpose 'Culture' covers a number of useful devices for enhancing a *sense* of teamhood, which the reps lack: uniform, for example (even if only a badge), common emblems of success (eg the MacDonalds 'service stars'), common motto or attitude to the product etc.

Question

13 and 14

We've included two questions on this particular model of Handy's because it is such a well-known and useful way of looking at the leadership of groups. You didn't need to know the particular framework, though: an awareness of any contingency approach would have let you piece it together. Look back at the notes to this chapter (3.3).

Givens ⟶ *Intervening factors* ⟶ *Outcomes*

- the group
- the task
- the environment

- group motivation
- leadership style
- processes/procedures

- group productivity
- member satisfaction

15

It's worth being realistic about group decision-making. Groups have been shown to produce less ideas - though better evaluated (4) - than the individuals working separately. As the Japanese approach to decision-making admits, group decision-making is slower (so 2 is out), but does mean that the result does not have to be 'sold' to members afterwards (3): there is a better chance of 'ownership' of the decision, rather than resistance or mere compliance. (1) is not, perhaps surprisingly, true: groups actually take *riskier* decisions than the individuals comprising them, because of the blurring of individual responsibility, and sense of security in numbers.

16

Straightforward. Members of an effectively functioning group will take an active interest (as opposed to (C)) in decisions affecting their work. (A) and (B) are healthy - see the comments to solutions 10 and 11 above. (D) may sound as if it detracts from group-mindedness, but where individual targets have been set, the group should enable and encourage that contribution.

17

If you thought this was obvious, good for you! The criteria for group effectiveness are *both* fulfilment of task objectives (which, if effective corporate planning has been carried out, will relate to the group's performance targets and those of the concern as a whole) *and* member satisfaction, where that contributes to the ability of the group to fulfil its task function, eg in the development of members' skills and abilities (3).

In fact, there is a certain ambiguity of group function, depending on whether it is looked at from the organisation's or the group members' point of view. Satisfaction of members' *social* needs, for example, would be an important function of the group from the members' point of view, and the group would be ineffective if it failed to offer that satisfaction. From the organisation's point of view, however, it would seem to have little direct bearing on fulfilment of task objectives, and would not be a criterion of group effectiveness. Tricky.

Question

18
Just to get some names straight. The Western Electric Company, at whose Hawthorne plant the investigations took place, started the studies themselves in 1924-27, and conducted the 'Stage three' interview programme. Mayo and his colleagues were called in after Stage One: Mayo is the name most usually associated with the research and with the Human Relations movement based on its findings. Roethlisberger and Dickson - a colleague of Mayo's and one of the original Company researchers - were involved in, and wrote the official accounts of, the research.

19
Again, straightforward, if you know this material as you should. The studies started out to investigate the effects of lighting on output (A) - but, as it turned out, output increased during the study, whether lighting was improved or worsened! This was attributed to (D) in the Relay Assembly Test Room stage of the research. The studies then changed direction and studied the effects of (B) and (C) in the interview and Bank Wiring Room stages.

20
An important phase of this famous research. The ability - and indeed tendency - of groups to restrict output (in spite of company incentive systems), to 'squeeze out' disliked ('officious') supervisors and to develop a keen group identity must be taken into account in group management. (D) refers to the tendency of the group to find informal ways of doing things and to the fact that the group 'fiddled' output reports to even out fluctuations.

10: MARKING SCHEDULE

Question	Correct answer	Marks for the correct answer	Question	Correct answer	Marks for the correct answer
1	D	1	11	C	1
2	B	1	12	B	1
3	B	1	13	D	1
4	C	1	14	B	1
5	D	1	15	D	1
6	D	1	16	D	1
7	C	1	17	A	1
8	B	1	18	C	1
9	A	1	19	D	1
10	D	1	20	B	1

YOUR MARKS

Total marks available ☐ 20 ☐ Your total mark ☐

GUIDELINES - If your mark was:

0 - 5
Oh, come now. If 'change' in any aspect isn't in your syllabus, you won't be worried unduly - but common sense and guesswork should have got you further than this. Concentrate, next time!

6 - 11
On the borderline. If you're pushed, look again at resistance to change and how it can be overcome, and the impact of new technology. That'll give you a firm foundation.

12 - 16
Very good: there's a fair share of real thinking to do in this chapter. As usual it's worth checking that if all your errors were in one factual area, that area isn't essential for your studies.

17 - 20
Enough said. You're well on top of it.

COMMENTS

Question

1

Change (A) may involve going back to past methods, or extending existing arrangements. Transformation (B) is change, but on a significant scale, and usually faster: it doesn't necessarily mean doing something for the first time. Growth (C) may also include covering old ground or enlarging activities and structures. Innovation (D) is by definition doing something entirely new. There is a view (eg Peters and Waterman - *In Search of Excellence*) that successful organisations are those which are 'continuously innovative'!

2

(B) - apathy, lack of interest, inaction - is the likely response. More important for managers are the possibilities for arousing (A), which can range from enthusiastic co-operation to mere compliance, and for avoiding or overcoming (C) - refusal to learn, working to rule etc - and (D) - deliberate 'spoiling' and errors, absenteeism, industrial action or even sabotage.

3

(A) will secure compliance, but probably not attitude change, or internalisation. If you pay people to change, they can justify acting contrary to their real attitude and will not experience the 'dissonance' or discomfort at their own inconsistency that would make them change their attitude as well as their behaviour. In any case, the incentive might be perceived as a 'bribe', which will not gain respect for the change. (C) may short-circuit resistance at the early stages of the changeover, but it is likely to resurface, probably strengthened by resentment at the lack of information and consultation and the use of pure 'position' power to coerce subordinates to change. (D) is not a good idea: the dishonesty will be found out and resented, and the results at best unpredictable. (B) alone should be effective: public commitment to a course of action makes it very difficult to renounce, and research studies show that those who instruct others in a new viewpoint change their own attitude more than those who simply listen. With the team leaders 'on her side', Ida has a better chance of team loyalty and group norms working in her favour.

4

(A) looks too much as if the change is a *fait accompli*, and as if management is trying to 'blind with science'. (B) is likewise an announcement that resistance is useless, and makes the change look more unreasonable than it may even be: it will secure compliance but not full acceptance. (D) is fudging the issue: it dosen't approach the nature and validity of the change at all, and is merely an appeal for subordinates to 'give us a break'. Why should they? (C) is the best way of 'selling' a change, by engaging subordinates' self-interest or combative instincts. If it is understood that there is a real problem or threat *and* that the change is a sensible solution, there will be a firm rational basis as well. Changes in crisis often face less resistance than routine changes.

Question

5

Pretty straightforward, once you've worked it through. The only potentially obscure connection is between 4 and (iii), but the creation of a new 'functional' authority intervening in line departments is bound to be resisted by line managers as an erosion of their power and invasion of their 'territory' - which is what organisational politics is all about. Note the variety of sources of resistance to change: there are still others, including habit, distrust, self-interest and low tolerance of change itself.

6

All four options are true statements about culture itself: but are they for or against change? (C) is what Peters and Waterman (*In Search of Excellence*) advocate as culture's role: it is clearly *for* rather than *against* change. (A) *might* work against change in order to maintain a sense of security and order, but cultural consistency does not imply or enforce static, unchanging organisation. Sweeping change in all areas is rare and dangerous in practice: change should usually be introduced from a basis of secure, unchanging (or slowly adapting) values and a firm sense of direction. (B) too might have a tendency to harden attitudes and norms - but precisely *because* of culture's role in attitude formation *and change*, it will be crucial in obtaining acceptance of changes. In fact, (D) is pretty clearly a source of resistance to change itself; a culture built on past norms and 'habits' and secure in its sense of success and invulnerability - 'the old ways are the best'. (Not necessarily.)

7

The scenario is actually an account of the famous experiment conducted by Coch and French in a pyjama factory. The non-participation group suffered inefficiency, conflict and resignations. The representative group had no conflict, and recovered efficiency moderately well. The total participation group 'won' as described (C) - as did the non-participative group members (at least, those who had not resigned) when *they* were switched over to the participative method: so the approach, rather than personality factors, was responsible. Bear it in mind when considering the role of consultation and participation in change.

8

Straightforward again, if you think about it. (D) means that there is little expectation of anything *other* than dictatorial change: those who might have resisted will have 'got out' or been squeezed out. (A) and (C) mean that even if autocratic methods *are* resented, there is little employees can do about it to the detriment of the organisation. (C), incidentally, would be the case where the employer had control over employees' livelihood in a time of high unemployment. (B) suggests that resistance or resentment *could* make itself felt, eg through disruptive action, withdrawal of labour, spoiling etc, which the change agent will need to avoid.

Question

9   You could have drawn on your study of Chapter 1 for this answer. Did you remember your organisation structures and cultures in this context of the 'adaptive' organisation? (B), (C) and (D) are all terms for the approach to organisation based on formality, tightly defined areas of authority, specialisation and rules and procedures. (A) was identified by Burns and Stalker specifically as a system of management suitable to conditions of change: it is flexible in its use of skills and labour, task-centred, and based on a flexible network of authority and communication - it requires employees with a desire for 'freedom of manoeuvre', a tolerance for ambiguous job descriptions, risk and change - like Ché.

10   'Divestment' means 'getting rid of' something, so an educated guess would have sufficed here. In strategic terms, it means selling off a part of the firm's operations or pulling out of a certain product-market area. *Growth* can be achieved organically or by means of a merger or takeover (A). It can be pursued in existing markets or products, or by diversifying (C) into new products, or by finding new customers for an existing/improved product (B).

11   No trouble if you know what entrepreneurship is. (A), (B) and (D) were the entrepreneurial aspects of managing identified by Koontz, O'Donnell and Weihrich (*Management*). It's worth bearing in mind that entrepreneurship exists not only in independent opportunists in business, such as Richard Branson, but in non-business operations and *within* organisations. There are internal entrepreneurs who pull together resources and strengths within their organisation to promote innovation: they are sometimes called 'intrapreneurs'.

12   (A) and (C) are pretty clearly encouragements to innovation, by giving financial and authority backing to innovation strategies and directing attention explicitly to defined innovation targets. (D) will also help. Personnel will need to devise innovation-related criteria for recruitment and selection, eg tolerance for risk, creativity and initiative, evidence of innovation in career history to date etc. Promotion policies may need to be adjusted so that innovation is rewarded and 'natural selection' populates upper levels of management with innovative individuals. Training may need to be provided in problem-solving techniques, brainstorming, technical or strategic areas to enhance the contribution of lower levels of the organisation. (B) may look helpful - injecting competition, keeping ideas down to earth etc - but in this context are more likely to stifle and inhibit innovation and creativity. Politics will inevitably intervene - there are significant opportunities here to 'look good'. Innovation requires the production of lots of ideas, and if they are knocked down at an early stage, there will be little incentive to take the risk again, especially if the proposed has been squashed by the proposer's peers (who have a vested interest in its failure), rather than management. (This is why brainstorming sessions do not allow criticism or evaluation, but simply production of ideas.)

Question

13 Step 1 has got to be identification of the need or desire to change (D): this is the stimulus to the whole programme. Some consideration of (C) would follow, and a list of alternative options would be evaluated in the light of (A) and (B) before a detailed strategy is formulated. The change manager would not be able to assess whether the change - or any change - were worth doing, unless he had first identified the problem to be solved, the opportunity to be grasped, or the cost to the organisation of *failure* to change.

14 This is quite a useful framework to remember, if you need to know about the role of the change agent in OD. It emphasises the flexibility of his position. (A) is the role of the consultant: it gives the agent a fair measure of control, second only to the expert/leader role, which is to plan and prescribe. (C) is the role of the problem-solver, involved mainly at the information gathering and problem definition stages. (D) is the consultant role. (B) is the analyst, the 'middle point' of the continuum between a directive and non-directive role: the analyst contributes expertise and data that the client does not possess, and identifies alternative options which are available - but does not evaluate or recommend. Any of these roles would be effective, given the right circumstances and relationship between the change agent and the organisation's management team - as long as *both* parties see the change agent's role as being the same one!

15 (1) may be an advantage by providing a perceived independence, 'neutrality' and fresh viewpoint - but it can also lead to the consultants being perceived as outsiders and 'meddlers'. (It will also take them time to learn about the organisation and acclimatise themselves, for which the organisation pays fees.) (2) may be an advantage in suggesting a wider range of practical options than would occur from the organisation's own experience - but may tend to an inclination to bring a standard solution to a problem, without considering its uniqueness and context. (3) can be an advantage because consultants are not tied by status and can discuss problems freely at all levels and without worry about the effect of change on their own career prospects and political standing - but it may also lessen their credibility in the eyes of employees, and may encourage a lack of conscience and responsibility. (4) is undoubtedly an advantage, where internal staff lack such training - but can be perceived as too acadamic, irrelevant to the real practice of management.

After all this, you may wonder why change agents are ever used, and how they manage. The problems, though, are mainly those of perception, which careful handling and communication will put right. Consultants will simple have to *avoid* (2).

16 An easy one, to get you thinking about new technology. (A) will be the purpose of improved stock control - reducing stock levels, wastage etc. (B) will be the purpose of the customer database - enabling information to be accessed quickly in response to enquiries, facilitating efficient ordering, invoicing etc. (C) will be the purpose of stock control (as part of the control system of the organisation) and of the improved management information system. So (D) is the answer. Note that there are other 'non-technical' purposes for technology too: the image it presents to employees and customers, keeping up with competitors, 'toys' for management to enhance their power and image etc.

217

Question

17 OK, (4) was given to you 'free': new technology will *always* affect work patterns in some way, because it will change the speed of working at least, if not the nature of the work, the task variety, the opportunities for social interaction etc. The important thing to realise is that new technology depends on *management choices* about how work is organised around it - which is why 1, 2 and 3 needn't *necessarily* occur: it's too easy to complain of the 'de-humanising' effects of new technology, when it is the work organisation, leadership and culture of the organisation that in fact create these effects.

Redundancy (1) is the trickiest one, but in fact it is often avoided, because technology tends to increase workload and generate new products and services, so the demand for labour is not necessarily reduced. Also, it takes time to implement technology *and* get it up and running *and* phase out old ways - during which time natural wastage may have achieved sufficient contraction of the workforce.

De-skilling (2) is less often the case than '*re*-skilling': process operations require *new* skills in the use and maintenance of the technology. A typist changing to wordprocessing for example, will need extra skills in file maintenance and security, and the use of the layout, communication and database facilities of the machine.

Enhanced job satisfaction (not (3)) may result from re-skilling in a perceived 'high status' field, together with frequent improvements in the work environment to suit the technology, and the reduction in heavy, dirty and dangerous labour, which is taken on by machines.

18 Changes to management practice may include more programmed decision-making, less supervision, working at home (with improved communications, portable computers etc). The extent to which such changes occur over time depend on the various contingencies mentioned. The progress of change is likely to be slower where human input and judgement is important in the work (C), and - ruling out (A), (B) and (D) - where the pace of change is itself slow (logically), where there are risks involved in relying heavily on electronic systems (because the organisation won't want to 'phase out' the human element - just in case), and where work is highly unpredictable and requires human input (because there are some things machines cannot do, or cannot be made to do quickly enough).

19 If you've ever seen a 'hi-tech' office or factory, you'll know about (A) - quite apart from the 'image' aspect, certain adaptations need to be made for new technology, eg in an office, for controlling heat, adjusting light, wire management. Some new technology is cleaner, safer and quieter than its manual or mechanical counterparts, eg printers and word processors. (B) will also change: information technology allows greater centralisation of decision-making, and a reduced need for middle managers (especially where supervision can also be reduced because work is more highly programmed). Machines will handle many clerical and technical functions, reducing these grades of staff, but there will be an increase in machine-skilled workers, 'knowledge' workers and contract labourers (a current trend) hired for defined periods or projects.

Question

(C) is a current phenomenon, with portability communications and 'networking' of computers allowing, (and space costs encouraging) working from home. (D) is a bit 'sneaky'. The way in which managers exercise their functions of eg planning and control may change, but the functions will remain the same: technology does not *absolve* managers from planning, control, co-ordination, leadership etc.

20

The question deliberately avoided the word 'systems' so that it wouldn't be too obvious. (B) is the answer. It was pioneered by Eric Trist and his colleagues of the Tavistock Institute, and applied in practice in a famous piece of research in the Durham Coalfields. The management had introduced technical innovations that were more efficient in themselves, but had organised the work around the technology so that the task was broken down into separate operations, and each team given a single operation. Previously the teams had had responsibility for the whole task, and allocated men to operations themselves: they had had autonomy, task variety and a sense of meaningful work. Trist was called in to find out why there was resistance to the technical change, and formulated his theory that the technical and social subsystems of the organisation are interdependent. Any given technical system can be run by a number of possible 'human' or social systems (patterns of relationships etc), and the needs of both must be considered.

11:. MARKING SCHEDULE

Question	Correct answer	Marks for the correct answer	Question	Correct answer	Marks for the correct answer
1	D	1	14	C	1
2	B	1	15	C	1
3	D	1	16	C	1
4	C	1	17	D	1
5	D	1	18	B	1
6	A	1	19	A	1
7	B	1	20	B	1
8	D	1	21	C	1
9	B	1	22	D	1
10	A	1	23	B	1
11	C	1	24	D	1
12	D	1	25	D	1
13	D	1	26	A	1

YOUR MARKS

Total marks available   26   Your total mark

GUIDELINES - If your mark was:

0 - 8
You're not really on top of this yet, are you? Or not trying? You should at least have basic recruitment and selection procedures at your fingertips. Go back to the notes to this chapter and check that everything looks familiar.

9 - 14
If your syllabus only covers recruitment and selection, you'll get by: just give the ones you got wrong in those areas another look. Manpower planning is worth some work, though, if you've got the time - especially if it's in your syllabus.

15 - 20
Not bad at all. You probably got the legal questions wrong - which you may not need to worry about - but for peace of mind, just make sure that you're on top of any of the other areas that you missed: they're all quite important.

21 - 26
There was quite a lot of difficult stuff here, so well done indeed. You may not need to know the legal provisions tested - although they're useful - so if these are the only areas you got wrong, you've got the rest of the topic well covered.

COMMENTS

Question

1

OK, we were just trying to reinforce the point. The manpower plan may consist of various component plans, according to the circumstances, embracing recruitment, training, re-development, productivity, redundancy and retention plans. The overall plan should include budgets, targets and standards, and should allocate responsibilities for implementation and control. Manpower planning is not just demand and supply forecasting.

2

The *demand* for labour will be forecast by considering:

- the objectives of the organisation, and the plans in operation to achieve those objectives - including proposed contraction, diversification or expansion (B); and

- manpower utilisation - ie how much labour will be required, given the expected volume of work and productivity or work capacity of different types of employee.

The *supply* of labour will be forecast by considering:

- the potential and structure of the existing workforce (skills (C), likely success of training schemes etc);

- the rates of wastage, based on the age structure (A) (anticipating retirements) and labour turnover statistics;

- the potential supply of new labour with relevant skills in the labour market, given trends in education, mobility etc. (D)

3

A bit of maths won't hurt. This is a very simple numerical example illustrating how demand forecasts and estimates of leaving and promotions can be used to determine recruitment requirements.

Opening staff		1,000
Wastage (30% x 600) + (10% x 300) + (5% x 100)	(215)	
Promotions to higher grade		
(10% x 600) + (40% x 300) + (20% x 100)	(200)	
Promotion from lower grade	—:—	
		(415)
Existing staff in this grade in 2 years' time		585
Staff required in this grade in 2 years' time		1,200
Estimated recruitment requirement over 2 years		615

Question

4

The point here is that forecasting is not an exact science, and that a significant element of judgement and risk is involved in manpower planning. Sudden increases or decreases in demand because of consumer fashions (A) can radically alter the manning levels required and affordable by an organisation: eg the boom in compact disc players, the 'stranding' of Betamax videos. The importance of leadership on employee morale (B) - and therefore likely productivity and stability rates - is difficult to quantify, and a sudden change of leadership personnel could significantly disrupt the manpower plan. Unionisation (D) offers an important reminder that manpower plans concern people and must be *negotiable*: particularly where redundancies are involved, or the erosion of demarcation agreements, the unions will need to be brought in. Improvements in information (C) at least facilitate trend analysis, modelling to test various assumptions, and faster access to wider range of accurate statistical information.

5

If you hadn't encountered the stability index before, it's worth taking note of this. The most common index used to calculate wastage is the BIM (British Institute of Management) Index =

$$\frac{\text{Number of employees leaving in a period}}{\text{Average number of employees in the period}} \times 100(\%)$$

But this largely ignores the importance of experience within the organisation, and the fact that people tend to leave early in their employment: length of service actually increases stability.

The stability index will alert the organisation if it is losing a significant number of experienced, longer-serving employees (2). This will be particularly important in a period of rapid expansion (1), because a seemingly low wastage rate may disguise a costly lack of stability and loss of core personnel. (For example, a company starts the year with 20 employees and has 100 at the end of the year: 18 of the original workforce resign. Turnover is 18% - based on year-end figures - but *stability* is only 10%!) The stability index gives an idea of the employees who are more likely to continue in employment within the planning horizon (3).

6

You had to sort out the main disadvantage (A) not only from a lesser disadvantage (D) but also from two potential *advantages* of labour turnover, (B) and (C). It is worth making the point that turnover does have advantages, and that the organisation need not find it unacceptable, until the costs get too high. Wastage makes room for progression of 'surviving' individuals up the hierarchy (B), which can be a source of motivation - and indeed long-term stability. It also ensures that the workforce doesn't remain static and simply grow old together - it makes room for 'new blood' (C). It *can* have a negative effect on morale (D), if it reaches very high levels and/or occurs with hostility on either side, eg resignations or 'sackings': it need not do so, however. The culture may be adapted to high through-flow of personnel, and factors such as (B) and (C) may alleviate the effects of lack of stability. There will, however, always be costs (A) involved in turnover, and these can be very high: there are *preventative* costs (retaining staff through pay, benefits, welfare, environment etc) and *replacement* costs (recruiting, selecting, training and allowing for initial inefficiency of new staff).

Question

7   (B) is wrong, because the promotion programme is just *part* of the manpower plan. (A), (C) and (D) are all part of the programme, along with design of performance assessment procedures, policies on internal promotion/external recruitment etc. (A), incidentally, is part of the process of determining the relative significance of jobs, so that the line and consequences of promotion are clear.

8   Straightforward enough, once you've worked out the relevance and implications of the four options. There are pressures to promote from within, from the familiarity of the promotee (A): he is a 'known quantity' to the organisation, unlike the external recruit, with whom it will be risking possible disappointment or incompatibility. Promotion of insiders is also visible proof of the organisation's willingness to develop its employees' careers, which can enhance motivation (B) and avoid some resentments. Promotees will not have to be instructed, coached, 'broken-in' and otherwise 'socialised' (C) into the methods, norms, politics, culture and personal relationships of the organisation to the extent that an outsider will. The great advantage of external recruitment is in bringing 'new blood' and a fresh viewpoint to potentially 'stale' situations: (D).

9   The choice of advertising medium will be the first stage at which pre-selection or 'screening' is taking place, because it will involve a conscious decision about the type of person the organisation wants to reach and hopes to attract an application from. A job ad in a particular professional journal, for example, will already have eliminated non-subscribers from the selection process. (A) should be formulated with the chosen medium in mind: it will be a close second. (The wording and information given should deter unsuitable applicants, ie should encourage 'self-selection').

10   It's too easy to rattle off the phrase 'recruitment and selection' without being clear which is which. This is basic stuff once you've got the sequence of events under your belt, though.

11   There is frequent confusion over this terminology. The following definitions were agreed between the Department of Employment and the industrial training boards.

(A) is the process of examining a job to identify its component parts and the circumstances in which it is performed.

(B) is a broad statement of the purpose, scope, duties and responsibilities of a particular job.

(C) is a product of job analysis, and is in fact defined by the question.

(D) is an interpretation of the job specification in terms of the kind of person suitable for the job.

Question

12 Job descriptions have a number of useful applications, providing information on jobs content, 'ready made', for detailed comparison in establishing salary structures (A), and as a yardstick for the measurement of jobholder ability, whether potentially in a job applicant (C) or actually, to identify areas for improvement (B). However, job descriptions have limitations - particularly for jobs where discretion, judgement and flexibility are required. Job descriptions quickly go out of date, and at best are only a description of a job 'frozen' at a point in time, without allowing for the dynamic nature of working life. Adherence to job descriptions encourages demarcation disputes and costly overmanning practices, stifling responsiveness to environmental influences, change and unexpected events. It is therefore not conducive to flexibility (D).

13 Like job evaluation, a job description addresses the job itself (including (1)), not the holder of the job at any given time. While it may specify what the job demands of the job holder - (2), (3) - it does not contain any judgements about the person in that job: that is left to appraisal, merit rating etc. So (D) is the answer.

14 You will find it useful to learn either the Seven Point Plan or J Munro Fraser's Five Point Pattern of Personality - but *not* bits of both mixed together!

7 point plan
- physical attributes (A)

- attainments (qualifications)

- general intelligence

- special aptitudes (eg for mental arithmetic)

- interests (B)

- disposition (or 'manner')

- background circumstances (D)

5 point pattern
- impact on others (including physical attributes, speech and manner)

- acquired knowledge or qualifications (including education, training and work experience)

- innate ability (eg mental agility)

- motivation (goals, demonstrated commitment and success at achieving them) (C)

- adjustment (stability, tolerance of stress etc)

15 (A) is unlikely to draw many applications: simply appealing to the wrong people. (D) will be expensive (in media and creative costs), considering that it will reach a great many irrelevant people, as well as a few potential applicants. Mann & Glevilles are not going to help an applicant for such a minor post to relocate to the area, and for the kind of salary and work offered, it's unlikely anyone from far away would think it worth relocating, so (B) will again reach a lot of irrelevant people, at higher cost (because of the large - though in this case, useless - circulation). (C) is a lower cost, realistic option. Others might have included school careers offices, the local job centre or an employment agency.

Question

16 Matt has indirectly discriminated against women by: (1) putting the job advertisement where the readership is predominantly male; (2) imposing an age limit which is disadvantageous to women, since many women in their 20s are hampered by domestic duties (according to a famous case against the Civil Service); and (3) asking non-work-related questions of the woman but not of the man, in the interview, implying different criteria for judgement of suitability, and probing for information likely to prejudice the woman's case.

(These are forms of indirect discrimination. '*Indirect*' discrimination occurs when requirements or conditions are imposed, with which a substantial proportion of the interested group could not comply, to their detriment. '*Direct*' discrimination is when the interested group is treated less fairly, usually deliberately, than another, eg if the ad had said 'Man wanted'.)

17 (D) is, in the end, fairly obviously a form of discrimination, but if you didn't know the main exceptions embodied in the Act - (A) (dramatic performances where the race of the character is specified), (B) and (C) - you would have had to think about it. An additional exception, or permitted form of discrimination, not mentioned is where personal services are rendered for the welfare of the group in question. Note that *positive* discrimination (ie favourable treatment for the protected group) is allowed only in training - not in recruitment and selection.

18 'Maximum' information (B) is *not* the point of interviews, although you might think so from the way disorganised or misguided interviewers conduct them. Squeezing as many questions as possible into the time allowed can restrict the flow of communication and unnerve the candidate, while a lengthy open-ended interview will be costly and time-consuming. And ultimately inefficient, because the *relevance* of the information to the selection process is the main criteria of interview effectiveness: unstructured, high-volume information may give the interviewer a good 'impression' of the candidate, but that will lead to a highly subjective selection choice. (A), by the way, is a more specific paraphrase of 'finding the best person for the job'.

19 Large panels have the great administrative advantage (A) of allowing a number of interested parties to see the candidate at the same time (rather than in separate interviews, with sharing of information and comparison of assessments at a separate meeting etc.) Time, accommodation and administrative support for the interview process is thus cut down. (B) does *not* tend to be an advantage, since formal, artificial situations give little opportunity for the candidate to demonstrate (C), (ie the extent to which he can develop rapport with others and will be a contributive team member). Panels are also inhibiting and stressful for many candidates: the pressures favour candidates who are confident, articulate and forceful - which may not be the attributes most relevant to the job, and may conceal underlying shortcomings. Questions tend to be more varied and random because there is no single guiding force behind the interview strategy: this is also stressful for the candidate, and may not elicit thought-out answers which do justice to his abilities, because candidates tend to have trouble switching rapidly from one topic to another (D).

Question

20 These are all common reasons for errors of judgement on the part of interviewers. Amon is committing contagious bias (B), whereby the interviewer changes the behaviour of the interviewee by suggestion. Amon makes it clear, by verbal and non-verbal clues, what he wants to hear, and the interviewee adjusts his answers to please him. The halo effect (A) is the tendency of interviewers to make a snap judgement based on first impressions, and then ignore all information which doesn't fit that impression. 'Stereotyping' (C) is lumping a candidate together with others of an assumed type or group and then attributing the assumed characteristics of that group to the individual: 'he's a Scot, so he must be mean'. Logical error (D) occurs when the interviewer simply draws an unjustifiable conclusion from the known facts: 'he's articulate, therefore he's intelligent'.

21 Straightforward. (A) tests general intellectual ability - mental agility, memory, logic etc. (B) predicts potential for performing a job or learning a new skill, testing for aptitudes, eg clerical, numerical, mechanical. (D) tests for a variety of characteristics such as emotional stability, extraversion, motivation, need for achievement. (C) measures ability to do the work involved: an applicant for a typist's job, for example, would be asked to take a typing test, and would be assessed on words per minute, errors, etc.

22 Interviews are notoriously the least accurate prediction of actual success in the job, so (D) is not a fair criticism. (A), (B) and (C) are, though, and you should bear them in mind if you find yourself advocating 'scientific' selection methods.

It has been shown that 'practice makes perfect' in tests (A), all the more if you know what the selectors want/expect you to say, in which case you can 'cheat' (B), especially on personality tests. Individuals tend to falsify the data in such tests, because it is in their interests to appear 'safe' or 'suitable' to the organisation, and it is not hard to do that: Whyte suggests that all you have to do is 'try to answer as if you were like everyone else is supposed to be'.

(C) is also a problem (and a controversial one): subjective judgements are made in the setting of tests and interpretation of results. Many tests are not culturally neutral, and can be tackled less successfully by particular groups - which is where bias (or discrimination) creeps in: traditional IQ tests, for example, are said to be based solely on the experience and vocabulary of white, anglo-saxon, middle class individuals. A famous example (which you may like to attempt yourself) is a question from an old '11 plus' exam paper. Which is the odd man out of the following?

MEASLES, STEAMER, LEAVE, OMELETTE, COURAGE*.

*Steamer - because all the rest (if you had a certain sort of upbringing!) have national connotations: German measles, French leave, Spanish omelette and Dutch courage!

Question

23 A simple point, but worth stressing. The identification of ability - and indeed all selection procedures - indicate *potential* for success (B): they don't *predict* or guarantee performance success (A), (D), although they attempt to get as close as possible. Lack of motivation or inclination, poor work relations, design of the job itself, changes in environmental factors, etc may not translate ability into performance.

In particular, capacity or being *able* to do something does not imply *willingness* or inclination to do it (C).

24 (D) is dismissal by reasons of non-capability, not redundancy.

25 'Dismissal' includes termination of contract (Troubel, Toyle and Bubbal), ending of a fixed term contract without renewal on the same terms (Hubble), and also resignation by the employee because of serious breach of contract by the employer ('constructive' dismissal). So everyone is deemed to have been dismissed.

26 Dismissal can be claimed to be *unfair* where there is unfair selection for redundancy (but this is not so in Hubble's case), and dismissal for pregnancy (*unless* it leads to non-capability), among other things: Bubbal and Toyle have, therefore been unfairly dismissed. Dismissal is *fair and justified* if the reason for it is: redundancy (Hubble), legal impediment (provided suitable alternative employment was offered), non-capability (provided adequate training and warnings were given), misconduct (provided warnings were given) (Troubel) and some other substantial reasons. Hubble was therefore fairly dismissed, as was Troubel.

In order to obtain *compensation* or other remedies for unfair dismissal, however, the employee must (i) be under the normal retiring age, (ii) have been continuously employed for one year (if engaged after 1 June 1985) or two years, and (iii) have been unfairly dismissed. (ii) disqualifies Toyle. So only Bubbal can claim compensation, re-instatement (getting her old job back) or re-engagement (getting a job comparable to her old one).

12: MARKING SCHEDULE

Question	Correct answer	Marks for the correct answer	Question	Correct answer	Marks for the correct answer
1	D	1	13	A	1
2	B	1	14	C	1
3	C	1	15	D	1
4	C	1	16	B	1
5	B	1	17	C	1
6	D	1	18	D	1
7	A	1	19	A	1
8	D	1	20	D	1
9	B	1	21	B	1
10	C	1	22	C	1
11	C	1	23	A	1
12	D	1	24	D	1

YOUR MARKS

Total marks available   24   Your total mark

GUIDELINES - If your mark was:

0 - 6 This chapter covers mainstream topics, so you'll need to do a bit more work. Start with the systematic approach to appraisal. That'll help clarify things.

7 - 12 You might scrape by at the upper end of this range. But since this chapter covers three topics, each popular with examiners, perhaps you could give the notes another look. Try applying them to your own experience.

13 - 18 Good. If your exam syllabus attaches particular importance to 'personnel' related topics, you may want to pay careful attention to the ones you got wrong, though.

19 - 24 Impressive. Enough said - you're well on the way.

COMMENTS

Question

1

The three main uses of performance assessment are: reward reviews (ie measuring the extent to which an employee is deserving of reward as compared with his peers - for example (A)); performance review (for planning and validating training and development programmes - (B)); and potential review ((C) - predicting the level and type of work the individual will be capable of in future, for promotion, planning etc). Job evaluation explicitly does *not* include any assessment of the performance of the job holder; it analyses the job content only. So (D) is the answer.

2

Howie's technique (B) is a simple method: fairly precise in defining criteria - though still subjective. Overall assessment (A) is an even simpler method, requiring the manager to write in narrative form his judgement about the appraisee. (C) adds a comparative frame of reference to the general guidelines: assessors are asked to select a level or degree to which the appraisee displays each given characteristic, expressed as points, grades etc. (D) measures appraisee's behaviour against 'typical' behaviour in the job. This 'typical' behaviour is defined by getting managers to report 'critical incidents' of success and failure in the job, and so working out what common - but acceptable - behaviour consists of.

3

A quick 'tour' through some aspects of the techniques available for assessment. If you work through (C), you'll piece it together. The combinations 3(ii) and 4(i) should have made the rest fall into place, even if you were less familiar with 1 and 2.

4

Of course, 'it all depends'. But generally speaking the subordinate's role will change (1), becoming more continuous, active and involved, since he is able to evaluate his own progress and success in achieving specific targets which he has also contributed to set (in a way that is unlikely with trait appraisal). The manager's role will also change (2) because of the collaborative nature of the process and because he no longer merely has to identify success or failure - the objectives themselves do that - but determine reasons for failure or opportunities arising from success: in other words he is less of a critic and more of a counsellor. Learning and motivation theories suggest that clear, known and particularly self-set targets are important in motivation - (3).

The effectiveness of the scheme overall (4) will, however, depend on the targets set (are they clearly defined? realistic?) and the commitment of both parties to making it work. Results-oriented schemes are less prone to ambiguity and moral connotations, and concentrate on what the individual 'does' rather that what he 'is' - which is the important thing. But they can still be fraught with problems at the interview, counselling and follow-up stages: if no action for the future is agreed or taken, for example, the scheme has not been effective at all.

Question

5

Three types of approach to appraisal interviews are commonly identified. Tel's approach is (B). It's a fairly participative approach, with the assessor taking on the dual role of critic and counsellor, and does not assume that the sole key to performance improvement is in the employee himself: problems in the job, technology or environment may be identified. (C) is a step further in this direction, where the assessor abandons the role of critic altogether: discussion is centred not on the assessment but on the employee's work problems, which are worked through together with the assessor/counsellor. (A) is the more one-sided approach: the manager tells the subordinate how he's been assessed, and then tries to 'sell' (gain acceptance of) the evaluation and the improvement plan. Peer rating (D) is where an individual is assessed and counselled by colleagues of the same level in the organisation hierarchy, rather than by his superiors: not the case here.

6

(A), (B) and (C) are useful criteria for assessing the effectiveness of an appraisal scheme. (A) suggests that it is relevant to organisational objectives (to improvement and development rather that simply praise or blame) and is understood by employees, who therefore do not find it 'threatening'. (B) suggests that fairness is built into the system: employees in each section are being assessed by the same criteria and against the same standards - which also implies that objectivity is being considered, and controlled. (C) is essential if appraisal is to be perceived as genuine, taken seriously by the organisation, and a collaborative exercise to which the appraisee is encouraged to contribute.

(D) is a double-edged sword: a link between assessment and reward may motivate employees to take appraisal seriously, but can also make it threatening if they fear that they haven't done well. Moreover, in many organisations promotion depends on seniority rather than performance, and pay depends on evaluated and negotiated pay structures with defined differentials (so that performance-related pay creates problems of equity, 'squeezed' differentials etc). Unless the connection between assessment and reward is real and immediate, the 'implication' that it exists will only undermine the appraisal system when expectations are disappointed.

7

All the information is relevant, so this is quite tricky. (A) is the least helpful of the items of information, because past performance is not an accurate indicator of whether the individual will be capable of handling a more senior job. Moving up the hierarchy demands different abilities and skills, less technical work, and more human relations (and eventually 'design' - strategic planning) work. Moreover, 'performance' is a function not only of ability but of motivation, experience and environmental factors: an individual whose performance is inexperienced, hindered by work practices and/or inhibited by lack of job satisfaction, does not necessarily lack *potential* for higher things in the future. Promotion purely on the basis of competence in the *present* job tends to push people upwards into jobs where they are no longer competent: this is the 'Peter principle' of LJ Peter.

Question

(B) is a more useful way of expressing past performance information. (C) will be important in gauging whether the individual will want responsibility, stay with the organisation, be motivated by the prospect of advancement etc. (D) will determine the purpose and application of the potential review.

8

The point of this is that 'induction' is much wider than first-day introductions and familiarising recruits with working conditions, rules, where the canteen is etc. It is an on-going process concerned with every aspect of the integration and initial development of recruits: its effectiveness should be reviewed after three to six months, or even a year. (The training and monitoring aspects will, of course, continue).

9

(D) is pretty clearly not the answer: it relates to initial integration into a working situation (see the comments on question 8 above). The distinction between (A), (B) and (C) is worth making. The definition given in the question for training (B) is that of the well known report 'The Making of British Managers' (Constable and McCormick, 1987). According to the same report, "Education (A) is that process which results in *formal qualifications* up to and including post-graduate degrees", and "development (C) is *broader* again [than training]. Job experience and learning from other managers . . . are integral parts of the development process".

10

(A),(B) and (D) have elements of truth in them, but betray the fundamentally negative approach of Phil E. Stein. (A) implies an abdication of line managers and supervisors from the process of defining training needs and priorities, coaching, guiding and monitoring - all of which they should participate in, since they know - perhaps better than Personnel - the job and the trainee, and they are responsible for his performance. (B) implies that training in itself is such a Good Thing that an organisation can't go wrong by just 'providing some'. But it can: training must have a clear purpose, and must take into account the performance needs and personal expectations and aptitudes of the trainee. It is too easy to run an old or standard training programme without considering learning needs, and suitability of teaching methods: training will be purposeless and inefficient, as in Phil E Stein's case. (D) is clearly an excuse for allocating inadequate resources to training: the benefits of training may be less easily quantifiable than the costs, but are significant for organisational health.

(C) recognises both *purpose* and *value* in training. It recognises that training is designed to solve and anticipate problems created by environmental changes - and also induces change by enabling developments and improvements.

Question

11 Simple, if you remember the training needs equation:

| Required level of competence (A) | minus | Current level of competence (B) | equals | The learning gap (D). |

The cost of training (C) will be considered, once training needs have been established, for the identification of practical training *objectives* (on which cost may be a constraint) and for the evaluation of alternative training *methods*.

12 Training objectives should be clear, specific and measurable: they should indicate how the trainee will be able to indicate that he has improved knowledge or skills. Effective objective statements are therefore expressed as targets for *behaviour* expected at the end of the course - ability to complete an action, demonstrate knowledge etc. (A), (B) and (C) offer no target achievement which can be quantifiably measured. (D) can easily be tested: its equivalent in a business scenario (eg a course in training management) might be 'to describe key stages in the training process', 'to prepare an acceptable training plan', 'to complete correctly the organisation's training assessment forms' etc.

13 Formal training may be less than effective because:

- the trainee may not be motivated to learn, because it seems as if the course is not directly relevant to his job, to the way things are done in his workplace (B);

- it is in fact often difficult for trainees to apply skills they have learnt to their jobs, because the culture of the organisation, the need for those skills and the informal work practices are not conducive to it (C);

- it is difficult for trainees to switch from the euphoria (frequently) and concentration of the formal teaching programme to the compromises and pressures of daily work life (D).

Formal training is, however, a way of making the connection between 'theory' and 'practice' *away* from the pressures of work: it is a 'safe' environment for the trainee (since he is expected and allowed to make errors in the interests of learning) and for the organisation (which can't afford those errors at work). So (A) is the answer.

14 Day-release is *off*-the-job training, a day per week. The others are all types of on-the-job training: coaching (3) is the obvious one - but note the variety.

Question

15 This is the other side of the coin from question 13. (A) and (B) are straightforward: training is conducted with less pressure and distraction in off-the-job training, and the trainer is less likely to favour his own 'pet' ways of doing things. You may have had to think about (C) and (D). On-the-job training does teach methods which are relevant to custom and practice (C) - but that isn't necessarily an advantage for learning 'pure' techniques and knowledge: the informal way of doing things may cut corners, compromise, foster biased viewpoints on areas of knowledge etc.

What *can* be claimed for on-the-job training is that it encourages the immediate *application* of new skills in the context to which they will have to be adapted (D); learning feedback will be work performance-oriented, the work group will be 'acclimatised' to the trainee's new abilities etc.

16 These are so-called 'experiential' methods, based on 'learning through doing' - though not necessarily on the job. (A) is where individuals take on roles and experience the nature of different interpersonal encounters eg interviews or negotiations. (C) is where groups are given a task, and the processes taking place in the groups are examined by the group and a trainer: this enables the group to explore relationships and share feelings. (D) is where groups are given a task, but may or may not be assigned a leader: the exercise is based on the emergence and function of leadership. The function of brainstorming (B) is primarily to draw out new ideas and suggestions from the inter-action of individuals in groups - not to study the interactions themselves.

17 An easier one, to start a little group of 'training evaluation' questions. Increased speed (A) and accuracy (B) will be measurable in terms of the amount of output meeting quality standards: cost savings will be identifiable in reductions in overtime or staff numbers, reduction in wastage of materials etc. (D) will be measurable, and will offer cost-savings in compensation and sick leave payments, down-time, staff replacements etc. (C) *is* a benefit of training, and may be suggested by improvements in labour turnover and absenteeism statistics - but the links from satisfaction 'backwards' to training (as being responsible for it) and 'forwards' to improved performance (as being a consequence of it) are not clear enough to satisfy the accountant in the scenario.

18 (A), (B) and (C) are part of the *'evaluation'* of training: what effect did it have on the trainees, on their job performance, on the organisation, on organisational objectives? Were the methods used appropriate? Cost-benefit analysis is an important method of evaluation, related to (C), in view of the organisation's objectives. *'Validation'* is an aspect of evaluation, and measures to what extent the stated objectives of the training programme (right or wrong) have been achieved: (B)

Question

19 (B) is also called 'job-related' evaluation: assessing the degree of behaviour change which has taken place on-the-job after returning from a period of training. It's not easy to evaluate the degree to which training has been responsible for changes in behaviour, however - especially where training in social skills, eg leadership, is concerned. (C) - 'reactions centred' evaluation - seeks to assess the reactions of the trainees themselves to the training experience: it's useful in evaluating training methods (did the trainees like them or hate them?) but rather subjective as a means of assessing the effectiveness of training itself. (D) isn't in fact easy at all, because by the time benefits (such as employee satisfaction or increased productivity) are identified in terms of organisational objectives, so many other variables (work environment, motivation, leadership style etc) have intervened that it is difficult to judge how far training was responsible.

(A) can, however, be assessed. Tests of knowledge (like Password) will indicate whether objectives such as 'to be able to identify validation methods' have been achieved. Gains in skill/proficiency can be gauged by measuring time taken, units produced or errors made, before, during and after training.

20 'Development' is part of the manpower resourcing plan, and therefore includes staff movement and progression (1) as well as skill/ability enhancement; (2), (3) and (4). Again, note that the range of learning situations is wide - including temporary promotion, guidance etc. If you paused over (4), remembering that education, training and development are to be distinguished from each other, well done - but:

Question

21

(A), (C) and (D) are important aims of *any* programme of management development. Formal off-the-job education and training was less popular for a while, a few years ago, because it was seen as being irrelevant to 'real' needs. (This was the root of the popularity of Management by Objectives and similar methods.) Recently, however, education - most notably in the form of MBA degrees - has had a great resurgence. In particular, the report 'The Making of British Managers' advocated education and training for its capacity to broaden the outlook of managers whose experience is solely in functional areas, without 'on-the-job' opportunities to develop general management skills (B).

22

Of course. (In fact the column headed 'On absence/leaving:' would probably be headed 'Possible successors' - but that would have made it *too* easy.) Management appraisal and development makes succession planning possible, by indicating and providing promotable material.

The other options are part of the overall manpower plan, too, but with different purposes.

23

Climie is in fact guilty of short-comings in *all* these areas. Once you realised that, you had to go back and decide which area came first in the setting up of the training programme. Training needs analysis comes first - and has not been carried out here, by all accounts, because the graduates' current competence and aptitude have been badly underestimated, and the requirements of their (managerial) positions have not been analysed - otherwise they would not be doing 'dull routine' tasks, and there would be no uncertainty as to the kind of training to be given. (The latter fault is merely aggravated by failures in (B) and (C).) Incidentally, even though the trainees are being well paid, 'reinforcement' is still a problem, since it includes *feedback* - positive and negative - on performance.

24

This highlights some of the important differences in the functional and general management position - and indicates why the *transition,* as the individual progresses up the hierarchy, can be so traumatic. (3), if you were stuck, means 'helping things get done' - co-ordinating interdepartmental activities, obtaining and allocating resources etc.

13: MARKING SCHEDULE

Question	Correct answer	Marks for the correct answer	Question	Correct answer	Marks for the correct answer
1	D	1	13	B	1
2	C	1	14	A	1
3	C	1	15	D	1
4	B	1	16	C	1
5	D	1	17	D	1
6	C	1	18	D	1
7	B	1	19	A	1
8	D	1	20	D	1
9	B	1	21	C	1
10	A	1	22	A	1
11	D	1	23	B	1
12	C	1	24	A	1

YOUR MARKS

Total marks available   24   Your total mark

GUIDELINES - If your mark was:

0 - 6 — If this area isn't in your syllabus, your needn't be too concerned. If it is, start with office layout and health and safety.

7 - 12 — If this area isn't in your syllabus, this is actually not bad. If it is, identify the topic areas you were unfamiliar with. Try office layout, health and safety - and perhaps stress and working hours if you've got time.

13 - 18 — Well done. This chapter covers quite a few topics, so this is a pretty good all rounder's score. If there were particular areas you got wrong, check (for your peace of mind) that they don't feature in your syllabus.

19 - 24 — Swot! (Seriously Well on Top of the subject...) Very good indeed, for this chapter.

COMMENTS

Question

1

A closed office layout (A) is one where small 'cells' are linked by corridors. Open plan offices (B) do away with walls and doors and allow 'freeflow' of people and work. Landscaped offices (C) are a variation of the open plan system which uses screens, cabinets etc to break up the open space and add a measure of privacy and protection from distraction: the main area of the office illustrated is of this type. A common practice, however, is (D), as illustrated, where landscaped office space is combined with a small number of closed offices for meetings, or for managers in more status-conscious organisations.

2

Lack of privacy (A) is usually perceived as a disadvantage in human terms, and is said to be a factor in employee dissatisfaction with working environment: it may particularly be a source of concern to managers, who may feel that they lack the status conferred by their own office. (B) is a double-edged sword, because although it facilitates supervision where it is needed, it also creates a tendency for managers to get unnecessarily involved in routine matters which they should simply delegate. (D) is an advantage for workflow and employee satisfaction - but also a source of distraction arising from noise, movement and social encounters. (C) is the great advantage of open planning. It has been estimated that a 33% space saving is possible, with additional economies on shared equipment and facilities, heating and lighting etc.

3

The internal environment of the work place is created by such features as heating, lighting, ventilation, decor, furniture design and noise. (A) is obviously not the problem - it has been ergonomically designed. As far as (B) goes, the office is perfectly acceptable: the colour scheme is that commonly recommended as warm and restful. Noise (D) is a surprising aspect, however: while sudden loud noises or intermittent noise is irritating and distracting, we do need *some* noise at work. Absence of all noise causes unease: some offices deliberately create noise where none naturally occurs, eg by transmitting low background music or sound. (C) is the problem in this office. Bulb lighting can cause strain to the eyes: strip lighting (fluorescent tubes) is kinder, and natural light ideal.

4

All four options are potential advantages of a well laid-out workplace, but (B) is not directly relevant to *workflow,* which is the movement of people, documents/information and work-in-progess within and between the different departments of the organisation. The requirements for (A), (C) and (D) might be assessed by the use of work study to determine where regular contacts and movements occur and how efficient they are.

Question

5

OK - (4) was meant to be the 'shocker'; the others you could have pieced together from your own experience and knowledge of office technology. Terminals give off heat (1) and even in purpose-built buildings, the effect of sun, people and machines can be underestimated. Paperwork - and human instinct - calls for high natural light (2) - but VDUs require different lighting conditions: anti-glare screens and office layout must resolve the dilemma. Furniture (3) is important in the tidy and safe handling of wiring and cables from machinery (ie 'wire management') and in 'ergonomics': computers keep people seated for long periods with little movement, so seating design, work surface height etc is important for comfort and health. And the mysterious carpeting (4)? Now that computers are moving out of special rooms, and into the open office, static electricity is becoming a problem and cause of 'blackouts' and errors in systems: static (and dust) in carpets is an element in this, and carpets may have to be treated or chosen accordingly.

6

(C) is the common description of ergonomics. It is relevant to both workplace layout (A) and machinery/furniture design (B) - but neither of these is its direct sphere of exploration. The research provides data which can be *used* in establishing conditions best suited to the capabilities and health requirements of the human body - which *are* the focus of ergonomic research. (D) is, loosely, a description of 'cybernetics': a pure red herring.

7

One for the 'afficionado' of work environment, perhaps, although your own daily experience should have helped. People strain to catch elusive 'messages' like (A). Like intermittent loud noise (C) and variations in noise level (D), they compete for attention, and can cause 'mental blinking' - shifts of attention and lack of concentration on the task. *Continuous* noise which is not expected to have any meaning or relevance - whatever its volume - is generally 'filtered out': workers have to put up with (B) in some situations (although sound-proofing is increasing), but say they 'get used to it'.

8

Monotony (ie the experience of stress through boredom, isolation and 'meaningless' labour) is *less* likely to arise if: (1) rest pauses are allowed (A), offering movement and variety; (2) workers are permitted the outlet of interaction with colleagues (C); (3) payment by results is used (B), offering some perceived meaning and purpose to the work; and (4) the work is grouped into whole, self-contained tasks with some variety - *rather than* the repetition of single, routine actions (D). So (D) is the cause of monotony here.

Question

9

Trial programmes have shown that short, frequent and flexible breaks are best. The Health and Safety Executive booklet for VDU users states: "Most types of continuous or sustained work may lead to a build-up of fatigue. In many jobs there are natural breaks where you can move about to do something different. Jobs should be designed to allow such changes in activity, but if this is not possible, short frequent breaks seem to prevent fatigue. Being able to choose when to take a break is preferable to having fixed rest break schedules." Bear it in mind when you're studying, too!

10

(B) and (D) are not among the more obvious advantages of shiftworking: in fact there are serious social, physiological and psychological effects associated with anti-social hours, disorientation and conflict with the body's normal 24-hour cycle. (C) will not be gained either: overtime is not necessarily eliminated by shiftwork (premiums for double shift and Sundays being common), and shiftworking itself is inherently unpopular, so that financial incentives will be required. The advantages to the organisation are that overhead costs can be spread over a longer productive 'day', and machinery/equipment can be kept up and running for longer periods.

11

Morale is enhanced (3) by allowing workers to plan their lives on a more personal basis, to fit particular needs and circumstances, and to vary their arrival and departure times without embarrassment or dishonesty. Stress - related to time-keeping through transport delays, or attendance in the event of personal time requirements - is also reduced (2). Pilot schemes also show that absenteeism drops (1), because trips to the dentist etc are fitted into the flexible time, and the idea that "I'm late for work/I've had two hours off - so I may as well not go in at all" is discounted. (4) may be unexpected, but Flexible Working Hours actually aid planning through transport strikes, traffic delays etc, because work is scheduled for the 'core time' - which benefits from more regular attendance - rather than for the uncertain morning and evening hours which might be disrupted: variations in hours are kept within limits clearly defined and acceptable to management.

12

Most people experience stress of some kind, at some time: there are simply some individuals who 'handle' it better than others. Along with workload, insecurity, change and innovation and management style, *personality factors* are important contributors to stress. Emotionally sensitive people (A) are pressured more by conflict and doubt, which insensitive individuals are able to shrug off. A highly developed sense of responsibility (D) and accountability exerts pressures to 'succeed', which may be particularly acute where there is uncertainty or risk eg in innovation situations. You may have had to think twice about (B): individuals who are seen to give in to pressure tend to invite further pressure from those who seek to influence them.

Question

The effects of stress are undoubtedly better handled from a basis of strong, supportive relationships with others (C). Such relationships will also help to reach co-operative solutions to situations such as role incompatibility or overload, where the individual will need to get together with others to resolve or redefine his role(s), reconcile the demands made on him, ask for help with his workload etc. Interpersonal competence can also offer a source of self-esteem from which to cope with insecurity.

13 Note that 'occupational health', the answer here, embraces not only protection against toxic substances, but also against noise, fatigue, stress etc. (A) addresses some of the latter issues only, and is a research science, not a practical programme of action. (C) are concerned with the prevention of accidents. (D) may include services to victims of occupational ill-health: welfare is essentially reactive rather than proactive in this area.

14 A fairly simple one, to ease you into the health and safety issues. Note the range of costs incurred by the prevention and aftermath of accidents: there are many more, including damage to equipment, replacement of the injured employee, administration of reporting and benefit payment procedures etc. (2) and (4) are consequences of accidents, so preventing accidents will eliminate the costs. (1) and (3) are contingency plans which will still have to be made 'just in case': moreover, they are provided for in law (Health and Safety at Work Act 1974 and Employers liability (Compulsory Insurance) Act 1969 respectively).

15 A fanciful question, you may think - but you should be able to identify common hazards in the office (maybe *your* office!), and counting them may have helped you to take them in better.

1. Frayed carpet
2. Obstacles in gangways
3. Obstruction of the stairway
4. Obstruction of a fire door (illegal as well)
5. Slippery floor
6. Standing on a swivel chair

16 (A), (B) and (D) are duties. (C) isn't: Safety representatives and committees have a purely advisory role, although the Act states the duty of employers to *consult* with safety representatives with a view to the effective maintenance of adequate safety. (The 'not later than three months' applies to the setting up of the safety committee once it has been requested.) Representatives derive their main power from their function of representing employees with inspectors of the Health and Safety Executive - which *can* impose sanctions on employers who fail to comply with safety requirements.

Question

17 The role of safety representatives (C) is purely advisory. Accountability for safety measures extends to superiors and managers 'on the spot': the supervisor may be personally liable if he has been negligent. Responsibility for ensuring that procedures exist, are known and are followed ultimately still rests, however, with the employer ie senior management. Under the 1974 Health and Safety at Work Act, responsibility also lies with the employee who has a duty to take reasonable care of himself and others, not to interfere intentionally or recklessly with machinery or equipment etc. So (D) is the answer.

18 Although an injured employee's damages may be reduced if his injury was partly a consequence of his own contributory negligence, due allowance is made for ordinary human failings (B). The employer has a duty to provide a safe working system (A), and to take reasonable care for employee's safety in all acts which are normally and reasonably incidental to the day's work (C). The employer is responsible in all these situations (D).

19 Yes, more detailed legal points - but the law is indispensable to coverage of health and safety.

It is no defence to show that there is no way of fencing the machine: the machine should then not be used at all (A). The employer is safe on the other counts. Fencing doesn't need to be kept in position during lubrication, inspection etc (B); a fence is sufficiently secure even though it does not prevent reckless employees from forcing it (C); and machinery is 'dangerous' only if it can be reasonably foreseen that injury to any person can occur in the ordinary course of use (D).

20 Yes, it looks like we're asking for a subjective judgement here. But looking at the statements listed:

(A)   is not quite true. The welfare state provides for pension, unemployment pay and other benefits, education, medicine etc but there are other welfare benefits and services that organisations could (and do) provide, such as counselling in times of personal distress, subsidised canteens, discounts in company stores, social activities, funds for private education or medical care where desired etc.

(B)   this attitude prevails in some situations: if an employee commits an offence outside work for example, it is not grounds for dismissal. It should, arguably, apply in other situations. In practice, however, it is impossible for employees to 'leave their problems at home', as a socially responsible organisation will accept.

(C)   is not true either. Organisations typically invest a great deal of money in their human resources, and any factor which retains - and may even enhance - that organisational asset is contributing to organisational goals. (Note too that social responsibility objectives may be part of the corporate plan.)

Question

(D) welfare *is* a 'hygiene' factor. It tends to be taken for granted, and does not positively motivate performance (although the *negative* effects of personal hardship or dissatisfaction should be alleviated where possible).

21

(C) carries an entitlement to 'reasonable' time off work - but it is *unpaid*, unless specific agreements have been made. ((A), incidentally, is a fairly recent extension of basic rights: Social Security Act 1986, which introduced Statutory Maternity Pay.) A further entitlement - not included in the question - is for time off to look for work or training during the notice period for redundancy.

22

Substantive rules are those which determine the terms and conditions of employment, such as (2) and demarcation (1), ie what work is done by what grades of staff.

Procedural rules are rules about the methods and procedures for

- arriving at substantive rules - for example, (4) - and for
- settling any agreements or disputes which cannot be resolved by normal negotiation. (ACAS, by the way, is the Advisory, Conciliation and Arbitration Service)

23

Lifetime employment (B) has for some years been thought, in the West, to make the difference in employee relations: it encourages loyalty and goodwill. It is now pointed out, however, (eg by Haruo Shimada and Hiroshy Takeuchi) that this Western stereotype is quite wrong. Only a quarter of Japanese workers employed by big companies enjoy anything approaching lifetime employment. Labour mobility is actually quite high in Japan: each year 13% of workers in all firms leave their jobs.

The factors that *do* contribute to employee relations in Japan are identified by Shimada and Takeuchi as (A), (C) and (D). The use of quality circles has been celebrated for their effect on quality, but is just as important for morale and communication. Information sharing is a key feature: most firms have joint consultation committees which chat (but do not negotiate) about all aspects of the firm. The use of first-time supervisors helps to erode status-consciousness and bridge the gap between workers and bosses.

24

(1) is the definition of a 'lawful trade dispute' under the UK Employment Act. (2), (3) and (4) are specifically excluded.

14: MARKING SCHEDULE

Question	Correct answer	Marks for the correct answer	Question	Correct answer	Marks for the correct answer
1	C	1	7	A	1
2	B	1	8	D	1
3	D	1	9	C	1
4	C	1	10	B	1
5	A	1	11	A	1
6	B	1	12	D	1

YOUR MARKS

Total marks available **12** Your total mark

GUIDELINES - If your mark was:

0 - 3

We put this chapter in as an extra source of more detailed questions for those who need to know about writers on organisations. If you're not one of them, don't worry about this. It is *does* include you, check the notes and comments: we've given you plenty to work from.

4 - 6

This chapter is intended for people who need to know about specific theories. If you don't come into this category, this is a pretty good score. If in doubt, check your syllabus. The notes and comments are fairly substantial, to help you revise the unfamiliar bits.

7 - 9

You've got a good grip on organisation theory. The nature of this chapter, though, is to test several different areas - so check your syllabus to make sure you haven't slipped up on something important.

10 - 12

There may be only twelve questions in this chapter, but it's a real test of your preparation all the same. Well done indeed. You're a true 'all-rounder'!

COMMENTS

Question

1

Schein's four models of individuals are well worth getting to know: they reflect the assumptions that organisations make about people, and therefore have implications for individuals' roles in employing organisations. They are not meant to represent real types of people, but people as organisations see them, for the purposes of designing motivation systems etc.

(A) is Schein's own view of what people are actually like. Individuals are variable and driven by many different motives; the situation will dictate which is uppermost at any given time. This means in effect that no single managerial strategy for motivation will work for all the people all the time.

(B) is influenced by a fairly wide range of motivations, from the needs for food and security at the simplest level to the need to realise his full potential as an individual. He is capable of maturity and autonomy and will, given the chance, voluntarily integrate his goals with those of organisation.

(D) looks for self-fulfilment in social relationships. His motivation at work will be not the job itself but the opportunity it offers to mix with other people.

(C), rational-economic man, is as described in the question. He's motivated mainly by monetary incentives - salary, fringe benefits etc. Belief in economic man is at the root of most incentive systems - even in an 'enlightened' age which recognises self-actualisation as man's 'highest' need.

2
and
3

We didn't make you unscramble all the possible combinations, but you had to know most of the theories to sort out the two questions set. Working through the list of terms:

- Benevolent-authoritative leadership is Rensis Likert's 'System 2' leadership style (not purely coercive, but still limited in the amount of delegation and communication practised). Systems 1, 3 and 4 respectively are:
  - exploitative-authoritative
  - consultative authoritative and
  - participative.

  This furnishes you with the answer to question 3.

- Coercive power is one of Amitai Etzioni's three kinds of power in an organisation:
  - coercive (eg in prisons),
  - remunerative (eg in most work organisations) and
  - normative (the application of norms or standards, as in professional or religious organisations).

  This furnishes you with the answer to question 2.

Question

- The socio-technical system is the basis of Trist's (and his colleagues') theory of organisation. It is a system of interdependent subsystems comprising the technology of work (including the way tasks are organised, as well as technology in the sense of mechanisation or automation) and human nature and relationships.

- Role culture is described by Harrison (and later by Handy) as a form of organisational culture based on formal jurisdictions and roles, ie a bureaucracy. Harrison's other classifications of culture are the person, task and power culture.

4 Straightforward, of course, if you know your theories. Specialisation is the great 'give-away': it is the cornerstone of Taylor's approach to work organisation, called 'scientific management' (C). Socio-technical systems theory (B) and neo-human relations (D) are both too concerned with human factors at work to be described as reducing the worker to an 'impersonal cog in the machine'. Systems theory (A) doesn't have these characteristics either.

5 Henri Fayol (A) was a French industrialist and an early writer associated with the classical school of management thought. He popularised the concept of the 'universality of management principles'. The others are all writers of what has been called the neo-Human Relations school, concentrating on human issues in motivation and leadership. Blake is famous for his 'managerial grid', Herzberg for the 'two-factor' theory of motivation, and McGregor most notably for his model of managerial assumptions about subordinates.

6 The answer is (B): work through the sequence of theories and you've got a useful framework for learning about Japanese management and Theory Z.

William Ouchi compared American (Theory A - (1)) and Japanese (Theory J - (2)) cultural values as applied to business organisations, and formulated an ideal cultural system (Theory Z - (3)) based on the 'family-like' qualities of large Japanese companies, but incorporating the best elements of Western practice.

It might be said that companies like IBM and Hewlett-Packard, or Marks and Spencer, are to a certain extent putting Theory Z principles into practice. Theory Z is in fact an extention of Theory Y, embodying more participation, mutual trust and integration of objectives. But you shouldn't have got side-tracked into thinking about McGregor's classification of Theory X and Theory Y, which are clusters of extreme management assumptions about the nature of individuals, not management strategies, or approaches to organisation.

Question

7

(A) is pretty clearly the answer if you recalled Blake's 'managerial grid'. The grid does not represent a continuum (C) from concern for task to concern for people, because it assumes that the two things are compatible: they can both be high or low at the same time. ('Tight' and 'loose' might in any case have suggested to you Handy's 'best fit' approach, which (C) describes.) The grid can be used in appraisal, to focus attention on the manager's approach, but does not indicate 'success' or effectiveness, so (B) isn't applicable. (D) is a pure red herring: 'matrix' and 'grid' might have led you astray, though, if you were reduced to guesswork!

8

The Durham Coalfield research is an important and fascinating study. The organisation designed by the *Coal Board* was called the 'conventional longwall method': so (D) is the answer. It wasn't the answer for the Coal Board, though. Prior to the technical innovation, miners had been used to working in small autonomous teams which were responsible for three tasks: each team member was an all-rounder and the team was flexible in sharing out different tasks. The conventional longwall method divided the three tasks (cutting, loading of coal onto conveyors, and moving the equipment forward) between three separate shifts: groups had to specialise, and since some individuals were more willing and able to do so than others, closer supervision was imposed.

Trist suggested that while the new technology must influence work organisation, the work group has social and psychological needs that must also be met. The method Trist introduced was called the composite longwall method, and was an application of a socio-technical systems approach (A), balancing the needs of the technological and social systems. The 'three task group' was restored, along with group autonomy: the method was thus group working that was *composite* (in the sense of flexible contribution of skills) and *autonomous* (in being allowed to allocate and schedule work within its responsibility): (B). It also utilised the smallest available social units in the organisation, ie primary work group (D).

9

(C) it is. Woodward was an important contributor to the socio-technical systems approach. She noted that production systems are associated with characteristic patterns of organisation: different *objectives* limited the techniques of production a firm could use (eg a firm developing electronic prototypes won't go in for mass production) and organisational structure tended to be linked to the *technical complexity* of the production system. "It appeared that different technologies imposed different kinds of demands on individuals and organisations, and that these demands have to be met through an appropriate form of organisation."

10

- Lawrence and Lorsch (A) are exponents of contingency theory. They compared the structural characteristics of a 'high-performing' container firm, which existed in a relatively stable environment, and a 'high-performing' plastics firm, which existed in a rapidly changing environment, and concluded that the most efficient structure was different in each case.

Question

- Burns and Stalker (C) identified the need for a different organisation structure when the technology of the market is changing and innovation is crucial to the continuing success of any organisation operating in the market. They contrasted 'organic' systems (suitable to conditions of rapid change) with 'mechanistic' systems (suitable to stable conditions).

- Peters and Waterman (D) were the authors of the popular and influential book 'In Search of Excellence', based on their observation of successful American companies. They suggested that 'excellent' can be defined as 'continuously innovative and adaptive to the demands of the environment', and put forward various structural and cultural measures for creating sensitive, flexible and responsive organisation.

- Gantt and Gilbreth (B) take us back to the 'scientific management' school - so they *don't* fit here. Henry Gantt, an associate of Taylor, did much work on the scientific selection of workmen, their training and development, and the formulation of incentive bonus schemes - although he's probably most famous for the Gantt chart, which depicts the relationship in time of activities in an overall project. Frank Gilbreth contributed to the advance of time and motion study techniques. For example, he made a study of 'wasted motions' (ie physical movements which aren't necessary to get the job done) and was able in one case to reduce the number of motions in bricklaying from 18 to 5 - doubling productivity without increasing the effort required!

11

(A), (B) and (C) are based on Drucker's useful comments on the scientific management approach. He was generally critical of it, in particular because:

- by breaking work down into its elementary parts, and analysing a job as a series of consecutive 'motions', (B) management tend to see the solution to their problems as being the allocation of each 'motion' to a separate worker. This is now recognised as *not* being a good idea (primarily because of the monotony and stress suffered by workers in eg assembly line work, which at best robs the organisation of the potential creativity and commitment of workers and at worst causes hostility and aggression). Job design is nowadays aimed at *reintegrating* tasks into whole, meaningful jobs.

- by divorcing planning work from 'doing' work (C), scientific management gives management a monopoly on information and knowledge, and allows no participation by workers in planning and target-setting. 'Development' is seen purely in terms of enhanced technical efficiency. Drucker suggested that this is a source of resistance to change. "Because the worker is supposed to do rather than to know - let alone plan - every change represents the challenge of the incomprehensible and therefore threatens his psychological security."

(A), however, was a point on which Drucker acknowledged the positive contribution of scientific management. "We shall never lose again the insight that human work can be studied systematically, can be analysed, can be improved by work on its elementary parts". In this sense, scientific management paved the way for the study, theory (and work improvements) that followed - including the Human Relations and neo-Human Relations approaches. (A)'s the answer, therefore (ruling out (D)).

Question

12 Herzberg (A) wrote the well-known comment about dissatisfaction and satisfaction: it encapsulates his 'two factor' theory of motivation: 'environment factors' and 'the job' (cf. job enlargement/enrichment etc) should have given you a clue, if not satisfaction/dissatisfaction. This is a good quote to learn, by the way: short and pithy, and eminently usable in an exam answer on this subject.

Weber (B) wrote the praise of bureaucracy. He is the organisation theorist most closely associated with the analysis of bureaucracy (although its modern critics, such as Crozier and Bennis, are now more 'fashionable'), so his name is worth remembering in this connection. Weber was impressed with the structure's accomplishments, and especially with the role of technical knowledge in bureaucratic administration. He was, however, ready to acknowledge its failings and deplored the 'little men, clinging to little jobs'.

Trist (C) was the greatest advocate of primary groups, which may have identified him as the second 'speaker'. Autonomy, whole tasks and flexibility are also the hallmarks of his socio-technical systems approach to work organisation and job design. (A 'sub-whole', by the way, simply means a meaningful group of jobs integrated to form a task unit, although still only a part of the whole production chain.)

So the silent party was Mayo (D), who - if he had got a word in edgeways - might have said: "Attitudes to people, as people, may be more important than such factors as rest periods, benefits, money etc. People are not merely instruments".

Further information

The Password series includes the following titles:

	Order code	
Economics	P01X	EC
Basic accounting	P028	BA
Financial accounting	P036	FA
Costing	P044	CO
Foundation business mathematics	P052	FB
Business law	P060	BL
Auditing	P079	AU
Organisation and management	P087	OM
Advanced business mathematics	P095	AB
Taxation	P109	TX
Management accounting	P117	MA
Interpretation of accounts	P125	IA
Financial management	P133	FM
Company law	P141	CL
Information technology	P15X	IT

Password is available from most major bookshops. If you have any difficulty obtaining them, please contact BPP directly, quoting the above order codes.

BPP Publishing Limited
Aldine Place
142/144 Uxbridge Road
London W12 8AA

Tel: 01-740 1111
Fax: 01-740 1184
Telex: 265871 (MONREF G) - quoting '76:SJJ098'